Contemporary China

Contemporary China

Between Mao and Market

François Godement

ROWMAN & LITTLEFIELD
Lanham • Boulder • New York • London

Published by Rowman & Littlefield
A wholly owned subsidary of
The Rowman & Littlefield Publishing Group, Inc.
4501 Forbes Boulevard, Suite 200, Lanham, Maryland 20706
www.rowman.com

Unit A, Whitacre Mews, 26-34 Stannary Street, London SE11 4AB,
United Kingdom

British Library Cataloguing in Publication Information Available

Library of Congress Cataloging-in-Publication Data
Godement, François.
[Que veut la Chine? English]
Contemporary China : between Mao and market / François Godement.
pages cm
Includes bibliographical references and index.
ISBN 978-1-4422-2537-4 (cloth : alk. paper) — ISBN 978-1-4422-2538-1 (pbk. : alk. paper) —
ISBN 978-1-4422-2539-8 (electronic)
1. China—Politics and government. 2. China—Economic conditions. 3. China—History. I. Title.
DS779.26.G6313 2015
951.05—dc23
2015006766

∞ ™ The paper used in this publication meets the minimum requirements of American
National Standard for Information Sciences Permanence of Paper for Printed Library
Materials, ANSI/NISO Z39.48-1992.

Printed in the United States of America

Contents

Introduction

China is a socialist state, according to its constitution. It is also the world's second-largest economic power, soon to be the largest in absolute value if not in quality. It has 271 reported billionaires and probably more than twice that in reality.[1] The seventy wealthiest deputies in the National People's Assembly account for a total of $90 billion in assets—far surpassing all other members of parliament around the world. Moreover, a third of the richest Chinese act as official advisers to the government of the People's Republic, which is led by the Chinese Communist Party (CCP). The marriage is certainly unusual, but it seems to be successful.

A SUCCESSFUL MARRIAGE

The party running the country can boast another success: it has eliminated the uncertainties that are usually associated with the history of political systems. It has regulated and even ritualized its operations at the top, portraying them as sacred, to the point of ruling out any surprises in its future history. During major public events, its leaders appear in black suits, red ties, and slicked hair behind tables laden with cups of tea. One of them made a bold suggestion once—he proposed ending the requirement to applaud at regular intervals in official meetings.

The seriousness with which China's leaders take their travel is unequaled around the world. President Hu Jintao did once make a state visit to the Seychelles (population twenty-eight thousand, the equivalent of a Chinese village), but it is unlikely he went for the snorkeling, the most frequent activity of visitors to this little Indian Ocean archipelago. In the main, Chinese leaders live out their existence and wield power out of sight from the general public, in a parallel universe. The political study of China, also dubbed Pekinology or Tiananmenology after the square that stands at the heart of the country, has become so dull that in the younger academic generation very few Western researchers focus on the Chinese political system. It is certainly more entertaining to study Chinese cinema, which tells beautiful or frightening stories. Or they might as well turn to easier subjects such as efficient urban planning and CO_2 traps. These issues lend themselves to harmless academic agreements with Chinese universities.

Yet the implications of China's one-party rule are no small matter. Indeed, they apply to an economic giant that has a growing influence throughout the world. China's mixture of a ritualized political system and a teeming economy is not an oxymoron, and it has precedents. For centuries, East Asia has experienced a rise in the court practices associated with neo-Confucianism—a Bible of recipes and rules instituting a dominant bureaucracy with a stringent collective code of ethics. China itself has inherited the formalism of the Ming and Qing dynasties. It is the most popular period today for major international art shows put on by the People's Republic[2] and was an inexhaustible source of iconographic inspiration for the Beijing Olympic Games and the Shanghai Universal Exposition.

But China is also the most individualistic society in Asia, at times descending into chaos. And it is a society that has owed much of its originality to hermit monks, Taoist sects, and many outspoken individual writers. The two trends can coexist or collide, leading to views of Chinese history as a succession of cycles. When the PRC's founder, Mao Zedong, finally died in 1976, it was an easy bet to predict a return of the Old Beijing Man, aka Chinese individualism. In a return to a fairly anarchic China, family, local, and community identities would count more than central authority and would of course supersede the imported ideology of Communism. Yet Leninism—as a technique of political power, not as an ideology—has survived Communism. The party-state has reinvented itself and even expanded with the help of modern control and communications technologies.

Hence China combines a Leninist form of government and a capitalist economy—a unique combination. Naive or self-serving Western observers long held the belief that a China going to market would also converge with the West's political systems. This hope was reinforced by the "1989 effect." A combination of Russia's Gorbachev laying down his power as if he were a modern Cincinnatus returning to his plow and Eastern Europeans seizing the moment to unseat their governments has made the fall of all Communist regimes seem inescapable. Unfortunately, the prediction also relieved us of the need to reflect on values, ours and those espoused by a Communism on the wane. It satisfied the intellectual laziness that summed up China's future with the word *transition*.

A RIGID TRANSITION

At the very least, this transition now appears endless. In fact, the theory of a continuing transition had advantages for China's rulers too. It was compatible with the needs of adapting the Chinese regime. It allowed the reduction of recent Chinese history to a blur, whether it be the human and political tragedies of the Maoist era (the *economic* mistakes are acknowledged) or the 1989 political crisis. At that time, Deng Xiaoping and conservative allies did away with or sacrificed the reformist factions. In the same way, the Dowager Empress Cixi had all but placed under house arrest the Guangxu Emperor and massacred his followers after a failed attempt at reform during the hundred days of 1898.

The events of 1989 spelled the death of political reform from above, but after an interval the theory of gradual transition made its return. To optimists, improvements in governance would lead smoothly to the same result as a major political change, without large-scale risk. To the pessimists, the fragmentation of China's bureaucracy, the continuing changes at the grassroots and within society, would render central power largely irrelevant. Again, no time limit was ever set for this transition. This was the compromise that allowed the regime and its backers to coexist with the advocates of change. History was replaced by ambiguity.

Of course, without a revolution and without reform politics, the transition and minute changes in governance failed to yield the results expected by optimistic international observers. Political reform froze at the top in 1989 and at the grassroots level (namely village elections) in the mid-nineties. For fear of a fiscal crisis, the government effectively recentralized and rebuilt its public economy after 1994. The global recession in 2008 put an end to international economic openness in many areas. This sudden shift in strategy in the year of the Beijing Olympics stemmed from a feeling of superiority over open-market economies and also from a fear of possible repercussions from the Western economic slowdown. Changes in the legal system had ground to a halt in 2006, and a counteroffensive protecting the arbitrary rule of the party-state started to take shape in 2009. In 2010, a wave of nationalist sentiment encouraged by official propaganda and media swept the country, a curious combination of resentment over the past and arrogance for the future, particularly with respect to neighboring Asian countries. This nationalist offensive eased in 2011, only to be succeeded by a move against the rule of law and the advocates of a constitutional system. Human rights activists were particularly targeted in the aftermath of the Arab Spring—again a fear of contagion. The issue of secret and arbitrary detentions now interfered with talk of a new code of criminal procedure.

A LOST DECADE

The words only appeared in its final year, but they spread around Beijing: the Hu Jintao decade of 2002–2012 was a "lost decade" for reform. Yet initially Hu Jintao and some of his close associates had played with options closer to the former reformist camp. Through their personal experience of hard times in Western China after 1965, they had identified the widening social divide with China's peasant population, migrants, and the inland regions. And their factional background within the party often placed them as heirs to more liberal leaders of the 1950s, particularly in the Communist Party's youth organization.

These intentions have lost out to what can now be called a mode of production. Karl Marx coined the term. The great man saw that economic structures dictated power arrangements that prevailed over any political ends or ideology. It now applies to China itself. A decade was perhaps politically lost. But it capped three decades of tremendous economic gains, altering the face of the country. China underwent a change in scale at the same time as imbalances in growth became more pronounced—vast migrations, huge investments made possible by forced savings owing to the lack of social protection or financial security, record industrial growth and exports with increasing social inequity, and a financial extraversion toward the US dollar symbolized by gigantic accumulation of currency reserves and a boom in investment abroad. With annual growth topping 10 percent and pervasive changes taking place, enormous tensions have built up, absent any progress in citizen representation. The environment, with a scale of damage never seen in human history, is a permanent reminder of an unsustainable, but apparently also endless, mode of production. Poisoned infant milk, cadmium-contaminated rice, fake medicine, record-breaking smog, and disappearing water supplies (alongside countless golf courses and manicured villas) are bringing the situation toward a climax. Particle pollution may be to China what vodka was to the Soviet Union—a life-threatening issue. But as with all human trends, it is hard to determine where the threshold is.

For all these reasons, the years from 2010 to 2012 were a particularly salient time to raise questions in China. The rise in domestic imbalances coincided with the risks from a global downturn. On top of that, nearly the entire Chinese collective leadership was up for replacement in the fall of 2012. At the apex of the Leninist power system is a group (Standing Committee of the Politburo, including its alternate members, heads of key party offices, and influential party elders) that has at different times comprised anywhere between five and thirty people. It is these individuals who make the decisions, and even among them it may be hard to pinpoint the real decision makers, who have varied over time. Mao moved from committee rule to autocratic power. Deng imposed reforms on his Standing Committee and Politburo colleagues by using, sometimes as hatchet men, the heads of central party offices—until he sided with conservatives against them. Hu Jintao saw an increasingly defiant group of party colleagues at the top. Xi Jinping, China's new paramount leader, seems to carry with him the Standing Committee—currently, seven people—over a publicly silent Politburo. Under his tenure, collective leadership is hardly mentioned anymore—and his moves against very powerful former leaders, such as Zhou Yongkang, China's former security czar, and Xu Caihou and Guo Boxiong, vice chairmen of the Military Affairs Commission under his predecessor—signal a return to personal power.

In short, life at the top is in precarious balance beneath the smooth public face. The renewal of the leadership—in itself a tribute to rules over power struggle—is an occasion when old alliances are torn and new ones are formed. Political debates—long kept under wraps by the principle of collective leadership—reemerge. And the vast society below senses the uncertainties within the "black box" above, and looks for confirmation in any signs that come to light of relentless personal or political struggles.

CHINA AT THE CROSSROADS

This book aims to shed light on some of the issues and personal or factional elements that emerged in 2010–2012. It cannot pretend to trace the actual turning points and decisions that were made, but only to take an educated guess at some of them. Anyone who claims to know the inside process of the Chinese Communist Party is bluffing. Like archeology and paleontology, Pekinology must extrapolate a whole monument or an animal from a mere column or a bone. But the past few years have yielded a wealth of signs and revelations. Among them are the appearance of publicly competing regional models; the fall of Bo Xilai, the most visibly ambitious of officials vying for power with a torrent of revelations; the party's about-face and recognition of the revolt of a rural community in Wukan (Guangdong); a revival of political reform, and open questioning of the development path and of so-called vested interests; an extraordinary succession of incidents, debates, and counter-moves in Chinese foreign policy, particularly with respect to its Asian neighbors; and lastly the appearance of strong competing currents in strategic thought. Such strong and public debates had not been heard since the period immediately preceding the Tiananmen crisis, a quarter of a century ago.

The debate and factional infighting were also fueled by concerns over the legitimacy of the party's rule. These must take Chinese society into account. Despite being capped by the Leninist power system and by extraordinary mechanisms of control and persuasion, Chinese society has its own dynamic, with an increasing freedom in social and private interactions. But it remains largely unorganized outside the party system, with very limited rights for nongovernmental organizations. Beyond local protests and a passion for information, society cannot lead the way. Instead, the party stakes its legitimacy on the ability to strategize and to foresee what lies ahead—in terms of domestic developments and international risks. The party can no longer rule every aspect of life, and some of its goals may not be met. But its decisions, usually taken by a very tight circle of top leaders, remain paramount. These decisions may later have unintended consequences, but they are implemented nonetheless.

REFORM AGAINST ONESELF?

There is, however, one major exception to this situation. The party can hardly move against its own interests. Mao Zedong in his time had extended mass movements and political campaigns to include party rectification—the correction of its own mistakes, which often implied the purge of cadres. The chaos that resulted from Mao's attacks on his own comrades has never been forgotten, and collective leadership has been instituted to avoid such struggle. But collective leadership also implies compromise, and today the sphere of vested interests close to the party has grown with the Chinese economy. It is not only 86 million party members, but also state enterprises and their employees; local governments and their relatives or private proxies; and to some extent, China's very real upper-middle class, after enriching itself in the past three decades, that constitute the new vested interests. They are both the supporters and the greatest danger to the Chinese regime. It is threatened neither from outside—China's partners wish above all for a stable China—nor by a hypothetical revolt from below. There are numerous reasons and occasions for discontent, and the social media carry these. But the party's hold on power is such that it snuffs out dissent in the social media as if these were brushfires. Effectively, the party has a monopoly on political representation, and dissenting views have to filter through its own apparatus.

This book therefore replays the incidents, debates, and stands taken in and around the CCP during those heady years of 2009–2012—when China was giddy with its growth in the face of the West's economic downturn, yet torn by competing interests and de facto political factions inside the party and the public establishment. The story ends with the ascent of a new strongman, Xi Jinping, who has initially collected more power and authority than any other leader since Mao Zedong. Debates and factional alignments have now been suppressed or pushed to the background, and this alone bears testimony to the enduring strength of China's political system.

Yet the cracks are likely to reopen, if only because choices will have to be made. China's strongest dilemma remains the same: keep what has been a winning formula but has led to increasing problems, inside and outside China, or change before the cost of change becomes impossibly high. Not surprisingly, the policy debates had run much ahead of a collective leadership that is above all risk averse. The reemergence of a strongman and more personal rule under Xi Jinping may open up the game, as it did under Mao's reign—for better or for worse.

NOTES

1. "Top 50 of the Hurun Rich List," http://www.hurum.net/usen/NewsShow.aspx?nid=151.

2. As exemplified in 2006 by a successful show at the Guimet Museum in Paris: "The Very Rich Hours of the Court of China (1662–1796)."

Chapter One

Inside the Chongqing Furnace

China is a country where apparent continuity encounters sudden and precipitous change, where individual behavior breaks through the collective veneer. It is a country where passions are rife. In unguarded moments, its political culture reflects the martial arts novels and television series devoured by the Chinese public, and some of it shows through its animated debates on the social media.

So let's begin with an improbable tale, recounting events that nonetheless took place in 2010–2012, and reached their conclusion in 2013. The place is Chongqing on the Yangtze River, once the capital of China at the time of the Sino-Japanese War. It is said to be one of the "three cauldrons of China"[1] for its unbearably hot and muggy climate. The two main protagonists in this drama are Bo Xilai, the political boss of this "autonomous municipality" with a population of thirty-two million, a contender for the highest office, and his right-hand man, local public security chief Wang Lijun. At the height of their glory the two men even suggested to the chairman of the Chongqing Writers' Union that their exploits be used as inspiration for a detailed story, a novel and a script for a television series.[2] The reader will kindly excuse the twists and turns in this story, but every one of them reveals an aspect of Chinese policy.

A PIECE OF FRIENDLY ADVICE

In late winter 2011–2012, He Guoqiang, head of the party's Inspection and Discipline Committee, in other words the party's internal police, addressed a group of delegates from the special municipality of Chongqing visiting Beijing to participate in the annual session of the National People's Assembly. In a seemingly bland comment, after reminding them of the three years he had spent previously as the Mayor of Chongqing, he warned the delegates against the sudden change in Beijing weather after a very cold winter: "The climate here is definitely very different from Chongqing, and delegates must watch out for their health."[3]

These few words were immediately tweeted by Weibo, the Chinese social network. Everyone found in them confirmation of what people were sensing in the political world: vicious factional infighting at the top of the party, the first public act of which had played out in the most incredible manner a few weeks earlier. On the evening of February 6, 2012, Wang Lijun, Chongqing's feared security boss, had disguised himself as a woman to leave his house without being recognized, and driven to the US consulate in Chengdu (Sichuan), 350 kilometers away. He stayed overnight but came back out "voluntarily" the next day, according to a terse statement from the US diplomatic staff.

Wang Lijun's move unleashed a storm. In the night a horde of policemen surrounded the consulate, including dozens of security vehicles from Chongqing. The mayor and second-in-command in Chongqing, Huang Qifan, confirmed he had left "by car with his secretary" together with two assistants to intervene at the consulate and "talk things over" with Wang Lijun "in the interest of national security." It also turned out that Qiu Jin, China's deputy minister of state security—Chinese espionage and counterespionage—then took Wang Lijun into custody outside the consulate after a direct altercation with members of the Chongqing Public Security Bureau, who had wanted to take him with them. The two men then flew first-class from Chengdu to Beijing. Despite the secrecy with which China is governed, this travel has been documented because the names of airline passengers and even their identity card numbers, on a flight that was code-shared with Air Canada, appeared in real time in the public domain via the airline reservation system. To date, that is the last time Wang Lijun has been seen or heard of in public. His trial in September 2012, closed to the public, resulted in a fifteen-year jail sentence—but more importantly provided the necessary testimony to further implicate his direct boss, Chongqing Party Secretary Bo Xilai.

THE COWBOY POLICEMAN

What happened at the consulate? Did Wang Lijun ask for political asylum? Such a request would have been unrealistic, for even the United States could not become embroiled in a confrontation involving a figure who was not a dissident but a high official of China's public security. Was he attempting to find a way to escape from his local adversaries, hoping he might be turned over directly to China's central government instead? We may have to wait twenty-five years to learn the answer, when America's diplomatic archives are opened.

Two days later, an uneasy statement from the Chongqing municipal government referred to a "therapeutic vacation" for Wang Lijun. A defensive rumor made the rounds, describing his allegedly bizarre behavior. This cowboy policeman had such a passion for autopsies that he put on his business cards the title of vice president of an international forensic medicine association. Wang was also obsessed with patents. He is said to have filed around thirty of them, including for a uniform with a magnetic field designed to protect every policeman, and another for an innovation facilitating organ transplants. But China's official media had also gone out of their way to praise him. In stories from October to November 2009, he was referred to as the "anti-mafia hero," Wang the "paratrooper," "Pure Heaven Wang." He was praised to the skies for his taste in inventions and his passion for autopsies. Photos were published of him in flattering poses—leaning against his car and dressed in camouflage with a machine gun and a walkie-talkie, or in a trench coat commanding an operation on the ground.[4]

The *People's Daily* is even said to have described him as the "guardian of the gates of Hell," an astonishing way to pay tribute to a policeman with a ruthless reputation.[5] The New China News Agency had applauded the internationally recognized specialist in forensic medicine and the psychology of organized crime.[6] Wang seems like someone straight out of a martial-arts novel, but his case is much more serious.

A FLASHY GO-GETTER

For ten years and since an initial position in northeastern China before arriving in Chongqing, Wang had been the right-hand man of Bo Xilai, the party secretary of Chongqing. Among China's leaders, Bo is undeniably the one who flaunted his ambition the most. He is the son of Bo Yibo, who should really be known as China's Suslov, the name of Stalin's most faithful and long-lasting subordinates. A chameleon in Mao's circle, Bo survived all the turns of the official line by becoming the party's political executor on major occasions. He was the one who in August 1959 sounded the charge against Peng Dehuai, China's minister of defense, who had dared express doubts about the Great Leap Forward, and who would subsequently be eliminated. None of that protected Bo or his family from a cruel fate during the Cultural Revolution when Jiang Qing, Mao's wife, took a dislike to him. Bo Yibo was persecuted (and denounced by his own son, Bo Xilai, a frequent occurrence at the time); his wife was driven to suicide. The old warrior made a comeback in 1978 and in the end became one of the "Eight Immortals," the former leaders who continue to carry weight with the current leadership. It was also Bo who, in January 1987, drew up the political indictment against Hu Yaobang, Deng's lieutenant convicted of encouraging political liberalization. He was also among those who encouraged the crackdown in May and June 1989, aimed in particular at Zhao Ziyang, the secretary-general of the party with more liberal leanings. Bo Yibo was therefore seen by many as a hatchet man for the party. In 1992, he made a key proposal to his colleagues: that the family of every leader be entitled to place one child (but only one) in the party's political machinery. Making himself a kind of trustee for the families of first-generation leaders of the party-family, he made certain that the number of "princelings" would increase at the topmost level of Chinese politics, thus creating a hereditary aristocracy. Bo Yibo died in 2007, leaving behind him a long list of those he had helped to purge and also of the children of his enemies, who would carry on their enmity to Bo's own son, Bo Xilai.

The young Bo Xilai started out as a player in the Cultural Revolution, as a Red Guard at sixteen and then as a victim of the Guards. With the help of his family pedigree, he rose quickly within the party apparatus. As the mayor of Dalian, the large Manchurian port city, Bo displayed administrative skills. He also was known to have a fondness for personal power, with a definite taste for publicity. He became minister of commerce and then a member of the Politburo in 2007. As such he was already a contender for its Standing Committee. Others were to be chosen over him, and Bo Xilai was appointed party secretary for Chongqing—a somewhat exposed position, as that metropolis on the Yangtze has long been reputed to be a hotbed of political racketeering and gangsterism.

There he carved out a new reputation, based on two policies that were to serve him well in terms of public relations. First of all, even before he arrived, Chongqing was designated as a new experimental model as part of the policy for developing Western China, the *xibu kaifa*. The state and the state-owned enterprises, backed by enormous investments, as had been the case in Shanghai's Pudong fifteen years earlier, wanted to attract international investments from multinational companies so they could expand the industrial miracle of the coast to inland China.

Salaries in Chongqing are twice as low as those in the coastal areas of China. Chongqing also was slated to experiment with a social policy based on public housing (along with huge private real estate developments) and on a newly devised policy of transferring peasant land rights, which is perhaps the only true originality of the much-hyped Chongqing model. Rural migrants could now exchange their original land, which could then be developed, for urban housing. The expenses involved are huge. For example, the local superhighway system is expected to reach 3,000 kilometers by 2015.[7] Parks and avenues have been planted with ginkgos, Bo Xilai's favorite tree. And the results have been on target. Growth in 2012 was up to 15 percent a year. Hewlett-Packard, Intel, Foxconn (the Taiwanese manufacturer of Apple, among others), and Bayer have set up operations in the highly subsidized industrial zones of Chongqing.

But Bo's talent didn't stop there. He launched a modern-day ideological campaign (television shows instead of political meetings) of "red songs," songs from the revolutionary Maoist era, thereby reviving a defunct political repertoire that clashed with the central government's slogans of harmony and civilization. He conducted his own public relations policy promoting the "Chongqing model," inviting prominent Western politicians, editorial writers, and sinologists. Above all, he launched a spectacular and brutal anti-mafia campaign that was to captivate Chinese public opinion. Bo imitated the "strike hard" campaigns against crime launched by Deng Xiaoping in 1983, backed by the combined actions of the courts, the prosecutors, and the police (*sifabu*). But the crackdown took on greater proportions. With thousands (some say tens of thousands) of sometimes spectacular arrests, he also prosecuted businessmen, developers, and local officials, including those at the highest levels of the security apparatus. In a China ravaged by government corruption, Bo Xilai became a great success in the court of public opinion, although his actions and propaganda greatly worried legal rights advocates.

VENDETTA AT THE TOP

It was at that precise point that the anti-mafia campaign led by the police chief and Bo Xilai's right-hand man, Wang Lijun, clashed with national policy. Two important leaders had run Chongqing before Bo Xilai. One of them, Wang Yang, who was close to the Hu Jintao–Wen Jiabao tandem and who like them came from Communist youth movements and not from a high-level family, launched the Chongqing experiment. He then went on to lead the large southern province of Guangdong, where he gained prominence as an advocate of economic reforms, allowing liberal voices to flourish. The other, He Guoqiang, is the chief of the party's Commission for Discipline Inspection. They were naturally upset about Bo's actions, since he was going after some of their former local subordinates.

There were even more personal reasons for the clash. It may in fact have been He Guoqiang who fired the first shot with the arrest of Wang Yi, the former private secretary (*mishu*[8]) of Bo Xilai's own father. Wang Yi had become vice president of a government investment bank.[9] A dispute arose with He Guoqiang from a conflict of interest concerning a large private pharmaceutical company.[10] Wang Yi was arrested in February 2009; he was actually condemned to death with a two-year stay of execution (in other words, a life sentence) in April 2010.

Bo Xilai has a reputation for being personal and brutal. There is an endless supply of stories to that effect. Believing his clan to be attacked by He Guoqiang, Bo is said to have reacted by launching the anti-mafia campaign. Soon the campaign implicated Wen Qiang, the previous chief of Chongqing Security. He was arrested as he got off the plane from Beijing in August 2009.[11] Wen Qiang was extremely close to He Guoqiang—so close he was considered a member of his family. Wen Qiang was sentenced to death and executed in August 2010.

Whatever the reasons for the anti-mafia campaign in 2009, it took from March to October of that same year for a central leader to approve Bo Xilai's campaign. The first to do so in October 2009 was Zhou Yongkang, the supreme head of Public Security and a member of the Standing Committee of the Political Bureau. In one year the campaign officially resulted in 3,348 arrests[12] and in what we now know to have been an increase in cases of abuse, torture, and arrests involving family members of the targeted individuals. These arrests proved especially upsetting in legal and human rights circles. Wang Lijun and Bo Xilai also arrested Li Zhuang, a lawyer who had come from Beijing to defend Wen Qiang, raising further the level of political confrontation. The scandal continued to reverberate, as Li Zhuang belonged to a law firm that was run by the son of another former top leader—Peng Zhen.[13] Intellectuals, the more liberal media, as well as other ruling families began to wonder just how far Bo Xilai would go.

THE GHOST OF MAOISM?

Bo Xilai had managed to worry everyone who feared a return of Maoism and the Cultural Revolution. His flashy campaigns took an ideological turn, creating a split among the leaders. Until 2009, it had been the central leaders most identified with economic reform who had made official trips to Chongqing to visit Bo Xilai—namely Premier Wen Jiabao, and Li Keqiang, generally considered his successor, whose trips focused on economic topics. In the spring of

2009, Jia Qinglin, a conservative reputedly opposed to the Hu-Wen tandem, had already come to extol the revolutionary tradition. After that, the official visits stopped. Starting in August 2010, the visits resumed, but leaders comprising the apparatus of political control were the main ones to visit Chongqing, starting with Li Changchun, the propaganda chief (August 2010), then Zhou Yongkang, chief of security (November). At the end of the year, Xi Jinping, the presumed successor to Hu Jintao, made a high-profile visit. Interestingly, he praised both the "red songs" campaign and the "strike black" anti-mafia campaign. A photo has survived where he benevolently looks at Wang Lijun, Chongqing's police chief. And in the spring of 2011, even He Guoqiang came, and then Wu Bangguo, speaker of the National Assembly, who took an especially close look at the social policy implemented locally. But the number one leader, Hu Jintao, who had gone to Chongqing just after Bo was appointed, never returned, nor has Wen Jiabao.

These visits became a clear vote in favor of the "Chongqing model," first of all for its economic and social benefits, but increasingly for the ideological revival and the crackdowns it publicized. Bo Xilai seemed to have found his way into the process of the political succession before the Eighteenth Party Congress slated for November 2012. In a pre-succession climate, when the leaders' acts and gestures are closely scrutinized by everyone, top leader Hu Jintao was undoubtedly subjected to pressure by a strong conservative wing within the collective leadership. The year 2010 was also marked by blatantly nationalistic statements on foreign policy and about the army. And starting in December 2010 and continuing into 2011 the country saw an increase in domestic political repression. The premier and a few leaders reputed to be close, such as Li Keqiang (previously mentioned) or Wang Yang, the Guangdong party secretary, seemed isolated or out of sync with these trends.

THE BO XILAI MYSTERY

This is the limit of what we know with any reasonable degree of probability. We shall see that the choices made by Hu Jintao are totally impossible to decipher. He has often been challenged by rumors at the highest level for the indecisiveness or the wait-and-see attitude he increasingly seemed to exhibit. But was this apparent passivity genuine or was it feigned? Was it a wait-and-see strategy, Hu letting several currents develop to better arbitrate his own succession? When Xi Jinping, Hu's presumed successor, paid a visit to Bo Xilai even though their fathers hated each other, was it a political alliance or a bid for inclusiveness? There are more questions than there are answers. What real chances did Bo Xilai have? This is a man who went further than any of his peers in self-publicity, and who seems to have so influenced some central leaders that they paid tribute to him in public. Was he really an advocate of a return to ideological Maoism, the same person who sent his son to Eton and Harvard, and who surrounded himself with a circle of public intellectuals? Did he inspire fear as the possible architect of a violent counterrevolution, or was he an opportunist who has just seen himself paid back in kind? And quite simply, do we know why Wang Lijun suddenly fled? How could the feared police chief of a giant city have ended up seeking political asylum in a foreign consulate? Was he taken hostage by Bo Xilai's adversaries, who might have unearthed some embarrassing piece of information? Had he been a pawn cast off by Bo Xilai, and did he suspect he was going to experience the same fate as his predecessor, Wen Qiang, who was executed in July 2010? Wen Qiang, his wife, and his oldest son had even undergone highly improper public questioning by journalists on the very day of his execution.[14] Another of Wang Lijun's victims in Chongqing, businessman Li Jun, later told the international press[15] about the weeks of torture endured in a clandestine military prison. He revealed his certainty, which was shared by other observers, that Bo Xilai's final target was his predecessor in Chongqing, Wang Yang—now the head of the large province of Guangdong and in the forefront in promoting reforms. In any event, to go through the door of the US consulate in Chongqing, Wang Lijun, the "anti-mafia hero" of 2009 through 2011, must have understood that he had no other option left.

A POLITICAL TURNING POINT

One major political consequence of the storm in Chongqing does stand out. In the weeks following the preposterous Wang Lijun episode in February 2012, official and media advocacy of reform suddenly increased in Beijing. From political reform of local elections to the deregulation of foreign currency controls, as well as a pragmatic compromise in China's foreign policy toward Asia and the positions taken by Wen Jiabao himself in the spring session of the National Assembly in favor of economic reforms, a shift was in the making. On February 19—that is, after the actual anniversary date—the party's official national press began to celebrate Deng Xiaoping's trip to southern China in 1992, when he revived the notion of openness and reforms. That anniversary, which falls in January, had aroused enthusiasm in favor of reforms, including political reforms, in the southern province of Guangdong, the province that was headed by Wang Yang. On the other hand, another campaign also began on February 19 to promote Lei Feng, a propaganda hero from the time of the Maoist era, and it was most probably a propaganda counteroffensive by conservatives. People's Liberation Army soldier Lei Feng, dubbed the "small cog in a big wheel" who gave his life for his country, died in 1962. But his personality cult was revived with the glorification of a beggar from Nanking who, after the Sichuan earthquake in 2008, is said to have donated the proceeds from his alms to the victims of the disaster.

At the National People's Congress, Wen Jiabao, choosing to respond to journalist questions on the case of Wang Lijun, suddenly gave it much greater political significance. In alluding to the scandal, he referred to the risk of "repeating the tragedy of the Cultural Revolution." He urged "Chongqing's current leaders to learn a lesson from the Wang Lijun scandal," and described the "liberation of thought" that occurred in December 1978 when the policy of reform and openness was launched. [16]

Thus two political trends seemed to be in opposition. Since 1989, we had been unable to get a clear picture of the clashes, if any, between factions or political wings among the five to nine members of the Party's Standing Committee or among the twenty-five members of the Political Bureau. Just as a deep underground fracture can cause a tsunami, the explosion at the foot of the mountain of the Wang Lijun scandal, a scandal involving a cowboy policeman who did not want to take the fall alone, caused a landslide at the highest level of the party. This case has provided a public window to understand some of the differences at the top, and how they play in personal or factional politics.

Where do the political spinoffs from the Chongqing revelations lead? There are some historical benchmarks. A study of Republican China (1911–1949) tells us that climate is not the only reason Chongqing is considered one of China's three "cauldrons." When General Chiang Kai-shek moved his government there during the Sino-Japanese war, the city became famous for its "private prisons" run by competing departments, all outdoing each other in terms of kidnappings. The Wang Lijun scandal can be seen as a reincarnation of that period—a dark corner of China suddenly impacting on national policy. But the history of the People's Republic also includes the Lin Biao case. Lin Biao was the minister of defense and the designated successor to Mao who, in September 1971, fled by plane and crashed in Mongolia on the way to Moscow. His downfall was a turning point toward the end of the Cultural Revolution. Although less prominent, the defection of the top security operative in Chongqing's mass campaigns has also brought the demise of a Politburo member and contender for higher functions.

THE DELAYED CONCLUSION TO THE BO CASE

Indeed, Bo's fall came right after the March 2012 session of the National People's Assembly, which saw Wen Jiabao's diatribe against the Cultural Revolution and in favor of the "liberation of thought." Bo Xilai was relieved of his duties and disappeared from the stage. He was subjected to an internal investigation by the party "for serious violations of party discipline." His wife, Gu Kailai, was arrested and accused of poisoning a British business consultant, Neil Heywood, who was working for the family's interests. Some highly valuable information (unverified, however) was to be provided to influential Western media—starting with the Reuters agency and the *Financial Times*—as well as a news site close to the government of Taiwan, WantChinaTimes.[17]

Jealousy, conflict over consulting fees associated with massive money transfers abroad, depression of a wife largely cast aside—nothing has been spared the Bo family, not even their son, Bo Guagua, who was studying at the best international schools (Eton, Oxford, and Harvard) while living the good life. The wealth of details emerging in March and April 2012 suggests a seamy underside. Heywood had a salary and fixed expenses paid by the family, but he wanted more. The family reportedly wanted to send a billion dollars outside China. Even under an oligarchy, that kind of money raises questions. Wang Lijun, the policeman with an interest in autopsies, reportedly took a piece of tissue from Heywood's body before it was cremated, and brought it with him to the Chengdu consulate. This made it possible to do a DNA analysis and provide proof of poisoning. The revelations expanded to include Bo and Wang's time in Dalian, the city port that Bo Xilai had governed before 2007, and also his highly active private life.

Political rumors have also involved other leaders who had supported Bo Xilai. Zhou Yongkang, China's security czar and a leading supporter of Bo's anti-mafia campaign, was reportedly the only member of the Standing Committee of the Political Bureau to oppose Bo's dismissal. Bo apparently cultivated ties in the army, ties in many cases inherited from his father, and also established a bridge with some ultranationalists. Common themes can be found with Liu Yuan, the son of the former president of the Republic, Liu Shaoqi, who has however emerged as a stalwart supporter of Xi Jinping after October 2012, and with the local chief of the army's logistic department in Sichuan province. Former leaders who still carry some weight with the Political Bureau (a tradition of the collective Chinese leadership since Deng Xiaoping) reportedly intervened to stop the political interpretations of the affair. Bo and his clan have been turned over to China's legal system—which allows holding them incommunicado. But political reformers have been denied in the end any gain because of it.

But one huge problem remained; there has simply not been a shred of evidence to back all these allegations leaked from China to various media. Not even the poisoning of Heywood has been satisfyingly demonstrated, let alone the exact role of Gu Kailai, Bo's wife. Only Wang Lijun's testimony at his own trial—and that represents just a few words—implicates Bo Xilai.

Bo Xilai's wife was tried and convicted in August 2012 for the poisoning of the British consultant Neil Heywood. The trial was held for seven hours before a hand-picked audience far from Chongqing and Beijing. Bo Xilai's name never came up during the trial, nor did the role played by Wang Lijun. Four policemen were sentenced to minor penalties for their involvement, and Gu Kailai was condemned to death with a stay of two years (which tells us nothing about her future: sentences are carried out almost entirely on an individual basis). Although during the trial the grounds for the murder were attributed to a quarrel over investments abroad, absolutely no link was established with corruption or with the "lapses in party discipline" that Bo Xilai was later accused of. Apparently, the government had chosen to dissociate an ordinary crime from its political implications.

Nothing can be taken for granted. The issue of trying a top leader over a criminal matter that also involves visible (if not exceptional) corruption is an explosive one. This raises the issue of the relative priority existing between the legal system, which is still a work in progress, and the law of the party, which does not provide for individual defense. Raising the specter of the Cultural Revolution, as Wen Jiabao did, means bringing history back to center stage. All of this threatens the efforts made by the collective leadership for nearly a quarter century, and the policy of "harmony" espoused by Hu Jintao. This policy was aimed at avoiding political surprises and at covering up conflicts at the highest level. The "black box" that has become the most outstanding characteristic of the People's Republic political system has opened up in this instance with Wang Lijun's surprise move.

The implications of the Bo Xilai affair and the comparison with other prominent figures whose family members have enriched themselves also cut through the fog surrounding the circle of senior leaders. The official press has recently taken to using the expression "naked officials" (*luoguan*) to designate those who have sent their families and fortunes abroad while retaining their positions in China.

Starting in early May 2012, rumors began to dry up and a lid was placed in the official media on any aspect of the story. Bo Xilai has descended in steps, one by one—losing his Chongqing post, Politburo membership, and CCP membership, and being turned over to the judicial system in late September 2012. This last decision was announced in the same public announcement that convened the Eighteenth Party Congress, confirming the central political importance of the Bo Xilai affair.

He was finally tried in September 2013 by a court in Shandong province: there is no obligation in PRC law to locate trials where a crime has been committed, and no clear hierarchy of courts according to the severity of the crime. Composed and physically fit, Bo struck a defiant chord by denying accusations against him ranging from bribery and embezzlement to abuses of power. He denounced the torture allegedly brought on him during interrogation, and reportedly wrote a letter to his family claiming innocence and expressing hope that this would be vindicated one day. But he did not appeal the sentence, and his declarations in court did not include a single revealing fact against any of the leaders who were his colleagues. The trial thus fit contradictory requirements: a demonstrated and public due process, even if somewhat rudimentary; Bo's tenacity in staging a spirited defense; and finally, his silence on affairs of the state, which may have been the only way for him to secure a life sentence as opposed to the death penalty.

NOTES

1. With Nanjing and Wuhan.

2. The plans confided to Huang Jiren, the president of the Chongqing Writers' Union, were highly praised in a report by the *Guangzhou Daily* on its website on July 12, 2010 (see http://news.qq.com/a/20100712/000080.htm, accessed July 14, 2012). The *New York Times* interviewed Huang Jiren, who mentions the plan for a television series (Didi Kirsten Tatlow, "Gang-Busting Cop Is One for the History Books in China," November 2, 2011, on http://www.nytimes.com/2011/11/03/world/asis/03iht-letter03.html, accessed July 14, 2012). The fall of Bo Xilai put an end to those plans.

3. Photographic report by Guo Hong and Du Yuan, Xinhua Agency, March 3, 2012.

4. These different articles were taken up again under a portrait of Wang published on May 27, 2011, by the Hong Kong website of Phoenix News Media when he was appointed vice mayor of Chongqing, http://newslifeng.com/mainland/detail_2011_05/27/6666545_0.shtml.

5. See Didi Kirsten Tatlow, "Inside China's Greatest Mystery," *New York Times*, February 12, 2012, ascribing to the *People's Daily* the origin of the expression "cold-faced Yama" from the name of the god of the Buddhist Hell.

We were unable to find the source, although the term appears in publications associated with the Buddhist sect Falun Gong, which is banned in China.

6. New China News Agency, dispatch dated October 17, 2009, http://news.ifeng.com/mainland/200910/1017, accessed on July 12, 2012.

7. For an area approximately the size of Massachusetts, New Hampshire, and Vermont combined.

8. This position is equivalent to that of a chief of staff.

9. The China Development Bank, run by Chen Yuan, who is himself the son of one of China's great leaders, Chen Yun.

10. Jiuzhitang Ltd., a Hunan company that manufactures flagship Chinese medicine products, is listed on the Shenzhen Stock Exchange.

11. The story of his arrest when he got off the Beijing-Chengdu plane is reported by the Chengdu evening daily, in an apparently enthusiastic and yet subtly ironic account of the exploits of Wang Lijun: (*Chengdu Wanbao*, "Dahei yingxiong da diao qian 'dahei' yingxiong"), as this title translates as, "The hero of the anti-mafia fight brings down the previous hero of the anti-mafia fight." http://news.ifeng.com/mainland/200908/0820_17_1311332.shtml.

12. Joseph Fewsmith, "Bo Xilai Takes on Organized Crime," *China Leadership Monitor* 32 (May 2010): 3, http://www.hoover.org/research/bo-xilai-takes-organized-crime.

13. Jean-Pierre Cabestan, "A propos du modèle de Chongqing et l'avenir de la réforme judiciaire en Chine," *China Analysis* no. 35 (November–December 2011): 25.

14. All these interviews conducted by the *China Youth Daily* on July 8, 2010, are accessible in English on http://www.zoneeuropa.com/s0100713_1.htm (accessed April 12, 2012).

15. "Chinese Infighting: Secrets of a Succession War," *Financial Times*, March 4, 2012, http://www.ft.com/cms/s/2/36c9ffda-6456-11e1-b50e-00144feabdc0.html#axzz3RwBpBMWc.

16. Press conference held on March 14, 2012, http://www.xinhuanet.com/politics/2012lh/zhibo/zongli/zfr_wz_2.htm (accessed March 14, 2012).

17. http://www.wantchinatimes.com.

Chapter Two

Rich Country, Poor People

In Beijing, carved into the stone of the outer wall of a posh apartment complex, there was a saying borrowed from Friedrich Engels: "Infrastructure commands the superstructure." Its developers undoubtedly understood the idea literally as a glorification of the construction and real estate business. Reviving capitalist growth in its purest form is of course the chief irony of post-Maoism in China. The Communist Party is in power, but it is capital that rules, most often ostentatiously. Sometimes details reveal everything. In the tempest that carried off Bo Xilai, a member of the party's Politburo, a minor argument arose among the foreign correspondents. Had his son, who took the daughter of the US ambassador out to dinner in Beijing, really picked her up in a red Ferrari? People had differing opinions, but the most level-headed among them issued a reassuring denial. Bo's family car in Beijing was reportedly a gray Bentley, and it is actually possible that Bo junior came with a friend in another car. [1]

If Marx came back to life in China, he would be feverishly writing a Book Three of *Das Kapital*, for rarely has a society, and a Communist society no less, exhibited so suddenly the workings of a consumer economy driven by profit and social inequality. But despite a populist and neo-authoritarian "left," Marx is not read much in China. The party can't be blamed for enforcing historical materialism in its own way.

EXPLOSIVE GROWTH

Talking about China without starting with its explosive growth is as hard as writing a novel without the most used letter in the alphabet, the letter *e*, as in *economy*. Of course the world has seen other miracles since 1945—from southern Europe to Japan, including Asian tigers and dragons. What distinguishes China from those previous "miracles" is the giant scale of the growth and the fact that it has constantly gathered pace for three decades, combined with the extraordinary inequality of wealth that has resulted. If China's thirty-one special provinces, regions, and municipalities were independent nations, they would have constituted thirty-one of the thirty-two fastest-growing countries in 2010 and 2011.

However, neither the scale nor the meteoric growth have completely broken with the Maoist era, which came before 1978, the era of reform. From 1949 to 1978 growth reached 6 percent a year despite the disasters of the Great Leap Forward (1958–1961) and the Cultural Revolution (mainly 1966–1971). The Maoist economy did have its high points and it did set some records, not all of which were faked. However, in appearance, everything separates the Maoist era from the era that followed after 1978. The former was characterized by planning and an economy of control, rationing, and special limits on the population. The political leaders and Mao, who started as first among equals and ended as a solitary tyrant, had absolute power and an existence entirely separated from that of the people. It was omnipotence coupled with blindness that explains the thirty-seven million deaths attributed to the Great Leap Forward (the toll taken by the Cultural Revolution varies a great deal depending on the source and may never be known). However, the leaders were rich only in terms of using state property and the political privileges their jobs ensured. In this case, as in other areas, Mao was an exception, wealthy from the royalties he received ad nauseam for his collected works; Kang Sheng, his henchman and secret police chief, was reputed to have poached a large collection of classical paintings. Late in life, Jiang Qing, Chairman Mao's official wife, took a liking to traveling by plane (a Trident imported from the United Kingdom) between Beijing and Hangzhou, the lake city in Western China. But Mao's personal physician reported disputes at the court over distributions of trousers.[2] As for the people, their labor allowed them at the most to save up for a bicycle or a watch. Corruption among the officials mainly took the form of banquets—*dachi dahe* (literally "eat and drink with excess") at the expense of their collective units. The trappings of power took other forms—in the absolute domination of others, in the cult of personality at the top, or in preferential treatment and abuses of authority at the grassroots level. The intensity of the deep-rooted hatred within the leadership was also due to the lack of monetary stakes—a void that left a lot of room for venting one's feelings.

What a contrast with today's China! The Bo Xilai scandal has revealed other issues: not only did the family acquire apartments in London,[3] but apparently over the years it transferred abroad a fortune of as much as $6 billion.[4] Of course, unto those that have, more shall be given. Nevertheless this figure must be considered carefully. Earlier, the assassination of the family's British go-between had been attributed to a dispute over his commission for investing a billion dollars abroad. Given the fairly limited social standing of that unfortunate intermediary, these amounts seem unlikely or should at least be proven. By contrast, the fortune attributed rightly or wrongly to the family of Xi Jinping, the successor to Hu Jintao, in a meticulous investigation by the Bloomberg agency seems much more modest: $345 million spread out among numerous relatives.[5] Even so, that sum represents seventy thousand years of average income in China.

LABOR, AN INDISPENSIBLE RESOURCE

These are impressive sums, especially since China is not a major oil-producing or commodity-producing country, resources that lend themselves naturally to kleptomania. There is no natural source of guaranteed income. To the contrary, China prospects for natural resources in the four corners of the globe, with the exception of coal and some metals. In fact, the details (no longer only rumors) suddenly coming out about the wealth of the families of senior leaders are one consequence among others of the Chinese political economy. Its chief commodity is labor, and it derives its growth from making profits. More than an economy of demand, the Chinese economy is an economy of supply. It supplies the labor force for the "world's workshop." This kind of production method presupposes a hybrid economy in which mobilizing labor takes precedence over the market economy, and in which the intermediaries and guardians of that organization receive an enormous guaranteed income.

These factors do not originate with the reform era but with the revolutionary era that preceded it. Maoist China was a system in which there was immense but hidden surplus extracted. The transfer of wealth was from the peasant population to the planned economy, to state enterprises and indirectly to their employees, who were provided with an "iron bowl of rice," in other words, a job for life. That transfer was based on the system of prices and not on levying taxes on individuals. By leaving the prices of consumer goods unchanged since the early 1950s while their production increased considerably, and by setting prices very low or through compulsory deliveries for crops, there was an invisible drain on farmer income. This enabled the state economy to invest huge amounts—as much as one-third of gross domestic product (GDP) on the eve of the 1978 reforms. The basic notion of accumulating capital, so dear to Marx, according to which industrial capitalism was built on the labor of the proletariat, was achieved in Maoist

China by relying on the work of collectivized peasants. The China of the reform era would apply the same approach to the labor force in the export industries.

AN INVESTMENT FRENZY

The reform era should be completely different from the first decades of the regime, and yet some features have remained identical. Two essential parameters were kept and even accentuated. One is precisely the rate of accumulating surplus (i.e., the equivalent of the savings rate, provided this includes the formation of gross capital by businesses, or in practice, their investments). This rate was set to fall in the first decade of reform, after 1978. But it has risen constantly since then so that it now exceeds 50 percent of GDP. This level has no international equivalent; it reflects an investment frenzy. The objective announced in 1979, the first year of the reform, was to bring it down to 25 percent. This objective has been forgotten. For better or for worse, economic predictions or forecasts, whether they are issued by international institutions like the World Bank or by the Chinese leaders themselves, who since 2008 have been announcing the aim of rebalancing growth with greater reliance on domestic consumption, are regularly denied by the facts, as evidenced by the very recent report by the World Bank, *China 2030.*[6]

This report is interesting in many respects since it constitutes a manifesto for economic and institutional reform endorsed by at least one current of thought in the Chinese leadership. It was published in March 2012 and is based on official figures until the end of 2010, and then on forecasts for the subsequent years. The report identifies over-investing as the number one problem in the Chinese economy, estimating it at 49 percent of GDP in 2010. It predicts a noticeable decline starting in 2011.

That is not what has happened at all. To counter the 2008 global recession, China's leaders rolled out a huge economic recovery plan, which was given a further boost by bank credit at the national level. It was boosted even further at the local level. In all, more than $1.5 trillion were injected into the domestic economy in 2009, an amount comparable to the issuance of monetary liquidities by the US Federal Reserve or the bank credit facilities of the European Central Bank during the same period. This recovery through public expenses and credit caused an uptick in investment rather than stimulation of domestic demand through an increase in household income.

The abundance of China's trade and financial surplus from abroad constitutes another source of credit and investment financing. With a current account surplus amounting to an all-time record of 10 percent in 2008 and still surpassing 5 percent of GDP in 2012, the Bank of China has to buy back dollars from Chinese enterprises and financiers to turn around and invest them abroad immediately. Without this strategy, China would be unable to withstand the pressure to revalue its currency. This is what is known as "financial repression"—an exchange rate kept artificially low with the state reexporting as quickly as possible any currency entering China. However, to buy the dollars held by Chinese exporters and financiers, the Bank of China has to pay with Chinese renminbi, which implies money creation. This implies a systematically expansionist monetary policy and extremely low interest rates. In turn, this monetary over-abundance feeds investment and speculation, first of all by the players who are the closest to the authorities—state enterprises that are either subsidized or that can borrow money under excellent terms, local authorities financing dizzying development plans, and real estate developers who are often fronts for government leaders and officials. As long as it has a foreign trade and a current account surplus, the Chinese government cannot control investments in the domestic economy.

The results defy the imagination. China has always held the record in terms of building up capital and investing in its economy, even by comparison with the other Asian economies. But it has gone even further in this area. Officially the rate of investment reached 49 percent of GDP in 2011 instead of slowing down. Since 2005, investment has increased by at least 15 percent a year. In the second quarter of 2009, this rate even increased to 42 percent. In the first quarter of 2012, it was still 19 percent, more than twice the country's economic growth.[7] Within three years, China invested as much as during the previous sixty years since the founding of the People's Republic.

INDIVIDUAL INCOME: THE RACE TO THE BOTTOM

At the same time, the amount of GDP accounted for by household consumption in China has fallen continuously, so that it now accounts for only 34 percent of GDP, another world record. Simply comparing these two figures shows why China is leading the pack in globalization. First, it provides unlimited financing for production capacities or economic infrastructures. Second, it is the international champion of the movement in the relative decline of salaries, way ahead of Germany and Japan, the other two mercantilist economies under which salaries accounted for a smaller and smaller share of the economy.

The latter figure concerning the percentage of individual incomes in GDP is surprising but it is also contested. The perception foreigners have of the Chinese economy is that "salaries are rising," an undeniable reality if one considers the tri-lingual financiers, engineers, or assistants employed by foreign firms and expatriates. But if a broader view is taken to include all industry workers, including those located in inland China, then the level of real salaries had changed very little before 2008. The hypergrowth in 2008—right before the global financial crisis—and again in

2010–2011, generated labor shortages for the first time in the coastal regions and in Beijing. The resulting increase in salaries must be looked at as it relates to inflation, which is considerable in the areas of food and real estate, as well as access to health care.

Let's take the example of Shenzhen, a mushroom city driven by the assembly industry adjacent to Hong Kong—a village in 1978 and today a city with a population of sixteen million. Shenzhen instituted a minimum wage early on. It amounted to around 280 yuan in 1996; today it is 1,500 yuan a month (around 180 euros at the May 2012 rate). But that is the minimum wage paid for seventy hours of work by the largest companies such as Foxconn (until the incidents of 2010). The giant Apple subcontractor employs 200,000 workers at one site alone in Shenzhen, and more than 800,000 workers in all. That said, prices have exploded, far beyond the official index. Housing costs 2,200 euros per square meter in Shenzhen, where construction is stretched to the limit, and much more in Canton, Beijing, or Shanghai. The income increases referred to in the press or in international reports apply to much fuller work schedules. Furthermore, migrant workers (250 million workers, accounting for 40 percent of urban labor, two-thirds of industrial labor, and 80 percent of construction projects) are often paid below the legal minimum wage.[8] Moreover, the increase in productivity (due to investments and to transfers of labor from a backward agricultural sector to the industrial sector) and the growth of the economy by more than 10 percent a year are outpacing salaries even faster. Even a substantial increase in the absolute value of salaries can coincide with a decline in their relative share of the Chinese economy. The stunning boom in the export industry combined with the strengthening of the state players and the maintenance of social discipline has created a dual economy.

THE LEADING LUXURY MARKET

One glance at the China of today is enough to explain the extent of the change and to confirm the rise in inequality. China is the world's leading luxury market. For example Lamborghini increased the number of its sales outlets there from six to twenty in 2012, and Chinese industry is buying out Ferretti, the Italian manufacturer of luxury yachts (owner of the famous Riva yachts and motorboats). Luxury brands also make a greater proportion of their sales in China than mass retail companies in the same sectors. One Chinese publication estimates at more than one million the number of Chinese millionaires in dollars. Another independent Chinese study (although funded by Credit Suisse, which was looking for signs on the market of "high potential" clients!) revalues the real income of the urban population, taking undeclared income into account. The richest 10 percent of urban households (around 70 million people) have a real income that is three times higher than government statistics indicate. Their nominal income is the same as that of wealthy Europeans, but with fewer taxes and a much lower cost of living and of available labor. Most of the income underestimation happens in the wealthiest 30 percent of urban households, or 200 million people. Moreover, the estimate does not apply to salaries but to other income sources. At the top, 2 percent of the population accounts for 32 percent of the income. That portion of the population even benefits from a scissors effect: it pays lower prices than in the developed countries, not only for goods but primarily for personal services, and it pays lower taxes. This means it can save 63 percent of its income, nearly two-thirds. It is a supreme irony that China has retained traces of the Maoist era: ownership and inheritance did not exist then. Today the inheritance tax is unknown, and property taxes are just starting to be introduced on an experimental basis. Wang Xiaolu, the author of this study, estimates that hidden income in 2008 accounted for around 15 percent of China's GDP.[9] Once included in total income, this "gray" income, which is the prerogative of a very small portion of the population, explains why China is the world's premier luxury market.

SOCIAL DIVIDE: A CHASM

Here lies the solution to an apparent problem: the low individual incomes as reflected in official figures do not tally with the flourishing and even at times frenzied consumption anyone can see. In short, China has definitely become a "rich country with many poor people"—*fuguo qiongmin*, as Chinese web surfers say, giving a different twist to the most famous maxim of the first Chinese modernization in the nineteenth century (*fuguo quiangbing*, "a rich country, a powerful army"). However, given the scale of China's population, this leaves room for a so-called "middle" class to emerge (in reality very much above the average) as well as a wealthy super-class with a standard of living matching the world's richest enclaves. At the other extreme, there are the migrants and those left behind in China's countryside. There are five million migrants in Beijing (including taxi drivers impoverished by the freeze in their rates, who often sleep in the vehicles), ten million in Shanghai, and fifty million in the province of Guangdong alone, the engine that drives China's industrial exports. Even when they qualify for residency permits (*hukou*) at their workplaces, the urban and rural social security systems are separate, and migrant workers remain tied to the system in their place of origin. Their children are often excluded from the public school system; therefore thirty million migrant children, separated from their parents, live in the country with older folks or wet nurses.

Other indicators have long shown an immense and widening gap. For example, health care accounts for only 2 percent of public expenditures but hospitals and doctors who take cash fees are ubiquitous. As a result, the price of medication can be higher in China than in other countries where there is a single public buyer that exerts a downward pressure on prices. On average, the rural population devotes more than 10 percent of its income to health care. In higher education, some indicators are pointing to the rise in social inequality. The elite universities are moving up to join the leading universities in the famous "Shanghai ranking" by Jiao Tong University, but access to basic education remains difficult; and in particular the commercialization of education (evening courses and private schools) is creating new economic barriers. A recent study illustrates the changes now occurring in the educational system. It identifies the social origins of students enrolled at Peking University, known as Beida (the most prestigious in the country) and the University of Suzhou (an average well-off city) from 1952 to 2002 (excluding the period 1966–1972, when the Cultural Revolution eradicated higher education). The study shows the predominance until the mid-nineties of students recruited from peasant and working-class families (37 percent) but chiefly from among the cadre class (31 percent), particularly "political" cadres under Maoism. The authors rightly point to this as proof of a social diversity for China's top-flight universities that is unmatched in the West.

However, during the last ten years of the survey (which includes incoming freshmen until 2002 or even 2003 at Suzhou), the picture changes. The percentage of incoming students from working-class families remains the same or increases, but the percentage from peasant families goes down at Beida. Social diversity remains striking. The percentage of children of cadres rises at Beida (from 31 percent to 39 percent). Within that top category, the percentage from families of "political" cadres (party and state) falls dramatically, while the percentage from families of "economic" cadres replaces it.[10] The percentage of students from intermediary categories—described as "specialized technical personnel" (*Zhuanye jishu renyuan*)—also falls dramatically. This study sparked a lively debate (more than 1,100 chat rooms on the web) because the issue of education and generational access to employment has become such a sensitive one. Of course this could be attributed to the trend epitomized by the *haigui* or "sea turtles," referring to the Chinese students who deviate from this path by attending foreign universities, sometimes as much for prestige as for training. This is the case of the children of many senior leaders, who generally attend the elite US universities but also the most exclusive public schools (i.e., private schools) in the United Kingdom, such as Eton or Harrow. It is no surprise that not many of them attend China's elite schools, since they've found something better. The case of Bo Guagua exposed the problem of the funding of costly tuition by opaque "foundations." But the best college students from Chinese universities often also pursue their graduate studies abroad.

In truth, this change in China largely follows the choices of the high-level elite families of Southeast Asia, for example, when it comes to sending their children to the United States or the United Kingdom (Japan being largely exempt from this trend because of the insurmountable barrier of the Japanese language, which makes study abroad so hard for Japanese students and puts those who do succeed at a disadvantage for jobs at home!). But those were often authoritarian capitalist countries. Today, China's elite and the Communist Party are being privatized, while many continue to view the legitimacy of the regime in terms of social justice and its implications in terms of educational and social advancement.

THE LARGEST PROPERTY TRANSFER IN HISTORY

There is no better illustration of the social revolution now underway than land and property. Both have undergone a radical (and undoubtedly irreversible) change, which benefited one generation and is now harming the next one. Let's begin with agricultural land. Between 1978 and 1984, the collectives were broken up while the purchase prices for their crops rose to an all-time high. Thereafter, the peasant class entered a much less profitable era. Under pressure from industrialization and urbanization, with the cooperation of the global markets and with China's accession to the World Trade Organization, the peasants saw their land bought out, either willingly or by force, by local governments seeking projects for profit. In nearly every instance, the price paid for the land was based on its agricultural value rather than on its commercial value as a building site. The recent example of the Wukan revolt in Guangdong shows that most of the peasants had sold their land there for 500 yuan per *mu*,[11] a pathetic sum.[12] The government learned from that trend and in October 2008 it granted permission to peasants leaving their land to sell the land use rights of the plots that had been allocated to them (initially, only for fifty years). This step toward the privatization of land was designed to facilitate rural emigration. In fact, as in Southern Europe during the Industrial Revolution, acreage located in mountainous regions or on hillsides is of no interest to buyers, and now it is only old people who live in the less-desirable villages.

Urban housing has also undergone a revolution since the decision by Premier Zhu Rongji in 1998 to sell public housing to the residents. This reform was greeted so enthusiastically that it is sometimes described as the largest property transfer in history. It benefited the first generation of buyers, who in many cases came out well given the subsequent rise in prices. The reform also marked a major shift toward investing in construction and private housing. Everything contributed to this. First of all, faced with insufficient tax revenues, local governments found a way to fill their coffers by creating wealth. Then, Chinese savers have found real estate as a new form of investment. Faced with the nearly total lack of a financial market, reliable investment vehicles, and low interest rates, these savers have now found an alternative to hoarding, for which China has become the leading country in the world (gold, silver, ivory, jade, etc.). Moreover, official statistics indicate that 80 percent of the Chinese are homeowners—admittedly an unreliable statistic since it also includes rural residents whose homes have little market value. The preference for real estate is driving a growing trend toward owning more than one apartment, empty if necessary. It is also becoming a basic criterion for matrimonial choices: no apartment, no wife, as the saying goes.

There are two consequences to this trend. One is the formation of real estate bubbles and the oversupply of housing. The other involves growing public debt, since local authorities make huge short-term gains by underwriting long-term borrowing.

Speculation is all the more striking as the supply of new housing is not necessarily where demand lies. In search of revenues, many local governments have created companies that borrow huge amounts to create housing developments that sometimes remain vacant; moreover the absence of property taxes also contributes to leaving apartments empty.

These economic risks are perhaps less important than the social consequences. With the enormous increase in the urban population, which rose over the 50 percent mark in 2010, and the rapid deterioration of older housing, overall demand remains much greater than supply, especially in the major cities. By 2012, Shanghai was catching up with Paris prices; Beijing prices were two-thirds those of Paris, and Canton prices one-third. This change has taken place in the amazingly short span of a single decade. Like many aspects of the Chinese economy, it is completely underestimated in official statistics. Analyses of growing income inequality in France since World War II have generally cited the key role played by inheritance and by inflated real estate prices since 1945, a historical low point for France's wealth.[13] In terms of inequality, China has made even greater strides since 1998, when the key choice to privatize housing was made. It will one day be seen to have played as great a role in Chinese history as the land enclosure movement in seventeenth-century England, which started industrial capitalism.

The social impact is massive, of course. Individuals actually borrow little in China to buy real estate. Instead, they use their savings, and often those of their close relatives, as a substitute for a nonexistent or rigged financial market. That factor, coupled with the lack of taxation, explains the extent of the construction boom. In Shanghai in 1978, every resident had four square meters of space. Today it is nearly thirty square meters, which is comparable to the figure for Paris. But more extreme trends can be observed. Near Hangzhou in a prosperous agricultural region, houses are springing up that measure hundreds of square meters on minuscule lots, financed by the savings of former peasants. As families have very few children, these vertical villas are full of giant television and computer screens and other gadgets. In Chongqing, where the government has invested heavily for two decades, there is hardly a single senior official who does not receive his luxury house or apartment measuring several hundred square meters. For the super-rich, marinas, where the yachts at anchor form a post card land-scape in front of palatial homes, have become the norm. Hainan, an old southern island where peasant families and fishermen still live, has become the country's earthly paradise for the Chinese super-class.

For the first time in 2010, the government has placed concrete limits on real estate speculation, for example by restricting credit for the buyers of multiple apartments. That measure has not proven sufficient, and the boom in real estate construction has continued unabated. In late 2011, cracks began to appear in the system, name-ly in the region of Wenzhou (Zhejiang), the very region known for the dynamism of its emigrants and exporters around the world. But the intensity of this local crisis is perhaps an exception. In Wen-zhou, "informal" (i.e., underground) credit is much more developed than elsewhere. The pause or the decline in real estate prices, no-ticeable in early 2012, did not directly threaten the national finan-cial system, as there was not the same pyramid of debt as in the United States or in Spain, for example. Like the stock exchange crises of traditional China in Taiwan or Hong Kong, China's real estate cycles punish small investors but they have not yet had the same impact as in the West. A decline in the consumption of steel, cement, aluminum, and copper will even be beneficial, not only for the rest of the Chinese economy but also for the world economy, as this drives down the price of raw materials.

LOCAL GOVERNMENTS AND FINANCE: A FATAL COMBINATION

There is nevertheless a fatal connection to the economy as a whole—through local finances. Since 1994, the date when most tax revenues were centralized at the national level, the provinces, municipalities, and districts have depended heavily on land sales and building permits to finance their enormous investment budgets. While provincial and local governments account for 80 percent of public expenses, since 1994 they have depended largely on revenue transfers from the central government or on their creativity in inventing new resources. In China local authorities do not have the right to issue bonds, so instead they create investment companies, which offer many more opportunities for corruption. Indirectly and through this form of "shadow banking," local public debt topped 26 percent of GDP in 2012, according to prudent estimates—far ahead of a central budget that appears highly conservative. One Chinese study refers to indebtedness equivalent to 150 percent of annual local tax revenues.[14] For the year 2009 alone, local governments borrowed around $600 billion. In 2010, the amount of land deals exploded to $4 trillion. It is these figures that explain the profusion of public investments, from highways to airports to prestigious buildings. But this is also pyramid financing. If there is a financial time bomb in China it is this connection between volatile earnings (because of their link to the land-price cycle) and longer-term debts taken out by local governments and the debt companies that front for them.

THE "NEW LEFT" AND SOCIAL INEQUITY

The connection between the centralization of tax revenue in 1994, privatization of housing in 1998, and local government initiative explains in large part the new wealth gap inside the Chinese population. Newcomers, and particularly the young, find themselves in front of a wall that has sprung up within less than a generation. This factor is more important than easy explanations based on corruption and inefficiency of a state overtaken by market liberalization and globalization. Yet such explanations are frequent in China; in particular, they are expressed by what is called the "New Left." It is one of the only trends of public opinion allowed in the official press, on the campuses of the big universities, and in Internet chat rooms. According to this school, it was economic liberalization and the market economy that caused the explosion in inequalities and imbalances in growth. The explanation ignores the role of the state itself—mobilizing income at the national level for state enterprises and encouraging local officials to create income out of speculative investment. Instead, the Chinese reformers, who would like to rebalance growth to focus more on the domestic economy and complete the transition to the market economy, are said by the New Left to be hand in glove with a new capitalist class. The New Left ignores the role that state policies and officials have played. Instead, it focuses on all defects of the present situation as if these were the sole consequence of market liberalization. Restoring an all-powerful state such as existed under Mao is seen as the only solution, based on its ideology of social equality. Yet Maoism was also synonymous with scarcity. Unequal growth, greatly biased in favor of official stakeholders and their well-connected friends, is nonetheless a growth of supply.

There is indeed one aspect of this new growth model that cannot endure. That is the endless overinvestment in production capacities and infrastructure, based on hopes for ever-increasing exports and higher returns from large economies of scale. In 2013, overinvestment in solar panels resulted in China producing three times what the world's market absorbed in the same year. The steel output by Hebei province was larger than the combined steel production of Europe and the United States. That model is a consequence of the political organization of the economy, which favors large investments. During the Hu-Wen decade, there have been attempts to reorient growth toward domestic consumption. Yet they pale in comparison with the frantic rush to invest amid mounting inequalities. When this cycle will finally end is the biggest question facing the Chinese economy.

REFORM: AT WHAT PRICE FOR THE PARTY?

Chinese society is stratifying. An insider super-class was born of necessity out of the party-state's will to retain a hand on the new economic opportunities it was creating. A higher middle class seized the once-in-a-lifetime opportunity of hyper-growth and housing privatization to get rich. The real middle class that does not own more than its own housing, in spite of its savings, faces a much more uncertain fate given rising real estate prices for first-time buyers and health care costs for the old. Lastly, there is a workforce whose revenue is racing to keep pace with the inflation in staple products, and that is facing competition from internal migration and industry delocalization in inland areas. These cleavages have appeared within a third of a century after the end of the Maoist-era caste system. Thus far, no public policy has dealt with them, and they portend much louder protests than in the first decades of reform. China's political leadership is faced with a momentous choice. It may keep pushing the existing growth model, based on a hybrid state and market capitalism and ceaseless global expansion, while defending political stability at all costs. But if that avenue closes, it must revamp China's political economy from top to bottom, with the risk of undermining its own political power structure and the support of the economic elites that have sprung up.

During the first decades of the reform, China successfully defied the well-known dilemma defined by Alexis de Tocqueville: the most dangerous time for an authoritarian government is when it starts to reform. While all major political reforms have been discontinued, growth through accumulation and investment policies have succeeded. But they have created powerful vested interests, which are supporters of the status quo.

This results in new obstacles to market reform. Individual leaders and their families are not the only stakeholders in a development model from which they take their cut. For the major state enterprises, government-owned banks, local authorities, and well-to-do urban classes, this model is essential for their prosperity. Inequality in China has reached the level traditionally associated only with Brazil. Can the CCP find a Chinese Lula[15] among its ranks? Can the party muster the long-term vision that is necessary to overcome the ties that bind it to such powerful interests?

NOTES

1. Officially, Bentley sold 1,839 vehicles in China in 2011.
2. Li Zhisui, *The Private Life of Chairman Mao: The Memoirs of Mao's Private Physician* (New York: Random House, 1994).
3. "Bo Family Bought Luxury Flats in London," *Financial Times*, June 27, 2012, http://www.ft.com/intl/cms/s/0/6dd9307c-bed3-11e1-bebe-00144feabdc0.html#axzzlzOMNWNPI.
4. Kenji Minernura, "Investigators Say Bo Xilai's Wife Admits to Killing Briton," *Asahi Shimbun*, June 22, 2012, http://ajw.asahi.com/article/asia/china/AJ201206220040.
5. "Xi Jinping Millionaire Relations Reveal Fortunes of Elite," *Bloomberg News*, June 29, 2012, http://www.bloomberg.com/news/2012-06-29/xi-jinping-millionaire-relations-reveal-fortunes-of-elite.html.
6. World Bank, *China 2030: Building a Modern, Harmonious and Creative High Income Society*, February 27, 2012, available on http://www-wds.worldbank.org/external/default/WDSContentServer/WDSP/IB/2013/03/27/000350881_20130327163105/Rendered/PDF/762990PUB0china0Box374372B00PUBLIC0.pdf.

7. Gavekal Dragonomics, *China Macro Chartbook*, May 2012, 9.

8. Stephen Green, "On the World's Factory Floor: How China's Workers Are Changing China and the Global Economy," *Standard Chartered Special Report*, January 2008.

9. Wang's study, carried out by the Foundation for Chinese Reform and supported by Credit Suisse, is available in various forms. Its best statistical presentation is: Credit Suisse, "Analyzing China's Grey Income," *Equity Research*, August 6, 2010. A version including the political aspects, namely the estimated percentage of hidden income accounted for by corruption, is also available: Wang Xiaolu and Wing Thye Woo, "The Size and Distribution of Hidden Household Income in China," December 25, 2010, available at http://www.econ.ucdavis.edu/faculty/woo/woo.html.

10. All these figures come from Liang Chen, Zhang Hao, Li Lan, Ruan Danching, Cameron Campbell, Yang Shanhua, and James Z. Lee, "Silent Revolution: Research on the Social Origins of Students at Peking University and Suzhou University, 1952–2002," *Chinese Social Science* no. 1 (2012): 98–118.

11. Around 60 euros for one-fifteenth of a hectare.

12. Interview at Sun Yatsen University in Guangzhou, May 2012.

13. Thomas Piketty refers to a phase of "primitive accumulation in France after 1945" in *Les hauts revenus en France au XXe siècle* (Paris: Grassat, 2001), 64.

14. Huo Kan and Wang Changyong, "Survey of the Black Hole of Local Indebtedness," (in Chinese) *Xin Shiji* no. 440 (March 7, 2011), quoted by Thomas Vendryes, "Chinese Local Authority Debt: The Makings of a Crisis?" *China Perspectives* no. 3 (2011), pp. 84–85.

15. President of Brazil, another economy with massive inequality, from 2003 to 2011.

Chapter Three

Separate Worlds

China couldn't seem farther from the Soviet style stagnation reminiscent of the Brezhnev era. It is undergoing a wrenching physical change, as it has become the world's largest source of man-made objects—of almost any kind. For a true grasp of the Bo Xilai/Chongqing affair, we have also to look at its backdrop: a sprawling mushroom city where arrests and suicides take place in the midst of luxurious homes and official apartments, a city swarming with major hotels and night clubs. But it is also one where the local party chief, we learned, chose to live in a military compound. "Us and them," perhaps the catch phrase of the old Soviet Union, applies to China as well.

A RESOUNDING SUCCESS

So far, China has mostly escaped the consequences of the 2008 worldwide financial crisis. It is impossible not to see this as a consequence of the control over its economy and its capital account. The country is led from the top by a party-state, and as one Western economist puts it, in China banks listen to the government. So it must be given some credit for these successes. Moreover, in what country does the prime minister feel forced to promise its foreign partners a *reduction* in trade surpluses? In what country must he demand a *reduction* in economic growth? Premier Zhu Rongji (1998–2002) often found himself in the former position and Wen Jiabao in the latter. Mr. Zhu's promise was never kept, and when Wen made his own pledge in 2012, few observers thought it would become a reality.

At the same time, the regime has touted its rise on the world stage, from the 2008 Olympic Games to space launches. It defines itself more and more often by the Chinese characteristics of its governance. Each of them may not be culturally Chinese, but their combination is unique: monopoly by the Communist Party combined with internal control mechanisms, a hybrid [form of] management that associates state policy with the appeal to private interests and market mechanisms, guidance of public opinion, and at least some responsiveness to deep-rooted social tensions. There are international polls that seem to indicate that 82 percent of the Chinese are satisfied with the "way things are going in their country today."[1] This percentage has remained steady since 2005. These results, for which no methodology is available, may be open to doubt in an authoritarian environment. But how can we not point out that of all the G7 countries, only Germany scored a 50 percent satisfaction rating? In France and the United States, the percentage in 2012 was 29 percent, according to the same study. In short, thanks to economic hyper-growth, the Chinese Communist Party is reputed to be much more popular than the governments of major democracies.

DOUBTS IN PUBLIC OPINION

Nevertheless, at the height of the patriotic fervor in August 2012 over the islands claimed by China and Japan, a Chinese web surfer asked a simple question on Weibo, the Chinese Twitter: "If your child were born in the Diaoyu Islands, would you prefer it to be

Japanese, Taiwanese, a citizen of Hong Kong or continental China?" Before the censor could respond, thousands of answers streamed in, ranking Taiwan first and continental China last, behind Japan! Patriotic consciousness does not rule out a very strong feeling of dissatisfaction and inferiority.[2] This points to the fact that polls conducted by international organizations in China should be viewed with caution.

In fact there is a growing feeling in China that every generation of leaders wields less authority than the previous one. As for the leaders, they display an obsession with security in keeping with their budgets. Often their words reflect the feeling of insecurity of a government intent on preparing for any contingency. China seems to feel threatened by the "three evils"—separatism, terrorism, and religious extremism—but also by a Western plot to undermine the regime. The domestic security budget at 702 billion yuans[3] in 2012, exceeded the military budget (670 billion yuans), which itself has been rising rapidly and steadily for a generation.

Why is certainty accompanied by such a strong feeling of insecurity? Why is an exceptional growth (in thirty-six years the per capita GDP has risen from $278 to $7,000 in 2013) combined with a feeling that nothing is ever enough, and why has there been so much criticism leveraged against the outgoing leadership in their final years of 2010–2012? There are several reasons for this. The central government is in fact less intrusive, leaving some leeway to society and local cadres. Decades of economic boom have also afforded local authorities and society a margin for action that was previously unthinkable. And the ascent of the "collective leadership" to protect the system from a personal autocracy such as Mao had imposed also implies dull and gray politics.

The government—and this is a positive development—intrudes less than before into the daily lives of the Chinese, especially their private lives. Therefore anyone not wishing to speak out or to go public can ignore the government, and will most likely be ignored by it. China has undergone in the past formidable "mass move-ments," phases of mutual denunciation and mandatory self-criti-cism as well as a nearly complete ban on individual interest and even individual psychology during the totalitarian era. Nowadays in many areas of their lives, the Chinese no longer see the hand of politics. Their private lives, their consumption, their entertainment, and their culture involve choices that were unthinkable only twenty years ago, including for urban dwellers the freedom to travel abroad. Freedom of speech outside of government premises and the public place is total. It is possible to live without giving a thought to either the regime or to sensitive topics as long as you do not engage in any public activity such as political criticism or denounc-ing abuses. Also off-limits are religions known to be independent, unofficial labor union activities, and of course the advocacy of other systems or parties. These restrictions matter, but they are far from the situation that existed in Maoist China and endures in North Korea.[4]

And so, like in the Soviet Union, the leaders and the led live in separate worlds. But in China, the leaders have allowed the popula-tion to live away from official requirements in much of its daily life. In 2004 during an official banquet in France, a French political figure asked President Hu Jintao what chance there would be of establishing a system whereby the Chinese president could be elected by universal suffrage. That is impossible, Hu reportedly replied quickly, for most Chinese did not even know his name. Since the death of Deng Xiaoping in 1997, the Chinese, including local cadres, are often heard to express their indifference to the affairs of the national leaders and the central state. Those leaders do not really influence their own existence, and any discussion or conflict at the top takes place behind closed doors. Between the local echelon units and the central government, there is a myriad of intermediary levels, which often exist chiefly for appointing offi-cials. Under the Maoist system it was vitally necessary to have "sponsors" and to belong to a network of political supporters in order to seek protection. Under that system, factional clashes spread from the top down. Patronage and the network of relationships—*guanxi* and *xitong*—are still important in China. At a higher level, namely the level giving access to the Central Committee, they remain more of a decisive factor than the performance criteria put in place by the Party Organization Department.[5] The party's Central Commission for Discipline Inspection can also decide to place any cadres in custody without any legal justification, thereby placing party members suspected of wrongdoings under a so-called "dual regulation" (*shuanggui*) outside the judicial system. Still, these actions are not based solely on factional affiliation, as was often the case with Maoist mass campaigns.

FAR FROM THE CENTER, LIBERALIZATION BY DEFAULT

The central government has always struggled to oversee and control the local echelon units. In the past this was done with mass campaigns encouraging the denunciation of abuses, during which local cadres were "rectified." Today quantitative criteria have been introduced to judge the actions of the cadres. Commentaries often present this method as new. It was reportedly introduced when the local governments were found to be unprepared for the famous SARS epidemic, the bird flu, in 2003. In fact quantitative targets have always been used by the party-state, whether for obvious economic goals or for more specific campaigns—such as the percentage of a given population they target. But creating an evaluation for the cadres based on a number of weighted criteria is indeed new. The well-known Party Organization Department is adopting the methods of human resource departments of major corporations. This step toward management based on objective criteria has its limits.

The apparent indifference of the local cadres to the national political debates is also a form of self-preservation and a façade to present to foreign partners. But the same conclusion is reached by a new wave of foreign researchers, political scientists or sociologists looking for change in China at the local level. They are confirming again an age-old theory on the Chinese bureaucracy—its presence and influence peaks at the top but tends to wane and even disappear at the grassroots level.

The economic boom and the development of a strong informal society favor the fragmentation of government entities.[6] Centrifugal forces also benefit local governments. This is nothing new in Chinese history. One of the greatest dilemmas of the imperial bureaucracy was control over local magistrates and its limited ability to act on a society too vast to be governed directly. Under Maoism, the central government often struggled against "localism" (*difangzhuyi*). It faced disastrous episodes (the end of the Great Leap Forward) or anarchy (at the height of the Cultural Revolution) when the state all but collapsed on the local level. But this time, the very success of reform, the opening up to the outside world, together with the withdrawal of the party-state from many areas of life, have modified the long-term balance between state and society. Even though the central government has vastly improved capacities, increasing local wealth has also created an immense margin for initiative by local cadres. The selling of land rights use for construction has brought in substantial income for local projects. The balance between public authority and individual autonomy has also shifted. Under Maoism, individual franchises were only an exception to the collective rule. Since 1978, any authority not explicitly claimed by the state has de facto withered. Society and the individual have made corresponding gains, even if these are not legal rights. By pulling back, the central government has opened the door to a local life featuring more diverse players: elected local cadres, judges and lawyers, and associations too numerous to be fully controlled from above.

The trend toward devolution of authority also has its negative side. Local governments are threatened by corruption and arbitrary rule, bringing back what Mao was already calling back in 1927[7] "village tyrants" (*tuhao*).

A SHADOW THEATER

On both counts—rebirth of the local society or abuse of power at the local level—the value of the central government is reduced. Its control over those who are in theory its own local agents is diminished, as local government becomes more complex. Nor can it prevent the stirrings of a civil society coming to life again. China is in any case a highly fragmented rather than a decentralized country. Until 1994 it nearly let its tax revenues slip through the fingers of the central government to benefit the local governments. Many analyses, starting with those by Chinese conservatives[8] predicted a breakup of the state or even the country, following an analogy with the former Yugoslavia. However, the state has regained control over taxes, and over other essential issues: ideology and censorship, territorial policy, and the principal economic levers. Yet nearly all careers, for cadres who are not at the top of the pyramid, are spent within one province only. It is not surprising that for a large number of these cadres, and for the urban elites focused on consumption and the global economy, national politics and its official framework are a shadow theater.

Hence liberalization is the result of both a devolution of authority to local levels and a process unfolding by default—everything that is not banned is at least tolerated. This has created a major secondary effect: national leaders and the party-state matter less in the eyes of the people. With the loss in top-down authority, central politics become less important. Chinese political culture is a theater stage: it can exhibit admiration for those who fight injustice and defend the poor, but also worship strength based on personal authority. Transactional politics and bargaining may be a frequent practice, but they are seen as self-interested and not deserving the same respect as absolute authority. Instead, individual revolt is romanticized, and personal authority idolized—all in the same breath!

Sometimes, these trends go hand in hand. To wit, the trajectory of Zhang Yimou, a talented filmmaker who first gained fame with *Qiuju, a Chinese Woman* (1992). This was the story of an ordinary plaintiff crossing all lines by appealing to high party officials for justice against local cadres. But Zhang then made the film *Hero* (2002), a hymn to the despot who united China and founded the Qin dynasty. Still, the theme was counterbalanced with praise for Taoist self-control. In 2008 Zhang Yimou became the official cast director of the Beijing Olympic Games, with its neo-classical set design inspired by the end of the Qing Empire. In twenty years, Zhang has gone from confidence in the integrity of at least high leaders to nostalgia for their imperial predecessors. This is a telling change. Current leaders no longer exude the initial aura of reform, which is often dismissed as just official rhetoric. And they cannot capture to their benefit the nostalgia for past despots and their supposed efficiency.

China's leaders should perhaps be given some credit for their loss of prestige. After all, modern democracies operate in a context where almost all politics is local and transactional, and where individual politicians do not command any cult—in fact, they rarely stay popular through their term in office. In China, a lack of interest in politics and its official standard bearers is actually progress—coming after an omnipresent dictatorship. Conversely, one need only look at the North Korean images of the funeral services in December 2011 for its "Dear Leader" Kim Jong-il, with the hysteria and tears forced on the public, to understand what China has come back from.

COLLECTIVE LEADERSHIP:
A PRECAUTIONARY PRINCIPLE

There is a third reason for the decline in reputation of the officials, despite the success of the reform and opening-up policies. The de-Maoization that followed the Cultural Revolution is not the complete negation of a political regime, but a rejection of some of the excesses brought on by Mao's. This is partial political liberalization. It has left room for his surviving colleagues to return to power in greater force, with a system of collective leadership that strictly limits initiative of all individuals, including the first among them. That trend has gathered pace with the implementation of internal party rules (both written and unwritten) and control mechanisms within the party system. Although Chinese official language speaks of "democracy" in this context, this is far indeed from a separation of powers, or even the notion of liability of the party-state before law. Even a law allowing any citizen to sue the state or its agents before an administrative jurisdiction does not exist in China.[9] Petition and appeal remain informal rights, although they are both widely practiced and fragile.

The revulsion at the consequences of Maoism, and the leaders' quest for security, both personal and political, has had increasingly serious consequences. All the members of the Central Committee appointed in 1956, before the storms unleashed by Mao in the party, were returned to their duties after his death. The list includes both those who had been purged and survived, as well as those who had been kept by Mao until his death. The only losers were those who had been promoted thanks to the Cultural Revolution.

THE END OF THE "STRUGGLE BETWEEN THE TWO LINES"

For the ordinary citizen, de-Maoization meant liberalization. For the party, it was a restoration. Rehabilitating victims was never done at the expense of the leaders in place before the Cultural Revolution, but of those activists and cadres who had been promoted by it. A classic case is the rehabilitation decided in December 1978, which benefited not only the victims of the Cultural Revolution but also those of the anti-rightist movement of 1957. A central leader, Peng Zhen, was put in charge of that "reversal of verdicts." Yet he and Deng Xiaoping had themselves been promoters of the anti-rightist movement. The removal of Maoist ideology from politics ended twenty-one years of upheaval and insecurity, returning the party to what it saw as its golden age from 1952 to 1956, its only period of relative quiet and stability within the bureaucracy.

Tiananmen and the crisis of 1989 represent the start of a second stage, which Deng Xiaoping had actually already begun in the fall of 1986. At that time he had already disavowed the political liberalization plans of one of his two key lieutenants, Hu Yaobang. On several occasions, first in the artistic and intellectual area, and then in the arena of political debate, Hu Yaobang had attempted to go further, and may have assumed that Deng would follow. But, in 1986 and in 1989, Deng sought Party unity with the conservatives at the expense of reformers, dumping successively his two main lieutenants—Hu Yaobang in January 1987 and Zhao Ziyang in June 1989. Deng saw high-level divisions within the party, the interplay of factions and open discussion, as responsible for the Tiananmen crisis. Conflicting views and indecisiveness had encouraged the demonstrators, endangering the regime. Indeed, today we forget that in 1989 the army was initially divided over the issue of martial law, much as it had been decided by Deng. The Standing Committee of the National People's Congress had the theoretical right, according to the Constitution, to revoke martial law. Some of its members attempted to call an emergency meeting. Just back from a trip to the United States, Wan Li, the more liberal chairman of the National People's Congress, was even delayed for some days in Shanghai "for health reasons" in order to prevent that possibility.

In short, from 1986 to May–June 1989, the party gave signs of breaking up. A legal coup nearly took place, which would have allowed the national legislature (which until then was a rump parliament) to stay a decision by the party. Against that risk, Deng reinforced even more the collective nature of the leadership to prevent the interplay of political factions or ideologies. One of the measures taken, as early as 1987, was to broaden the definition of state secrets, focusing first of all on information regarding top-level debate—which until then had leaked quite liberally to the Hong Kong media, for example. China's "black box," or the secrecy surrounding decision making at the top, was born then.

Gradual reforms and the opening-up policy would resume in 1992. Deng then started a race for foreign investment, and his designated successor, Jiang Zemin, would raise the level of China's international cooperation. But rallying around a "central core" of leaders and maintaining silence regarding differences at the top have remained the rule. For a second time after the experience of the Cultural Revolution, historical memory—this time concerning 1989—has been erased from the official accounts. To prevent the upheavals inherent in the system of "line struggles" practiced by Mao, the party outlawed them, and any memory of them.

THE "BLACK BOX"

With Hu Jintao's rise to power in 2002 another step has been taken. Deng himself had identified and promoted Hu within the so-called "fourth generation" of leaders, but Hu also had to make peace with the veterans of the previous generation, starting with Jiang Zemin himself. To date, all the rumors since 2002 concerning the closing of Jiang's personal office, his illness, and his imminent death have turned out to be unfounded. Evidently unlike Deng after 1984 and even Jiang, Hu has only been first among equals within the collective leadership. By emphasizing the procedures and customs (such as the age limit) of the collective leadership, by recommending "harmony" over any other value, Hu has attempted to limit even more the political risks inherent in the party's internal conflicts.

That approach has paid off. With no constitutional separation of powers, which are all subject to the party, China has enjoyed a second decade of political stability. It has even introduced the appearance of predictability regarding the political succession process. As early as 2007, observers were convinced of the names of the successors implicitly appointed for 2012 (Xi Jinping and Li Keqiang) after two five-year terms for the leading tandem. True aficionados of Chinese politics were betting instead on the names of their potential successors—in 2022, for what would be the "sixth generation" of leaders! Leading the pack, Hu Chunhua, the head of Inner Mongolia, from the party's Youth League, and Sun Zhengcai, the head of Jilin (northeastern China), former minister of agriculture, were set to race to the finish line by 2022. A time machine has been invented, returning the party to the year 1956. Observers credit the same time machine with controlling the future as well, mapping out in advance not just one, but two successive cycles of power, each lasting ten years each.

There are sociological analyses of top-level politics, the most popular opposing "princelings" or children of high-level leaders with those who have gone up the ranks from the party's Youth League, a key entry point in official politics. There are also generational analyses (after revolutionaries come engineers, and after engineers, managers or law graduates). But next to nothing had been learned about the discussions at the top of the party since 1989, and nothing since 2002. If any remaining factional alignments were as strong as the cleavage between conservatives and reformers before 1989, there is no way to know this. Politics at the center of the country has become a "black box."

NOTES

1. Poll 2011, Pew Global Attitudes Project, Pew Research Center, http://www.pewglobal.org/database/?indicator=3http://www.pewglobal.org/diatabase/?indicator=3&group=11&response=Satisfied.

2. This poll, which can be viewed on http://vote.weibo.com/vid=1960887&source=feed (accessed August 23, 2012) was also reported by Helen Gao, "Diaoyu in Our Heart: The Revealing Contradictions of Chinese Nationalism," *Atlantic*, August 22, 2012, http://www.theatlantic.com/international/archive/2012/08/diaoyu-in-our-heart-the-revealing-contradictions-of-Chinese-nationalism/261422/.

3. This figures includes both law enforcement expenses and also the more extensive expenses for the "preservation of stability or '*weiwen*,'": for example, surveillance of the Internet and public opinion. It also includes local government expenses.

4. Juan Linz, the dean of the transitional school of political science, wrote a good description of this slow change by European regimes: Juan J. Linz, *Totalitarian and Authoritarian Regimes* (Boulder, CO: Lynne Rienner, 2000).

5. Victor Shih, Christopher Adolph, and Mingxing Liu, "Getting Ahead in the Communist Party: Explaining the Advancement of Central Committee Members in China," *American Political Science Review* 106, no. 1 (2012): 166–87.

6. Kenneth G. Lieberthal, "The 'Fragmented Authoritarianism' Model and Its Limitations," in *Bureaucracy, Politics and Decision Making in Post-Mao China*, ed. Kenneth G. Lieberthal and David M. Lampton (Berkeley: University of California Press, 1992).

7. Mao Tse Tung, "Report on an Investigation of the Peasant Movement in Hunan," 1927.

8. Wang Shan, *Di sanzhiyanjing kan Zhomgguo* [The third eye looks at China] (Taiyuan: Shanxi People's Press, 1994).

9. In France, the right for citizens to challenge state actions in an administrative court—not in ordinary justice proceedings—was affirmed only in 1873, eighty-four years after the French revolution. See http://www.legifrance.gouv.fr/affichJuriAdmin.do?idTexte=CETATEXT000007605886&dateTexte=.

Chapter Four

Crossing the River, or the Impossible Political Transition

Occasionally, news or rumors leak out from high-level government circles regarding the leaders' children ("princelings") being put in charge of the economy or enjoying a lavish lifestyle; and occasionally their private lives spill over into the public sphere. Mistresses are an inexhaustible topic of discussion, but, until recently, below the supreme echelon of government. The eighteen simultaneous affairs attributed to Liu Zhijun, the railway minister overthrown in 2011, set an all-time record. On the other hand, in 1999 the mayor of Daqing (the oil city in northeastern China) was accused by an investigative journalist of keeping twenty-nine mistresses at the same time.[1] There is also the saga of the French-Vietnamese Li Wei, nicknamed "public mistress" by China's leading financial weekly. She became a rich businesswoman after her alleged affairs with a governor of Yunnan, a vice mayor of Beijing in charge of the Olympic Games, the CEO of Sinopec (the company with the second largest market capitalization in the world at the time), the minister of finance, and others, many others.[2] Many of her lovers are now in prison for corruption, often for life, but Li Wei was given safe conduct to Hong Kong.

THE PREFERENCE FOR STABILITY

This Chinese version of human excesses in the political realm is no substitute for a good political analysis. The antics characterizing private lives merely emphasize the colorless nature of politics. Here the notion of an inexorable "Brezhnevian stagnation" makes sense, at least from a political standpoint. The Hu-Wen collective leadership government increasingly shielded itself from the discussions swirling below it—unlike in the 1980s when, in the Maoist tradition, competing wings of the party either inspired or provided protection from the media and from public intellectuals. The fact that it became impossible to discern the individual positions of the leaders is obviously one way to keep the peace among them. Hu Jintao in particular insisted on cultivating ambiguity. The fact that the central leaders are far removed from local affairs and society facilitates their de facto immunity.

Exceptions to this immunity have been rare, reflecting the persistence of personal factions. They appear in periods of political tension. In 1995, Chen Xitong, the Beijing party boss, a native of Sechuan like Deng, was purged for corruption just as Jiang Zemin was freeing himself from the grip of Deng's close associates after Deng's death. In 2006, Chen Liangyu, the Shanghai party chief, a close associate of Jiang Zemin, was accused of corruption at a time when the Hu-Wen tandem was shifting its focus to growth and investment in inland China as opposed to Jiang's Shanghai and coastal faction. Chen Xitong and Chen Liangyu were accused of corruption and sentenced to prison, while lower-level officials often receive death sentences. No official mention was made of any departure from the official line, or of any factional activity.

Stability, pacification, risk avoidance—every generation of leaders since the end of the Cultural Revolution has further refined these guidelines. All in all, for a Leninist party whose political culture is rooted in violence, these concepts represent the equivalent of the principle of precaution forbidding risky scientific experiments in democratic societies.

MANY CONFLICTS, LITTLE VIOLENCE

This brings us to a paradox: The heirs of the turmoil of violent revolution that caused millions of deaths after the Communist takeover are now the embodiment of order and stability. This is reminiscent of the doctrine of political Confucianism, which prefers order to justice—precisely what the Chinese had rebelled against from the time of the May 4, 1919, movement until Mao's famous maxim launching the Cultural Revolution: "It is right to rebel."

There is no doubt that Chinese society fears two forms of chaos (*luan*). First of all it fears a void in government or public administration: barbarity lurks on the margins of order. The second has to do with factional struggle and civil war, whether it be the Cultural Revolution or the conflicts among independent kingdoms—or whenever more than one power center existed and mobilized society to their own ends.

Through an extraordinary reversal, the party-state can now make use of this fear of chaos. It stands as a guarantor of order in opposition to a violence that is inherent in society and against the political unrest that would result if a full-fledged democracy were established. Because Mao had manipulated the "great democracy"—that is, appealing to the masses and inciting them to violence—the very idea of social or political conflict was discredited by his successors.

Yet China is still prone to conflict, especially in society's relationship with local governments, as witnessed by the steady rise in the number of "mass incidents," a generic term applied to riots, as well as demonstrations and strikes. The figures do as much to reveal the rigidity of the institutions as the propensity for public protest, whether violent or not. In 1993, the police identified fewer than nine thousand such incidents. In 2005, eighty-seven thousand.

In 2010, for lack of government statistics, a well-informed sociologist estimated the number at one hundred eighty thousand.[3] Many of these incidents are related to the defense of individual or collective rights.

This explains why in some cases public opinion believes the use of violence is justified. Thus, some extremely violent individual acts have become popular causes in the past few years. Yang Jia, an out-of-work youth who, after being arrested and beaten by the police in Shanghai in 2008, took it out on a police station and killed six policemen, was viewed with surprising sympathy before being sentenced to death and executed. Indeed, police brutality is feared by the population. Deng Yujiao, a young woman who stabbed one of the local cadres who raped her in a hotel in 2009, was acquitted after an Internet campaign defending her. More seriously, a series of brutal attacks on nursery schools between March and May 2010, again perpetrated by single individuals, caused dozens of victims among the schoolchildren. The authorities had to forbid publicizing these acts in order to prevent copy cats. This epidemic can undoubtedly be explained by the extreme frustration of a society where marriage is contingent on financial resources and lineage.

The surge in Internet forums has also led to the boom in "human flesh search engines" (*renrou sousuo*): specialized sites where vigilantes by the thousands surf the web, unleashing manhunts against targets introduced by one of them. The resurgence of Maoist mass movements is evident here; even the party's official phrasing once referred to the "excesses" of such movements. The importance and number of protest movements, the existence of cases of extreme violence, and the virtual unleashing of passions on the social networks reveal a society still in the grip of strong tensions.

Although prone to conflict, especially with authority, on the whole Chinese society is not that violent. After rising for thirty years, the number of serious crimes remains low. However, as is the case for many statistics, the figures for homicides vary in what can only be described as sheer fantasy. Unchanged, falling, or rising? In 2005, 31,000 homicides were supposedly reported, including 20,000 murders—a round number from the Ministry of Public Security repeated in the Blue Paper on the Law of China's Academy of Social Sciences, and frequently quoted since then. But in 2008, a UN report identified 14,811 homicides based on China's official statistics, or 1.1 homicides per 100,000 inhabitants.[4] That rate would be below the rate of 1.4 reported in France in 2008, four times lower than India, six times lower than in Indonesia, twenty times lower than in Brazil, and so on. As usual with China, the figures are still uncertain. Thus China is announcing a rate of close to 90 percent of homicide cases solved. But this figure is strangely incompatible with the announcement made by the Ministry of Public Security of a national campaign ending in 2011 with the arrest of twelve thousand murder suspects.[5] Whether there are 14,000 or 30,000 homicides a year in China, this rate is below that of nearly all the other emerging or developing countries, and also below that in Russia or the United States.

SOCIETY'S MORAL AWAKENING

Traditionally, Chinese society is considered passive and publicly indifferent to violence or suffering. The great progressive writer and critic Lu Xun has denounced this culture of indifference (*kanke wenhua*), for example at public executions, which people attended without saying a word. But we must beware of hasty generalizations. The culture of indifference still exists, but the social networks have also created a culture of righteous indignation opposed to that very traditional passivity. In October 2010, the tragedy of Yue Yue, a two-year-old girl run over in Foshan by several vehicles in a row while no passersby intervened, was revealing—thanks also to the surveillance cameras on location. A few months earlier, the discovery of another child in a railway car forty-eight hours after the Wenzhou high-speed train accident (and very shortly before the train was hastily buried at the site) also stirred emotions. These stories have made the rounds in China, arousing collective revulsion at the state of a society that shows no mercy toward the weak. Passivity and inaction in the face of the suffering of others are in the Chinese tradition. But indignation on the social networks is something new, and it is reviving the criticism of traditional society and authority. The tragedy of the earthquake in Sichuan in 2008, where thousands of children died in schools built with cheap bricks, aroused indignation that the authorities had trouble quelling.

Chinese society is also returning to some forms of charitable activism to make up for the government's shortcomings. One has only to look at the nongovernmental organizations and volunteers rushing to help the victims of the 2008 earthquake in Sichuan. The Chinese are going back to the tradition of private charity. In pre-Communist China, philanthropy from the rich—particularly the merchant class, which wanted to gain consideration—coexisted with a more general passivity in Chinese society. During the great famines of the first half of the twentieth century, merchant associations, churches, and local Red Cross units were very active—much more so at the time than in Japan, where the legacy of feudal distinctions resulted in stronger barriers among social categories.

Hence it is misleading to present Chinese society today as being intrinsically chaotic or amoral and the authorities as the only uniting principle liable to contribute order and stability. Yet by presenting itself as a bulwark against chaos the regime justifies the political status quo and the preference for a "harmonious society" as an alternative to the interplay of political and social forces. Moreover, like any state, it retains a legal monopoly on the use of violence, a most effective political deterrent against protesters.

THE DEATH PENALTY: A MISUNDERSTANDING

The situation with regard to the death penalty in China is a good illustration of the responsibilities of society versus those of the government. But here a misunderstanding persists. People believe that China makes such a common practice of applying the death penalty because society is very much in favor of it, like in Asia as a whole. According to the proponents of culturalism, values in Asia are completely different from values in Europe, where the death penalty has been abolished, and even in the United States, where there are highly conflicting opinions.

Yet this prejudice is correct on one point only: it is true that the death penalty is widely applied in China. But the consensus concerning it is much more limited than one might believe. The death penalty is still more prevalent in China than in any country in the world. The Dui Hua (Dialogue) Foundation estimates the number of executions at five thousand in 2009, only seven hundred of them[6] showing signs of government involvement. That figure fell to four thousand in 2011, owing to the mandatory procedure for the review of individual sentences by the Supreme People's Court established in 2007: well-informed sources reveal that this measure alone has cut in half the number of executions since it was adopted and that the Court quashes around 10 percent of the death penalty sentences handed down.[7] In 2011, as a result of an official debate on the use of the death penalty for economic crimes, the number of death penalty counts fell from sixty-eight to fifty-five. This reduction includes relatively minor offenses such as stealing historic art works or VAT tax fraud! By way of comparison, the courts of Victorian England had two hundred counts for sentencing someone to death (including cutting down trees and destroying rabbiting terriers, etc.), and the Qing dynasty criminal code listed eight hundred fifty, including defending the family order.

But is the death penalty really that popular? Some rapid and relatively unscientific opinion polls taken in 1995 and 2005 seemed to indicate so. Yet a recent and much more serious survey conducted in Beijing and in the provinces of Hubei and Guangdong refutes these impressions, unless they indicate an important recent change.[8] For want of a valid system of measurement for China as a whole, the survey indicates that public opinion in these three regions is only 57.8 percent in favor of the death penalty. That percentage is lower than in the United States, far below that in Japan and South Korea, and even below polls conducted in Europe: in Europe, opposition to the death penalty became the majority view only after it had been abolished. When the question is asked by category of crime or criminal offense, a majority appears to favor the death penalty only in cases of murder, rape of a minor, and drug trafficking. For all other criminal offenses, from terrorism to espionage, including rape, corruption, fraud, and tainted medicine or food, public opinion is largely opposed to the death penalty. Two-thirds of the Chinese also claim not to know the number of capital executions in their country—and rightly so since that information is kept secret. Two-thirds of the respondents also feel this figure should be made public. When asked about the suggestion to abolish the death penalty (with life sentence as an alternative), most Chinese approve abolishing it. The slight majority in favor of the death penalty can be explained primarily by the need for vengeance; therefore approval is concentrated on blood crimes. In traditional China, most people believed in the notion of vengeance—*bao-chou*—and that still holds true today.

This means our cultural prejudices about Asia have to be reconsidered. Death-penalty cases are down considerably, even though the death penalty has not been abolished.[9] In Singapore, the country more inclined to use capital executions than any other country in the world, the number has been divided by ten since 2005, and as of 2012 the death penalty is no longer automatic for drug trafficking or for unpremeditated murder.[10] This measure followed an unprecedented local opinion campaign to obtain a pardon for a young drug trafficker from Malaysia.

In what way are these Chinese and Asian debates on the death penalty important for the political system? They reveal a society different from what was prescribed by tradition—and Western public opinion. There is no longer such a thing as "traditional" society, no obvious consensus in favor of the rigorous exercise of authority. Despite the many political and social conflicts in China, the stereotype of a society so violent that it needs the protection of a dictatorship must be reconsidered.

The division of opinion on the death penalty also reveals defiance toward the authorities. A large majority of Chinese believe the death penalty is applied more to the poor than to the rich. Does opposition to the death penalty in crimes other than murder or drug trafficking also reflect such distrust? A recent case could illustrate the reasons. In Wenzhou, a region known as the capital of clandestine loans in China, a rich businesswoman, Wu Ying, reported to have become at age thirty-one the sixth-richest person in China, was threatened with execution for her role in clandestine financing. Such financing is a scourge throughout the system, and Wu Ying incriminated the local authorities. More than anything, her death sentence was undoubtedly a way to silence her for good and to punish the person responsible for bringing the scandal to light. In March 2012, Premier Wen referred to her case, pointing a finger at the networks of clandestine lenders and urging the courts to "seek the truth in the facts." Then Wen launched the offensive against Bo Xilai and the methods inherited from the Cultural Revolution. In April, the Supreme Court struck down the death sentence against Wu Ying. This raised the hopes of legalists and reformers. In May, the same local court once again sentenced Wu Ying to death but with a two-year stay of execution, suggesting the possibility of a commuted sentence. On that date, the regime hushed up any debate following the Chongqing affair. The timing is telling. Wu Ying's

fate, symbolic of death penalty issues, has changed with the ups
and downs at the highest level of the party.

IMMUNITY AT THE TOP

At the top, in any event, the regime has banned executions, whether
legal or not. Since 1978 not a single leader has been killed, and
important cadres are rarely sentenced to death. That is also why the
thirteen death sentences handed down during Bo Xilai's anti-mafia
campaign were a source of concern in Chinese political circles.
Even the lives of the ultra-Maoist "Gang of Four," tried in 1979,
were spared. Since then, in the rare cases in which senior leaders
have been dismissed, they have usually remained members of the
party. Only two midlevel cadres have been executed, both for corruption: a deputy speaker of the National Assembly in 1998, and a
director of the food and drug safety agency in 2008, after fraud and
poisoning scandals that rocked the country. As we have seen, this
trend does not hold for subordinates, but there again, death penalties are generally commuted. Below that level, the death penalty is
frequently applied.

In short, the regime no longer uses the old methods of political
struggle against itself, nor does it resort to physical eliminations
within the regime. On the other hand, ordinary justice remains
harsh indeed and is based on the fear of violence and social chaos.
One can only assume that stability and legitimacy depend on a form
of immunity for leaders, who contain their factional and personal
differences within limits.

But by putting a stop to the mechanism of political campaigns
and the mass mobilization associated with it, the party has also lost
its levers of ideological influence over Chinese society. Of course
the instruments of coercion are there and, as we shall see, they have
been thoroughly updated to include more sophisticated control and
communications technologies. The "material incentives" (*wuzhi*

jianli), marginal bonuses during the Maoist era, have become a compelling basis for legitimizing the regime on the grounds of its economic growth. But Maoism had governed China with the help of mass movements driven by ideological campaigns. Those campaigns targeted real or imaginary opponents, rallying most of the population against them while at the same time promoting the "activists" (*jijifenzi*), in other words the most determined and unscrupulous of the participants. The verb "to struggle" had become transitive as in "to struggle someone"—that is, making him a target of a mass movement.

At times that strategy had an effect bordering on magic, creating a mass catharsis. It often called for manipulation and deception, and scapegoating was a vital component. That was how politics operated for two generations of Chinese, from the civil war to the Cultural Revolution. During the latter period, in particular, that strategy gave most of the educated urban youth the illusion of freedom along with the notion that they had a political role to play, such as fighting "bureaucratization" (*guanliaohua*). It also provided a Manichean interpretation of the new society, one with an absolute view of good and evil.

The people who restored the collective leadership and the party of 1956 banned both the "great liberties" of the Cultural Revolution, in the name of which so much violence had been committed, and brought security to the vast majority of the population. The very engine of change during the Maoist era—the group dynamic based on the "mass line," manipulation and violence—was set aside.

However, one might ask: What about the fact that the regime itself openly practices violent repression in some cases, such as the Lhasa demonstrations in March 2008, and the community riots in Urumqi in July 2009? In the former case, the regime argues that it reacted to violent demonstrations, which is correct, even though that does not excuse the crackdown against the Tibetan clergy. In the latter case, it is undeniable that the clashes between Han and Uighurs in Urumqi turned violent on both sides, with fatal knifings and lynchings. Death sentences were handed down on both sides of the ethnic barrier. Bearing the marks of modern-day communitarianism rather than classic separatism, these incidents originated with the lynching of Uighur immigrants wrongly accused of rape in a plant-dormitory in Guangdong, three thousand kilometers from Urumqi. The Han responsible for the incident was also sentenced to death. In this case the regime justifies the violent crackdown on the grounds of preserving stability.

Because of the preference for stability and risk avoidance as well as the rejection of party-line struggles, the regime has curbed the reform process undertaken after the Maoist era. The official slogans were the first things to go. The Maoist regime had worshiped at the altar of the will. Deng's successors, more so than Deng himself, replaced it with the worship of precautionary experimentation. At the outset, this meant a reform method in stages. In the end, precaution and conservatism won over. Party unity coincides with the search for the greatest common denominator within, which increasingly involves vested interests.

THE INVENTION OF A SLOGAN

The ambivalence between change and the status quo is reflected in the very slogans of the times. Just think of the origin of the most famous watchword of the reform era, which is often wrongly attributed to Deng Xiaoping: "Crossing the river by feeling for the stones" (*moshi guohe*). The wording is a masterpiece of political balance and ambiguity. The precaution in this policy is obviously opposed to Maoist adventurism (even though Mao himself introduced the practice of experiments designed to become models for the entire country). This practice is also opposed to radical reform—the big-bang or shock therapy approach to liberalization recommended after 1989 for Russia and Eastern Europe. Even so, it does suggest crossing to the other side of the river. The slogan is intentionally cryptic and actually plays both sides of the river—expressing hope for a new era on the one hand, and hope for maintaining control of the party on the other hand.

However, China is still fording the river, despite or because of its economic successes. Thirty-five years after Mao's death, the party, the regime, and its high-level institutions have changed very little. The market economy is still dominated by powerful government players, and economic openness has even declined in the past few years. With a few notable exceptions, society can no longer even refer to the tragic aspects of the Maoist era. Ranging from the mass campaigns of the first year until the Great Leap and the Cultural Revolution, most have been hushed up. Since then, the Tiananmen Square protests and massacre of 1989 also have become taboo. Those events are associated with a generation of leaders who were either active or passive accomplices. By closing the curtain on those aspects of the past, the regime has seen to it that new generations will know nothing of them. This way they can accept an indefinite present in which the blossoming of the individual exists side by side with collective censorship. Thus the transition has become endless. Between two banks of the river, with Maoism on one side and the rule of law on the other, the entity crossing, in this case the collective leadership, has stuck the boat in the middle of the river.

This was not always the case in the collective history of Chinese Communism, which was known to heap praise on other long crossings. For Maoist China the Long March was the equivalent of the battle of Thermopylae for ancient Greece—a heroic symbol. It is also an epic myth replete with adventurous river crossings by guerillas on the move. One incident in particular, said to involve the taking of a chain bridge over the Dadu River in 1935, is immortalized in numerous paintings and illustrations celebrating the exploit, and emphasizing audacity and speed, as opposed to the risks of procrastination. In truth, it matters little that the last witnesses found after 1976 refer in the end to the complicity between a local warlord and his officers, who reportedly left the bridge poorly defended; the fight did take place but it was a minor skirmish. [11] The myth served as a political weapon used by Mao to extend the role of activism and willpower well beyond the Communist takeover, imposing an "uninterrupted revolution" (*buduangeming*) on his colleagues and his country.

Thus, choosing the image of crossing a river was an unusual contrast meant to symbolize the China of reform and openness. The expression "feeling for the stones to cross the river" has come to symbolize the supposed gradual and pragmatic nature of reform in China since 1978.

However, as is often the case in the repertory of official Chinese maxims, appearances are deceiving. *Moshi guohi* was in fact used for the first time in 1950 by a veteran of the regime, Chen Yun, to indicate the need for caution in establishing the new Communist regime at the local level. He used the metaphor again in December 1978, this time to criticize the "small Great Leap Forward" (*xiao dayuejin*), launched in February of the same year by Hua Guofeng, Mao's designated successor, with an ambitious ten-year production plan. Hence the expression in itself does not mean a reformist policy, but an end to the Maoist-era policy of voluntary mobilization. Moreover, Deng Xiaoping never used it in public. Chen Yun, the only one of the first generation of leaders trained in political economics, was a strong advocate of the plan and the state, even though in 1962 he encouraged consideration of Khrushchevian reforms. He had defended the revamping of the Chinese economy in the middle of the Great Leap disaster, speaking then of "taking the entire country as a chess board." He also fought the shift to a new market economy. He was famous for summing up relations between the state and the market with the metaphor of the cage and the bird: the cage must be big enough to allow the bird to fly, but its door must remain closed. Starting in 1985, he came to oppose many of the economic liberalization measures taken by the reformers. Thus it is the cautious advice from someone totally lacking in a spirit of adventure that has come to symbolize the method for change.

REVERSIBILITY, A WEAPON OF THE PARTY

This kind of misunderstanding is encouraged both by the ambiguity of classical Chinese maxims—*chengyu* or expressions generally containing four characters—and by ignorance or by the failure to remember the context from which they are often drawn. China's political history is replete with such misunderstandings, but at times they were deliberately encouraged, including by Mao. Thus his famous liberal maxim of the spring of 1956, "May a hundred flowers bloom"—the anti-rightist campaign that was to follow in June 1957 denounced on the contrary "poisonous weeds" and persecuted hundreds of thousands of intellectuals and cadres deemed "right-wing."

Mao was accustomed to that game. When Edgar Snow, the famous author who told the story of the Long March, went to visit him in 1970, he described himself modestly as "a solitary monk walking under his leaky umbrella." When reading that, foreign sinologists believed that Mao was about to die. Snow was unable to understand the different possible meanings of an expression delivered through an interpreter. By referring to the monk under an umbrella, Mao used a Taoist metaphor making a man who is directly exposed to Heaven the equal of any emperor. The expression undoubtedly refers to the founder of the Ming dynasty, the former wandering monk and rebel Zhu Yuanzhang, known by the name of Emperor Hongwu. There is another verse Mao was fond of: *wufaw-utian*, or "without hair and without sky" or tonsured like a monk.

As the character for "law" is pronounced *fa,* the expression also means "without law and without sky," in other words all-powerful. The dictator was an anarchist when it served his purposes, harking back to the imperial privilege of practicing his own private religion.

Mao is not the last of the leaders to have included ambiguity as well as reversibility in his statements. As heirs of the system, some current leaders may also engage in political double talk to leave themselves the option of choices and reversals (sometimes to the point of caricature and perhaps not without a certain irony). It is worth noting that during his trip to the United States in February 2012, Xi Jinping, at that time the presumptive successor and himself the son of a top leader, resorted to exactly the same expressions. Discussing US-China relations at the White House, he explained: "We can only do what Mr. Deng Xiaoping said: 'Cross the river while feeling for the stones.' Or what Secretary of State Clinton once said: 'When you're facing a mountain, you find a way to cross it. When you're blocked by a river, you find a bridge to the other side.' A Chinese pop star sings: 'May I ask where the road is? It's where you take your first step.'"[12] None of these sayings is original. The first one, as we have seen, is not from Deng Xiaoping. The second one, although attributed by Xi's speech to Hillary Clinton, is a more or less faithful paraphrase of the Mao of the Long March—and his voluntarism. And lastly, the third one, attributed to a pop singer, makes special reference to one of the best-known quotes by the Taoist philosopher Laozi.

The most famous statement by Deng Xiaoping, a master of hidden meanings, is "It doesn't matter if a cat is white or black if it catches mice," which Deng said during the famine of the Great Leap Forward to justify the disastrous return to individual agriculture (many collectives having collapsed at the local level). It contains other misunderstandings, even though none is as misleading as the Maoist maxims. The context was that of a temporary retreat from collectivism in June 1962, not an apology for market capitalism. In fact it was during the Cultural Revolution that this expression was termed a capitalist blasphemy in order to better criticize Deng. In foreign policy, Deng's famous *taoguangyanghui*, generally translated as "hiding one's talents and waiting for the right time," is in fact even more ambiguous. Literally it means "fleeing clarity and seeking obscurity,"[13] which one will agree is hardly conducive to international trust. It was published on or after September 1989 (around the time China was on the defensive after the Tiananmen crisis), and it is not even certain that Deng himself said it.[14]

The Communist Chinese generation of steel, the generation that lived through the civil war and established the dictatorship of the proletariat, was well versed in the ideological struggle, its slogans and its sudden reversals. After Deng, his successors did not use the same instruments. Doubtless, they were aware of the danger that one of those instruments might revive the old methods of struggle and violence.

LEAVING BEHIND THE REVOLUTIONARY LIE

Hu and Wen have not launched any major movements, either for reform, like Deng, or to "correct" the cadres and the ideology, like Mao. On the other hand, since they promise less, their political attitude means progress compared to their predecessors. Hu and Wen are ambiguous, but they have not indulged in lies as a political weapon. This is reminiscent of an old debate between French philosophers Maurice Merleau-Ponty and Jean-Paul Sartre on "bourgeois morality." For Sartre, "bourgeois" morality was only a façade and therefore did not exist, while Merleau-Ponty preferred quoting La Rochefoucauld: "Hypocrisy is the homage that vice pays to virtue."

People often fail to appreciate the exception represented by Jiang Zemin himself, Deng's successor, who was also a colorless leader but without drastically changing course. Their predecessors had been chameleons under Mao. For decades, Mao had designed a strategy around his ability to shift with lightning speed from "right" to "left" on any subject, going so far as to hold well-known sting operations such as the party's first internal rectification movement in Yenan, during which in 1941 and 1942 a number of intellectuals who had rejoined the CCP were encouraged to express themselves and then punished, or the Hundred Flowers campaign of 1956–1957, which ensnared a generation of students, intellectuals, and urban cadres in the subsequent anti-rightist crackdown. And lastly the Cultural Revolution and its Red Guards, who were first used against Mao's rivals and then rejected in turn. In July 1968, when leaders of five groups of Red Guards came to complain to Mao about the "black hand" controlling the counterattacks on them from a distance, Mao lashed out, "The black hand, that's me."[15] His alter ego, Zhou Enlai, who had become the iconic protector of the survivors of the intellectual establishment after the Cultural Revolution, was just as complex. His reputation as a protector was due to the fact that during the Revolution he chaired the Central Case Examination Group, which decided with the utmost meticulousness on the targets of the movement and their fate. Zhou had the power to spare some people because he exercised his sentencing power first.[16]

These abrupt changes are not only personal attributes; they are part of the revolutionary political arsenal. Deng Xiaoping himself is the product of an implacable history. He fought in the Sino-Japanese war as a political commissar of the Second Field Army led by Lin Biao, Mao's heir apparent, who was purged in 1971. Suddenly, after 1978, Deng was to use the officers from that same group, which had lost favor after Lin Biao's downfall, to help him control the People's Liberation Army over competing factions. As the first leader joining the central authority since 1949 and a close associate of Mao's, he, along with the mayor of Beijing, Peng Zhen, was put in charge of the anti-rightist campaign, in other words the purge of hundreds of thousands of intellectuals.[17] Whether by luck or design, at the time of the first differences over the Great Leap Forward unleashed by Mao, he, along with Chen Yun, missed the Lushan meeting in July 1959. It was the most important senior echelon debate in the history of the People's Republic since 1949, ending with the disgrace of the minister of defense, Peng Dehuai. Deng was highly favored by Mao in the months that followed, and only later would he come to criticize Mao. Much later, in October 1986, Deng Xiaoping's own lieutenant, Hu Yaobang, expressed concern about the fact that Deng was dragging his feet on political reform and the separation of the party and the state. Hu even led a campaign for political liberalization, namely in the Shenzhen special economic zone. Two articles came out in the local press that added fuel to the fire. One of them called on Deng Xiaoping to retire.[18] That article is considered one of the main reasons for the fall of Hu Yaobang in January 1987. The other article, published in the local organ of the Communist Youth League, was nearly as important. It tells about the Lushan episode and Deng's absence on that critical day when Mao crushed the critics of his personal power over the party. In other words, when Deng withdrew his support for political reform, Hu Yaobang reminded him of his previous ambivalence. One cannot help noting that it was also in Shenzhen in August 2010 that Wen Jiabao called for the revival of political reform.

Compared to Mao or even to Deng, Jiang Zemin and the Hu-Wen tandem have been peaceful political leaders, whether by inclination or by necessity. China's international claims did not lead to any major armed confrontations, despite the irritation and the many incidents it caused. Open conflicts and political mobilization were systematically avoided as a means of resolving rivalries within the government. Ambivalent political speeches were also the sign of an increasingly centrist approach in Chinese policy. This was combined with an effort to design standards and rules to guarantee a collegial government, balancing the different echelons and giving the government a tight control over a more limited area, releasing others from its grip.

But this effort to regulate the course of history and abolish what authoritarian regimes fear the most—the unexpected—has been challenged on two fronts since 2009. First by political reform, the advocates of which now spoke out more loudly than ever, and second by nationalism, which began to exert visible pressure from within and outside the leadership.

NOTES

1. The report by journalist Jiang Weiping published in July 1999 in the magazine *Qianxian* [Avant-garde] in Beijing is available in English at Committee to Protect Journalists, http://cpj.org/awards/2001/jiang.php#jiang1. Thereafter, Jiang Weiping spent six years in prison and now lives in Hong Kong.

2. Profile in *Caijing*, February 19, 2011, http://blog.caijing.com.cn/expert_article-151485-17010.shtml, accessed February 11, 2012.

3. Sun Liping, a professor at Beijing University, *Jingjiguanchabao*, February 25, 2012.

4. United Nations Office on Drugs and Crime, *Global Study on Homicide: Trends, Context, Data* (Vienna: Author, 2011), 94.

5. Xinhua dispatch of December 17, 2011, http://www.china.org.cn/china/2011-12/17/content_24181121.htm.

6. "After One Year, Dui Hua Uncovers 700 Executions in China," Dui Hua Foundation, November 27, 2010, http://duihua.org/wp/?p=2383, accessed February 12, 2012.

7. "Dui Hua Estimates 4,000 Executions in China, Welcomes Open Dialogue," Dui Hua Foundation, December 12, 2011, http://duihua.org/wp/?page_id=3874.

8. Dietrich Oberwittler and Qi Shenghui, "Public Opinion on the Death Penalty in China: Results from a General Population Survey Conducted in Three Provinces in 2007/08" (Forschung Aktuell/research in brief 41, Freiburg, Max Planck Institute for Foreign and International Criminal Law). Undertaken by four European universities, this survey can be viewed at https://www.mpicc.de/en/forschung/forschungsarbeit/kriminologie/death_penalty.html (accessed February 24, 2012).

9. David T. Johnson, "Asia's Declining Death Penalty," *Journal of Asian Studies* 69, no. 2 (May 2010): 337–46.

10. Sharon Chen, "Singapore Plans to Exempt More Criminals from Death Penalty," *Bloomberg*, July 9, 2012, http://www.bloomberg.com/news/articles/2012-07-09/singapore-plans-to-exempt-more-criminals-from-death-penalty-1-.

11. Shun Suyan, *The Long March: The True History of Communist China's Founding Myth* (New York, Anchor Books, 2008), 140–48.

12. Speech by Xi Jinping, February 14, 2012, http://www.whitehouse.gov/photos-and-video/video/2012/02/14/state-department-lunch-honoring-vice-president-xi-jinping-china#transcript, English text viewed on February 27, 2012.

13. Jean-Pierre Cabestan, *La politique internationale de la Chine* (Paris: Presses de la FNSP, 2010), 34.

14. M. Taylor Fravel, *Strong Borders, Secure Nation: Cooperation and Conflict in China's Territorial Disputes* (Princeton, NJ: Princeton University Press, 2008), 134–35.

15. The dialogue from the meeting of the capital's five Red Guard leaders with Mao on July 28, 1968, is reproduced by Song Yongyi (ed.), *The Chinese Cultural Revolution Database* (Hong Kong: Chinese University, Hong Kong), CD-ROM.

16. Michael Schoenhals, "Central Case Examination Group, 1966–79," *China Quarterly*, 145 (March 1996): 110–11.

17. Yen-lin Chung, "The Witch-Hunting Vanguard: The Central Secretariat's Roles and Activities in the Anti-Rightist Campaign," *China Quarterly* 206 (June 2011): 391–411.

18. *Shenzhen Daily News*, October 21, 1986.

Chapter Five

China Inc., the Hybrid Economy

China has its share of dissidents and political liberals. By far the more effective in achieving a measure of change are the legal activists, who at the most aim to separate the legal system from the party, and at the least work for the respect of the system's own rules. Yet it is in the economy that most of the debate about reform, and most of the transformations of the past three decades, have happened. This is for a very simple reason. Deng Xiaoping and the party have closed political options early in the reform era—some would say as early as March 1979, when they put a stop to the so-called Wall of Democracy in Beijing, and certainly again in June 1989, when the Tiananmen demonstrations threatened their rule. They separated economics, where innovation and liberalization were possible, from politics, where party rule prevailed over any other consideration. This led to market developments, which were often taken as a transition to a full market economy—a status that China claims toward its international partners. China's growing interdependence with the global economy also caused a shift to international norms, from car emission standards to international trade rules.

But even in the economy, the momentum for change has slowed down and reversed in some cases. To liken China's development model to other globalized economies is to misinterpret it. There are important restraints on any move toward a free market economy. Some of them have to do with developmental goals to build a strong economy and a strong country. Others serve special interests that are largely intertwined with the country's power elite, guaranteeing income and investment resources for the state economy at the core, while opening the periphery to the global economy.

Some of these restraints are a legacy from the past. Chief among them is the residential permit system in force since the 1950s—the *hukou*—which still exists in spite of massive migratory trends across the country. The *hukou* has long ceased to be an instrument to tie down the people to the land. But it has created across the urban and industrial sectors two classes of citizens, permanent residents and migrants. Internal migrations remain more managed than they appear. Provincial-level labor bureaus and even education departments manage immigration through contracts stipulating salaries and working and social conditions. They are very different in practice from those afforded to permanent residents. Backed by an immense reservoir of rural population (250 million more people will leave the countryside in the next decade or so), the *hukou* system has allowed for what is the textbook condition for capitalist accumulation according to Karl Marx: an abundance of cheap and mobile labor.

RESTORING A STRONG STATE

Other major decisions were made in favor of the state economy under Zhu Rongji, who served as prime minister from 1998 to 2003. Zhu often gets international credit as an economic liberalizer for having led China's final negotiation to enter the World Trade Organization and inspired the adaptation of China's laws and norms after China's entry in 2001. But it is a mistake to see him as a paragon of a free market economy. Zhu was as much a builder of a modern state and its economic underpinnings. In 1993 and 1994, he reversed the trend that had previously seen tax revenues flow more and more toward local administrations, and less and less toward the central government. His major tax reform returned local budget resources to the central government. Local government units were left to get by with the equivalent of pocket money from various duties and fees—or with subsidies by the central government, of course. In 1998, during the great Asian financial crisis, Zhu also completely restructured the SOEs or state enterprises. The bloated state sector was running up an ocean of red ink and was much less dynamic than the JVs—joint ventures enterprises with foreign capital—or China's smaller private enterprises. Zhu merged the SOEs to establish large firms analogous to the Korean *chaebols*, while leaving most of the light industries and consumer products to the private sector. He also did heavy job-cutting throughout the state economy, and canceled much of the debts from its losses and those of the state banks by creating separate debt-management companies. Those reforms came to be symbolized in 2003 by the creation of the influential SASAC,[1] which manages the state's share-holding over major SOEs. The oversight, coupled with the nomination of senior managers by the party's Organization Department, goes well beyond what would be the norm for public firms in an open economy.

Having again mobilized resources with his tax reform, and having created the tools to control the state economy, Zhu Rongji would also launch major industrial policies. The drive to expand new sectors such as information technologies, chemical industries, and alternate energies has come from these reforms, which gave again the state a very strong hand over the economy.

CHINA'S INDUSTRIAL GIANTS

Fifteen years later, the results are astounding: fifty-seven Chinese companies are included among the world's top five hundred companies featured in the 2011 *Fortune* magazine ranking. They are nearly all SOEs—or in some cases thinly disguised agents of the developmental state, such as Huawei, the telecommunications giant that is officially owned by some of its employees. The profits of the state enterprise sector have risen 25 percent since 1998.[2] These enterprises have three distinctive traits in common. First, with a few exceptions, SOEs are definitely *not* China's main exporters: that role is held by foreign or jointly owned firms and by China's private sector. The state sector's share of exports has dropped from 57 percent in 1998 to only 15 percent in 2010. Instead, the large SOEs are in upstream activities holding natural monopolies or state concessions. They are strictly regulated in terms of market access and prices: oil, gas, nuclear energy, electricity, transportation, telecommunications, information technology, and above all financial services. In these sectors, state enterprises are in a lucrative monopoly or majority position. State or state-controlled enterprises account for at least 80 percent of the investments made in major cities. Conversely, the state sector plays a negligible role in exports of the consumer goods for which China is world leader. Yet the principal 138 state enterprises in 2008 took in 77 percent of the profits from China's industry as a whole. The top ten state enterprises accounted for two-thirds of these. Sinopec and China Mobile (the mobile telephone giant) alone achieved a third of all the profits reported by the state enterprise sector. The bonanza also applies to wages paid out. Salaries in the financial, tobacco, oil, and natural gas sectors are ten times higher than in the textile industry, for example. They continue to rise more rapidly than in other sectors, as do employee housing subsidies. On the other hand, for the top 992 SOEs taxes are only 10 percent of their turnover, compared with 24 percent for private companies.[3] It is these figures that support the judgment of Chinese liberal economists and foreign competitors alike: the public economy is expanding again at the expense of the private economy. In Chinese: *guojin mintui*, or literally, "The public [sector] advances and the private sector retreats."

PAMPERED STATE ENTERPRISES

The same study looks at the indirect subsidies received by the state enterprises, such as nearly free-of-charge land use, and special interest rates (1.6 percent versus 4.7 percent for other companies). Without these subsidies, the state sector would actually have been running a deficit since 2001. These Unirule Institute figures would seem to be a gold mine for trade negotiators from other countries— as they are a flagrant indication of distorted competition.

With one important reservation: the recipients of these subsidies are usually not China's star exporters, but the mostly domestic state enterprises. They, their managers, and employees gain from the prices set by the state, from subsidies and from their commanding position in the economy. The Unirule study also identifies these sectors, which were also pinpointed by Wang Xiaolu's pioneering study on hidden income, as the most prone to corruption.[1] A mere visual inspection corroborates this. Of China's fifty-seven state enterprises in the *Fortune* 500 in 2011, only eleven did not have their headquarters in Beijing or Shanghai. It is also there that the most obvious signs of accumulated wealth are found. A Chinese tax collector looking for external signs of wealth would definitely not dismiss provincial clusters of wealth or the coastal ports, where there is also money to burn. But his quest would take him inevitably to the heart of the system, to those two global cities under state control—Shanghai and especially Beijing, with their processions of black limousines. Audi sells half of its global production of black A6s in China with prices starting at 40,000 euros. There are reportedly seven hundred thousand of them on the streets of Beijing. The short-lived decision by the Chinese government to remove Audi and BMW from the list of makes authorized for government contracts in February 2012 was extremely interesting from several standpoints.[5] Announced at a time when the European Union was starting to demand access to China's public procurement, this Chinese move could in effect hold the German automobile industry hostage to trade policy with China because quite simply, public offices and firms are the main buyers for these high-end cars. In the end, the decision was not confirmed, but it would not in any case take all high-end vehicles away from the servants of the state. The now revived Red Flag (Hong Qi) brand is adapting high-end Toyotas and Audis and is planning a Chinese equivalent of the Rolls.

A POLITICAL ECOSYSTEM

Chinese capitalism is private in spirit, but it is part and parcel of a system that is primarily public in nature. Half of China's new billionaires made their fortunes in real estate, and the ownership and devolution of land is strictly controlled by the state. Whether true or false, the information on huge sums allegedly invested abroad by the deposed leader Bo Xilai did not really stir up controversy. This is because public opinion is already convinced of the worst. In any event, the scale is plausible. Thirty percent of the thousand wealthiest people in China hold official positions—and five of the top ten hold senior public titles.[6]

Despite China's dynamism and the taste for competition, what we are looking at is a thoroughly political economy that gives the lie to Friedrich Engels's famous saying: in China it is indeed the political order that commands the economy and not the other way around. More than a developing economy, an emerging economy, or even a market economy, China is above all a political ecosystem. The most perceptive analyses revolve around its relationships rather than its formal "socialist" definition. It is in these relationships that the Leninist strings of political and administrative control assert their strength. In its study, the Unirule Institute traces the history of relations between the state and enterprise, emphasizing the connection between state control and private management in the *guandu shangban* system of late Imperial times. Inspired by the reformist restoration of the state in the last third of the nineteenth century, this system hinged on "supervision by civil servants, and management by merchants." A twenty-first-century version has emerged, whereby the party's Organization Department for personnel moves, and SASAC, the state's supervising agency over large SOEs, exercise control and create policy for the key domestic economy sectors.[7]

It is therefore no mere coincidence that the Chinese economy includes two diametrically opposed sectors: on the one hand, a domestic-based swath of large state enterprises that appear to be highly profitable, and on the other hand, a web of private or semi-private companies that are more engaged in international trade. The spirit of mercantilism and the hand of the state can also be seen in the official designation of eleven strategic industrial sectors, and in the constant push for innovation policies and technology acquisition. But not all policy is an industrial policy. In the oil sector for example, companies like Sinopec and Petrochina charge very low prices for gas at the pump, often below global production prices for oil. This makes their refinery and distribution business unprofitable. But cheap gas is part of the social compact with farmers using engines, taxis and truckers, as well as increasingly with the affluent middle class. China now produces eighteen million cars per year, almost all of them sold at home. In this case, price setting is a social tool.

To the contrary, in other cases such as mobile phone use, prices are quite high, taking a toll on what was at last count in May 2013 1.13 billion users. And for export, the primary subsidy is land management—giant investments in ports, airports, highways, and in-

dustrial development zones—making it easier for Chinese produc-
ers to access the global market. The example of high-speed trains
designed for individual travel by the Chinese is tempting but misleading. The trains charge prices that are out of reach for the average Chinese, and their construction has resulted in $340 billion in
debt (5 percent of GDP!).

THE LEGACY OF MAOISM

In fact, the era of opening up and reform has reproduced many
traits characteristic of the Maoist era, adapting them to the circumstances. The state fashions development by investing in infrastructures. This includes balancing the coastal economy with the *xibu
kaifa*, China's version of America's western frontier, in this case
inland China. The system of state-owned firms creates guaranteed
income from the different echelons of the party-state down to its
employees. The financial system, chiefly through credit allocation,
is biased toward the well connected, and that applies particularly to
real estate and construction. The system evokes the "cronyism" that
was long criticized in Southeast Asian economies, or rent-seeking
capitalism, Latin American style. The behavior of China's wealthy
classes, who have become global travelers and indulge in capital
flight, certainly is close to Latin American standards—where social
inequality is also huge.

But the regime has not only favored the well connected. It has
also gone out of its way to attract foreign investors looking for
abundant and cheap labor. And the largest group of foreign investors remains the overseas Chinese. Small businessmen from Hong
Kong reproduce their low-end production of mass-market consumer goods (the famous "Hong Kong model" of the 1960s) even in
remote inland areas of China. Austere Taiwanese capitalists have
relocated and bolstered their electronics industry. Asian, American,
and European multinational companies (the latter more focused on

the Chinese domestic market), have made a fortune with cheap labor.

Under Maoism, the peasants paid indirectly for the industrialization drive. Very low prices for agricultural products and very high prices for the inputs they needed and for the most basic consumer goods were imposed on them. Capital was extracted from them stealthily, if not painlessly.

The reform era has brought a new chapter of this capital accumulation story. It is now achieved by three means: one is low industrial wages, another is the high savings rate induced by the lack of social protection and retirement pensions. And finally, state control of the financial system, and so-called "financial repression" (the storing of foreign currencies reserves, which implies abundant creation of domestic money), produce very low interest rates on deposits and savings generally. To endure, this system needs some restrictions in place. The private capital markets, and for instance life insurance and mutual fund products, should not be too important. This forces the Chinese to save large amounts of their income to deal with contingencies or plan for large purchases. These savings are cornered by the largely public banking system. Or they go into real estate—which is also tightly held by local officials and their beneficiaries. Social barriers such as the *hukou* system must also stay in place. They guarantee a dual labor market—whereby immigrants are paid low wages while permanent urban residents often enjoy a higher and guaranteed income. Social support for the regime is to be found in a middle class, which is middle class in name only, since it is location and status rather than skills that bring in substantial income. The arrangement also requires large sectors of the economy—from financial services to land and real estate—to be closed to foreign players. There is therefore no foreign alternative to uncompetitive interest rates and returns, and ordinary savers cannot move to international markets. This being China, where no barrier is airtight, and much energy is invested to get around rules,

the most savvy investors—which is synonymous again with the
well connected—do actually find exit routes abroad for their
wealth. But so long as they are in the minority, this does not threat-
en China's current account and capital balance, which are fed with
large inflows from abroad.

Of course, these barriers also hinder competition and reduce
economic efficiency. Labor and capital are both hyper-abundant,
and resources are often squandered. The proposals for reform rely
more often than not on the elimination of these barriers. But such a
change not only clashes with the immediate interests of the party-
state and its main clientele today. It also goes against the grain of
Chinese history, which has often favored statism and social management over the market and free enterprise.

IS IT A STATE OR MIXED ECONOMY?

One may go back in history to the very foundation of China's
political economy. Without harnessing hydraulic resources (rivers
and canals, navigation, irrigation, and flood control) and without
the state that makes it possible, neither the country's agriculture nor
its population centers would ever have grown to the extent they
have for more than a millennium. A follower of Engels in the
Second Socialist International, Karl Wittfogel, coined the concept
of "oriental despotism"—an authoritarian ecosystem inherent in
that hydraulic civilization. Without the financing and upkeep of
these utilities, or without the public granaries that can ease the
effects of drastic weather irregularity over China's great plains, the
Chinese population would never have become so large. The two
capitals of the Song dynasty, Kaifeng and Hangzhou, reached a
population of one million each—a figure inconceivable without the
material support of an efficient government, and which surpasses
all Western cities of the same era. Not even the Great Wall (which
in truth functioned as the biggest toll-barrier ever built and as a

restraint against outward migration) or the famous salt tax can do justice to the influence of the Chinese state. For instance, the Manchu Qing, China's last dynasty (1644–1911) set up large hospitals in Beijing for its Manchu inhabitants (easily 40 percent of total city population), with a public management system that kept full medical files on them. An intricately designed system of military colonies made it possible to conquer and populate the West, with Han settlers in very arid regions. These policies created a nation well before the advent of the West and the contemporary era.

China's demography itself is anything but natural. It has been wrongly seen as an illustration of Malthusian theories, with the balance between population and resources determining either population growth or demographic crisis. In fact, we are now discovering an age-old capacity, both by the state and within society, to regulate births, either through contraception, infanticide, or forced celibacy, or by social eugenics that have long favored clan chiefs and heads of families.[8]

The vision of Chinese society as individualistic or even anarchic or chaotic applies to a long interregnum, a period of a hundred and fifty years when the State collapsed and the elites went into decline, from the end of the eighteenth century to the Warlord era of the 1920s. With the People's Republic, the strong state returned. With the revenues it collected, it renewed the accomplishments of the so-called "celestial bureaucracy" of the High Empire era, before the nineteenth-century decline. Even the collectivization drive has precedents, such as the "equal fields" reform, an experiment in agricultural egalitarianism that started in the fifth century and was renewed by the Tang Dynasty. One has to admit that there is a historical background for talking about a "Chinese model" of public management with some features of collectivization.

However, this interpretation leaves out one essential fact: the economy and society of China were constantly faced with the state or market dilemma. Commercial and banking networks, grain markets and public price regulation, inter-province quarrels involving protectionism over free trade—all these were present, as well as a mixture of private business and public initiatives or oversight. It might be more accurate to call China's traditional economy a "mixed economy," after the term used for post-1945 France.

What's more, China has outpaced any other country but exceptional city-states such as Hong Kong and Singapore in terms of participation to the world economy. And this trend isn't completely new either. In the sixteenth century, China's exports of tea, ceramic ware, and miniatures brought in silver that came ultimately from the mines of the New World. Europe used the silver to pay for imports from China, and this filled the coffers of China's imperial administration. Thanks to a positive trade and current account balance, the Ming dynasty had found the means to finance itself while lightening the tax burden on its population.

These developments associated a role for the state with the entrepreneurial spirit that characterized merchants, craftsmen, and even commercial farmers. China's rural gentry was a socioeconomic class, based on a mixture of meritocracy and economic success, rather than a hereditary aristocracy. There was no official religion: while the emperor had his private forms of worship like everyone else, Confucianism was more of a secular moral philosophy. This left the state free to focus on the economy and society.

The balance between state and market is matched by a balance between social destiny and individual opportunity. Chinese feudalism, serfdom, and traces of a caste system gave way in modern imperial times to a much more fluid society. The "wheel of fortune," originally a Chinese expression, describes graphically how families can climb the socioeconomic ladder through educational achievement, business acumen, and sheer clan cohesiveness. Of course, they can also go down this ladder just as quickly if these virtues are forgotten.

Our instant measure of inequality does not fit the criteria of Chinese traditional society either. Buddhism teaches that equality exists not within a single generation but across several generations. This optimistic morality does not need the promise of heaven to suggest salvation; it combines submission to the destiny of the group with individual hope. The fine line that exists between the collective and the individual is rooted in Chinese culture, just like the fine line between state and market.

Why bring up this mixed legacy at a time when China's economic miracle of the past three decades seems to have broken with all precedents? The explanations given for this miracle are often simplistic. Either they assume that the turn to market drove China's growth, or that this growth reflects the capacity of the state as demiurge. The former case implies a transition to a free market economy. In the latter case, China is seen as a paragon of state-controlled mercantilism. This simplification is not confined to foreign observers only. A generation of Chinese economists suddenly trained in US universities has embraced economic liberalism as a reaction to socialist economic dogma. *Caijing* (Finance), the leading magazine promoting free market reforms, jokingly described the 2008 law instituting open-ended employment contracts as a "French-style law," alluding to a famous rigidity in the French labor market.[9] Conversely, under the guise of a new socialism, a neo-Maoist left now defends the state-run economy, based on special interests and an incestuous relationship with party cadres.

Yet China's economic policies are dual. This dualism has been revived after two wild swings. One occurred in the 1920s with the breakup of the unitary state. The other phase, occurring between 1958 and 1972, saw a totalitarian state inflict untold damage on the economy and society. China has returned since to a dualism that also explains the tension and debates in China's path to growth, which is historically unique. Without exception, other Communist countries have remained poor (Vietnam may emulate China on a smaller scale). The fast-growing economies of postwar Asia never reached the height of state involvement that exists in China. Nor have they suffered from as much social inequity. Even at its heyday, the so-called "iron triangle" of Japan (i.e., the collusion among politicians of the Liberal Democratic Party, senior public officials, and large firms) until the late 1980s, or the *chaebols* (large groups) in pre-1998 South Korea never achieved such a dominant position. The paradox is that China's private economy, involving more foreign participation than either Japan or South Korea, is also extremely dynamic.

CHONGQING VS. GUANGDONG: WESTERN CHINA VS. THE WEST

After 1989, and even more so under the rule of Hu Jintao after 2002, the political implications of social and economic line debate were hushed up. The looming succession in 2012 has allowed for an opportunity to reopen them. Divisions and rivalries at the top provided an outlet for expressing divergent views. Two implicitly competing "models" appeared on the political scene. First, starting in 2009 the "Chongqing model" appeared, extolling a city run by Bo Xilai. In a countermove, the province of Guangdong, run by Wang Yang, was also held up as a "model." The irony was of course that Wang Yang, another contender for a top job, was the party official who had actually started the Chongqing experiment before Bo Xilai, and who then moved to Guangdong. Indeed, this competition involved much posturing, but major differences did indeed exist. Guangdong, which along with Shenzhen is the original cradle of the policy of "opening up" to the global economy, has made no secret of its attempt since the 2008 global financial crisis to switch from labor-intensive industries to high technology. It has many ties with Hong Kong, and higher learning is encouraged. The ambivalence of the local Cantonese to the central government is reflected in a form of local liberalism. Within sharp limits, it has nonetheless favored the development of private nongovernmental organizations (NGOs), particularly for social assistance. A pilot reform adopted in May 2012 simplified the registration of NGOs, and in July 2012 they were allowed to compete for public contracts in welfare-related sectors. It was indeed hoped that the NGOs would be more effective than public administrations. This boom in privately managed social services (or the delegation of public services, Chinese style) was also an indication of political and economic liberalism. Guangzhou and Guangdong province were among the first to establish legal minimum wages. Yet they lagged behind in government funding for social policies, particularly the provision of housing, which is generally left to private developers.

Chongqing is quite a different case, which cannot be reduced to the controversial figure of Bo Xilai. In the 1990s, Sichuan was made into a hub for the political development of Western China. Then Chongqing city was separated from the rest of the province and received a windfall in government investments: real estate construction and state-owned firms dominated the local economy by the end of the 1990s. In 2007, a plan took shape to turn Chongqing, like the Pudong district in Shanghai, into a new center for multinationals and export industry. The plan also provided for a twofold social policy: in addition to a boom in public housing, peasant migrants leaving rural areas could sell their plots of land (which would then become factory or building sites!) in exchange for the right to housing in the city. Some other features—the revolutionary "red songs" campaign, the gingko trees planted at enormous cost across the city, a violent anti-mafia campaign—were indeed the work of Bo Xilai at the height of his power. But there was a rational economic and social core in the Chongqing model that existed before Bo Xilai.

What were its goals, and is it a viable model of public management and social economics? The Chongqing model is first and foremost a second wave for China's industrialization and export drive. The land allocated to companies such as HP, Foxconn, Bayer, and others is leased at very low prices. A huge pool of rural labor guarantees salaries that are less than half of salaries on the coast. In 2011, Chongqing's minimum monthly salary was next to last in China (870 yuans, or around 100 euros[10]) just ahead of the impoverished province of Shaanxi. Transportation infrastructures make up for Chongqing's geographical distance from the coast. The municipality has plans for three thousand kilometers of superhighways by 2015; traffic on the Yangtze River is containerized. There is even a plan, promoted by Bo Xilai during his tenure, for a Eurasian rail freight line originating from Chongqing: in 2014, the first carriages have started the line all the way to Dusseldorf. This kind of push is designed to extend China's fast growth well beyond its demographic downturn (the overall labor force is expected to decrease starting in 2013). It involves industry relocation within China, lowering again the cost of labor. If Chongqing is as successful as Shanghai has been with Pudong, it could mean another decade of Chinese export growth, especially since Chongqing is not alone. Chengdu, Sichuan's provincial capital, is in competition with it. Even China's Far West, as far as Urumqi (Xinjiang) is now connected by a superhighway leading straight to Beijing.

The Chongqing model also aims to correct some of the social inequity in China's fast growth path, by controlling issues such as land and housing at the outset, and by helping rural migrants instead of discriminating against them. This aspect of the Chongqing model is attractive, and should in fact give pause for thought to the promoters of economic liberalism from the Deng Xiaoping era. Yet if the transfer of land rights from countryside to city is unique, the urban public housing policy is very similar to Hong Kong and Singapore, two free-market economies with a strong central government. It also follows a national policy introduced by the central government under Wen Jiabao.

Transfers from the central government have in fact heavily subsidized Chongqing development. Isn't the Chongqing model artifi-
cial, like so many Maoist utopias? Since Bo Xilai's downfall, revelations have swirled around the cost of developing the municipality.
They seem to echo the denunciations of some Maoist-era propaganda mirages, following the death of the Great Helmsman. Of course,
local economic growth has been enormous—possibly as much as
26 percent for the year 2011 alone. Two hundred of the *Fortune*
500 global companies are reportedly active in Chongqing. Investment in Chongqing amounted to 76 percent of local GDP in 2011.
By comparison, the flagship province of Guangdong invested only
26 percent of its GDP. Conversely, exports from Chongqing still
accounted for only 12 percent of its GDP in 2011, compared with
65 percent for Guangdong. The city's budget deficit reached more
than 10 percent of local GDP for the year 2011 alone; and this
assessment did not include public expenditures below city level.
Public debt reached three times yearly revenue (which depends
largely on subsidies from the central government and land sales).
After the fall of its political patron, the Chongqing model looked
like a balloon ready to pop.[11] Perhaps for that reason, the central
government has stepped in even more heavily, bringing in addition-
al cash and credit.

The Chongqing and Guangdong models display two opposing
sides of the Chinese economy. The state economy embodied by
Chongqing spends lavishly while Guangdong relies on its export
industries, often operated by foreign or private capital. Chongqing
owed its development to subsidies from Beijing, to borrowing from
public funds, and to income from transfers of land for construction;
its pace could not be maintained, but neither has it been allowed to
crash. In May 2012 the influential China Development Bank,
which financed the overall policy for developing Western China,
announced that in addition to the $20 billion already loaned, it
planned to commit more capital, for the specific purpose of contin-

uing the construction of the city's superhighway network. If the world is vast enough and rich enough to absorb another wave of Chinese exports, the Chongqing project will appear prophetic. If not, it could symbolize the pride and overreaching of the local governments in China. In any event, it cannot possibly serve as a model for the rest of inland China because it is too much of a financial drain.

UNSUSTAINABLE GROWTH

China's growth is prodigious, but is it sustainable, and on what model is it based? The answer to the first question must be yes. Its reserves of productivity are huge, as much of the population moves from the farms to plants, a move that easily outstrips the aging of the labor force. Aging of course poses a serious social question, owing to inadequate pension and savings systems. But that very lack of security for individuals leads them to fund a gigantic nest egg for the state, which is another driver of growth. China has built the best transportation infrastructures in the world—American style turnpikes, European style fast rail lines, and the leading harbor and airport infrastructure in the world. The country can afford to ward off the risk of a global (or even a domestic) financial crisis, because of the continuing disconnect of its capital markets, with control over foreign exchange, curbing of financial investments, and limited currency convertibility.

Yet the sustainability over time of this model is threatened by several new developments. The free-market reforms of the 1980s and the globalization of the 1990s have led to huge gains for part of the population, which has also benefited from the quasi-legalization of private property. These gains are no longer available to the younger generation, for which the entry cost to the property market is now too high. The global reach of China's export industries has allowed the largest wave of development in human history. But it is also generating huge inequalities. The guaranteed income enjoyed by the party-state's organizations and their clientele can be sustained during a phase of rapid growth, but it is less sustainable if growth slows down and real income declines. In effect, the party has created a new ruling class and privileged social strata around it. How can it check itself and these excesses in the absence of democratic control and contested elections?

The Chinese model also has external limits: foreign markets cannot absorb indefinitely the overcapacity created in China by cheap capital and labor. The steel industry, the solar panel sector, and shipbuilding are primary examples. China's model also creates a voracious appetite for energy and raw commodities. China is therefore feeding global price inflation for natural resources, and is also the first to suffer from it. Part of the boom in imports and domestic consumption is actually the result of an increase in price for these imported resources. These external limits are also physical. The extraordinary deterioration of the environment in China is such that it will be forced to switch to a "green" economy based on energy savings and the use of alternate sources. Yet until 2014, nothing had been done to curb the increase in coal consumption or oil imports. After attempting to eliminate its dependence on coal in the late nineties, notably because of accidents in the most marginal coal mines, the government gave up. At its height in 1960, French coal mines produced 57 million tons. Coal mining in the United States is still rising, at 1.1 billion tons in 2011, and India produced 1.3 billion tons in the same year. But in 2015, China will produce 4.1 billion tons of coal. It is already the world's second-largest importer of oil, and it is planning to buy 400 million tons of crude oil by 2015. That is more than half the *total* consumption of all twenty-seven European Union countries in 2010.

Sometimes the excesses of the Chinese model, on the financial and on the resource side, feed on each other. In the summer of 2011, global copper prices experienced a record spike, driven by

Chinese purchases, which accounted for 40 percent of global consumption. But that peak was due not only to the need for copper, or even to direct speculation over its price. In fact, Chinese real estate developers, endangered by increasing government limits on real estate lending, had woken up to an alternate method. The state, in the name of "economic security," encourages borrowing for the purchase abroad of raw materials. Speculating on an indefinite rise in commodities prices, the developers began to make forward purchases of copper on these loans. In the short term, they could use the money from these loans to keep their real estate projects going. In the longer term, they figured on a steady increase of the price of copper—fueled by their own purchases!—to repay the loans when the forward purchase contracts came due.

Thus a compulsive appetite for raw materials, snowballing credit, and semipublic real estate speculation can feed on each other. In the first half of 2013, a new way to avoid lending restrictions inside China emerged: companies artificially marked up the price of their exports—toward Hong Kong, a key destination, their value rose by 93 percent year on year. This increase was not real. Instead, it allowed the firms to borrow money on the new renminbi capital markets abroad and to repatriate it under the guise of these inflated exports. Similarly, Chinese banks have begun to market so-called wealth-management products to their customers, which are really based on the returns from lending to the real estate sector. The similarity with pre-2007 US subprime lending is striking, and the amounts collected in a very short time—until the government reined in these practices in June 2013—are staggering.

In 2008–2009, the Chinese government rolled out fiscal stimuli and lending—all told, an estimated $1.5 trillion—to fight off the recession brought by the West's financial crisis. The move worked to perfection, since Chinese growth took off again and left behind all competitors, including other emerging economies. But it cannot be renewed on the same scale. The officially low rate of central government debt hides several time bombs: the debts of local governments, the debt that comes from so-called "shadow banking" credit, and unfunded pensions: the population over age sixty-five will triple by the year 2035.

ESCAPING FROM THE SUCCESS TRAP

These uncertainties have revived the debate on economic reform. On the one hand, there is the power of vested interests, from major state-owned companies to the many beneficiaries of the real estate market and of a financial system based on cozy relationships. They want the same growth model, based on exports and privileged access to financing, to keep going: "If it ain't broke, don't fix it." You don't change a winning strategy. The crisis in the outside world, particularly the West, should serve as a warning on growth prospects. But it is tempting to ascribe this crisis to the breakdown of the free-market system, and to endorse a statist Chinese model with heavy incentives and redistribution in the form of subsidies. Theories of a Western financial plot are propagated freely in China as is shown by the publishing success of a trilogy entitled *Currency Wars*.[12] Fascinated by the saga of the Rothschilds, the author, Song Hongbin, draws inspiration from Western conspiracy theorists to rewrite the history of international finance. His first volume appeared in 1997, a year before the global financial crisis. Song claims on the Chinese back cover of his book that he has worked for Fanny Mae and Freddie Mac as a "senior adviser." He says he has worked on the design of the automated auditing system of US real estate loans and in the risk analysis of mortgage-backed securities (MBS). Thus this Chinese author found himself by accident at the heart of the subprime loan industry in the United States—the time bomb of the major crisis of 1998. Yet he saw only past and present financial conspiracies as an explanation for world history.

The perception of an unprecedented economic crisis of the Western economies has also encouraged China's "new left," a motley group that advocates Maoism and nationalism as cures for the inequity of China's development. It explains the appetite for Bo Xilai's "Chongqing model." Thus, noted economists of China's "new left" like Cui Zhiyuan[13] or Wang Shaoguang have seen in Chongqing the renewal of Chinese socialism based on a strong state focused on redistribution.

Conversely, liberal economists, officials of China's central bank, and former premier Wen Jiabao, saw in the Western financial crisis a threat to the expansion of Chinese exports, and therefore to the Chinese path of growth. The most eloquent among them is a sociologist from Tsinghua University, Sun Liping, who has lashed out against "special interests" and recommended a resumption of major top-down reform, rather than continuing a policy of incremental change. He, along with others, has stressed that the "new left's criticism of economic liberalism, which it holds responsible for mounting inequity and corruption, is misplaced. These ills are the results of the limits placed on reform, and the incapacity of the Party-state to check itself. The results of the reform have often ended up benefiting ruling families, clans, and corporate interests."

At this point, the issue becomes directly political. By denouncing the illusion of stability as a danger, by explaining that imperfect reforms are better than no reform at all, and by stressing the success trap that delivers the economy to vested interests, the reformers inevitably begin to challenge the control of the party-state. Even from an economic perspective, calling for independent regulatory bodies, or demanding that the law be enforced above and beyond the interests of the party, is a departure from the party's basic operating rules since 1949. Cutting the umbilical cord between forced savings and the distribution of credit or subsidies means revolutionizing the political economy and hence politics. Most economic reformers have managed to confine their criticism so that it never reaches the point of a direct challenge to the government. They are biding their time, in the hope that gradual change will solve the problem. As long as growth remains robust, the losses and defects of China's growth model will be absorbed. However, any sudden slowdown in growth (due either to a global recession or to a breakdown in the domestic financial markets) would quickly bring these hard choices to the fore and create an explosive political situation. It is to ward off this crisis that Xi Jinping, Hu Jintao's successor since 2012 and a much stronger leader, has resorted to a mixture of authoritarian control, checks on corruption and special interests, and deregulation of new sectors such as personal finance and service industries. The hope is that this controlled change will cushion the fall of the sectors that traditionally have led China's growth, such as construction, real estate, coal, and steel.

NOTES

1. Commission for the administration and supervision of state assets.

2. Xi Li, Xuewen Liu, and Yong Wang, "A Model of China's State Capitalism," The Hong Kong University of Science and Technology, May 16, 2012, available to the public on http://igov.berkeley.edu/sites/default/files/55.Wang_Yong.pdf, accessed May 28, 2012.

3. "Guoyou qiye de xingzhi, biaoxian yu gaige" [The structure, performance and reform of China's state enterprises], Unirule Institute of Economics, April 12, 2011.

4. Wang Xiaolu and Wing Thye Woo, "The Size and Distribution of Hidden Household Income in China," available at http://www.econ.ucdavis.edu/faculty/woo/woo.html, pp. 15–16.

5. "China Removes Audis and BMW Cars from Official List," *Telegraph*, February 28, 2012, http://www.telegraph.co.uk/news/worldnews/asia/china/9110647/China-removes-Audis-and-BMW-cars-from-official-list.html.

6. The Hurun China Rich List 2011, is no longer available on the Hurun website. It is cached however at http://img.hurun.net/hmec/2011-08-23/201108231121093254.pdf.

7. See Kjeld Erik Brødsgaard, "Politics and Business Group Formation in China: The Party in Control?" *China Quarterly* 211 (September 2012): 624–48.

8. See James Lee and Cameron Campbell, *Fate and Fortune in Imperial China—Social Organization and Population Behavior in Liaoning, 1774–1873* (Cambridge: Cambridge University Press, 1997), 55–57.

9. Camille Bondois, "Economic Publications Attack 'French Style' Labor Law," *China Analysis* 17 (January–February 2008): 14–17.

10. *Lingdao juece xinxi* [Information for decisions by leaders] 42 (October 2011): 26.

11. The "true accounts" of the municipality of Chongqing are described by the Chinese press in May 2012: see Chan Yang, "What Remains of the Chongqing Model?" *China Analysis* 39 (July–August 2012).

12. Song Hongbin, *Huobi Zhanzheng*, vol. 1 (Beijing: CITIC Press, 1997).

13. Professor at Tsinghua University, Cui has had an advisory position in Chongqinq and published the most intelligent defense of it: Cui Zhiyuan, "Partial Intimations of the Coming Whole: The Chongqing Experiment in Light of the Theories of Henry George, James Meade and Antonio Gramsci," *Modern China* 37 (November 2011): 646–60.

Chapter Six

Reform without Elections

From the moment Hu Jintao rose to power before 2002 until his term was renewed for another five years in 2007, he disappointed those who had expected him to take up the torch of political reform. Absent information on debate at the highest level, it is hard to blame him personally for this lack of momentum inside the collective leadership. Wen Jiabao picked up some of these hopes in the next five years, from 2007 to 2012. He was the only one of the central leaders to speak out forcefully on a number of occasions in favor of political liberalization. Yet he also disappointed. His wording remained ambiguous, although his accents were strongly put. Were they truly his own thoughts or merely a clever variation within the political dogma of the party, a song in line with United Front tactics and intended to woo the gullible? Did he truly advocate political liberalization, or was he simply "China's best actor," as the intellectual dissident Yu Jie has called him?

As early as 2007, Wen called for a resumption of political reform. On the anniversary of the May 4, 1919, movement in 2010 at Beijing University, he extolled "the spirit of democracy." In August of the same year in Shenzhen he referred to the need for political reform and intellectual emancipation, criticizing the "overconcentration of uncontrolled power." This was widely taken up in the official press. In September 2010, during a CNN interview, his responses proved more cautious in terms of substance but highly combative in terms of form. "Political reform is a point of view put forward by Deng Xiaoping a long time ago," he said. He made a distinction between the phase of taking over power and the phase of exercising power, but reduced political reform to a commitment to act "in accordance with the Constitution and the laws." This is much less audacious, since it is not so much a call for changing the political system as for enforcing the laws as they exist. However, Wen was unusually passionate about it, emphasizing that the law must be obeyed by all "without exception," and vowing to defend these ideas "unfailingly and unyieldingly, against all odds until my dying day." What did Wen really mean, and who was the implicit adversary targeted by his statement?

WEN JIABAO AND POLITICAL REFORM

First of all, Wen was right to point out that his own words are not original with him. Resurrecting the 1954 Constitution in 1982 and adopting a state of laws (if not the rule of law) was the path chosen by the party-state after arbitrary Maoist rule. Free elections were nevertheless ruled out. The paradox of the 1954 Constitution has often been noted. The power structure outlined by this text is inspired by the philosophy of the Age of Enlightenment and as such is universalist in nature. But this language also echoes the 1936 Soviet constitution written under Stalin, in that its lofty words mask absolute arbitrary rule. However, its authors included constitutionalists from the era of Republican China, and leaders such as Deng Xiaoping and Hu Yaobang. They would incorporate again the same general principles into the 1982 Constitution. [1]

In August 1980, Deng Xiaoping gave a famous speech on reforming the party and the state, in which he criticized the "excessive concentration of power in the hands of the Party committees that purportedly strengthen the centralized leadership."[2] He went on to recommend separating the party from the state, and calling for a "balance of powers" (*quanli zhiheng*). In so doing, he legitimized political reform and justified the action of his chief lieutenants of the 1980s, Hu Yaobang and Zhao Ziyang. In 1986, at the same time as a campaign of political liberalization was launched (the "Double Hundred Flowers"), Hu Yaobang carried on with the separation of the party from the state. After his fall in January 1987, his successor Zhao Ziyang took up the torch, but more discreetly, by having the same speech by Deng republished before the Thirteenth Congress of the CCP. It was Hu Yaobang's death in April 1989 that sparked the first Tiananmen demonstrations.

Wen could hardly have been unaware of the fact that this chain of events had been interrupted by force in 1989. Nor could he have been unaware of the contradictions in Deng's remarks. In March 1979, Deng also proclaimed "four cardinal principles." They included the dictatorship of the proletariat and the leading role of the Communist Party. Although rarely discussed before 1989, these principles were suddenly to be revived at that time. Wen had also come close to breaching a taboo by distinguishing between the act of taking power in a revolution and the exercise of that power. That was tantamount to declaring the end of the Chinese revolution, a proclamation never really made in China, where Mao advocated uninterrupted revolution. In any case, the party reacted in 2004 by explicitly strengthening its hold over the state. One leader, Zeng Qinghong, referred then to the "painful lesson of the loss of power in the Soviet Union."[3] His directive, aimed at strengthening the party's leading role, resulted again in utterly interchangeable roles for the party and the state. In the end, Hu Jintao elected to regulate the operation of the party but not to separate it from the state or to uphold the rule of law as it would apply to the party.

Starting in April 2010, Wen took an even bolder position by paying a highly personal public tribute[4] to Hu Yaobang. Taken together, Wen's statements had a clear purpose. His remarks were indeed cautiously based on the stance taken by Deng from 1980 to 1989, recommending a resumption of the political reform process that had been interrupted since Tiananmen. With this approach, he attempted to promote a legal system based on the remnants of the liberal principles expressed at one time or another in the People's Republic. The fact that this was phrased as an evolutionary rather than a revolutionary proposition did not mean it was completely devoid of impact.

AGAINST A MAOIST REGRESSION?

The philosopher Karl Popper has characterized as unfalsifiable theories those that cannot be disproved by any event. Wen's words sound as if they were designed to belong to that category. They cannot be described as heterodox and yet they are bold in terms of form and context. Evidence of his audacity lies in the reactions they aroused. An editorial on the first page of the *People's Daily* signed by a fictitious group with a revealing name (Zheng Qingyuan, a near-synonym of "making a correction"[5]) attacked "western-style democratization" and the doctrine of the separation of powers. It was an indirect attack and not aimed at the actual words used by Wen, but the timing was close enough. Another Beijing paper stated on its website that this fictitious name was that of the collective leadership itself.[6] Some later said that it was Hu Jintao himself, frustrated with the political offensive by Wen, who put together the anonymous writing group.[7]

Several incidents in particular ensued. In December 2010, the day before the Nobel Prize was to be awarded to the dissident Liu Xiaobo in Norway, some intellectuals and legal experts were silenced. Then several of them were threatened by Security with being "buried alive." The most detailed testimony comes from Yu Jie, an intellectual who happened to be the author of the book describing Wen Jiabao as "China's best actor." His interrogators told him, "If the leaders give us the order, it will take us only one night to arrest the two hundred intellectuals who represent a threat and half an hour to bury them alive." Every literate Chinese is familiar with the story of Qin Shi Huangdi, the founder of the Qin dynasty, who unified China in the year 221 BCE. In his fight to impose the Legalist School, he had the manuscripts of the classical Hundred Schools burned, and 460 scholars buried alive. He was also chosen by Mao as a model of opposition to "old-fashioned Confucian ideas." During the Cultural Revolution, Mao created the slogan "Let's burn the books and bury the scholars alive."[8]

Another case in April 2011 provides a further indication. The artist and activist Ai Weiwei, kidnapped and held in secret for eighty-one days, invoked the law with his interrogators. They also threatened to bury him alive, telling him, "Do you know that Liu Shaoqi before his death was holding a copy of the Constitution in his hand? When it comes to illegality, things haven't changed in this country since the Cultural Revolution." The case of Ai Weiwei was an affair of state, especially since, as the son of the Communist poet Ai Qing, he was personally known by many of the leaders. Not coincidentally, Ai Weiwei was finally freed and placed under house arrest in August 2011, on the eve of a trip to Europe by Wen Jiabao.

At the same time, a proposal also appeared in the bill to reform China's code of criminal procedure. Under this proposal, it would be legal to detain in secret for six months without outside notification anyone suspected of violating state security. This issue became in 2011–2012 a symbol of the clash between the advocates of legal reforms and those who, to the contrary, wanted to return to a more absolute arbitrary rule, such as had been implemented under Maoism.

Did Wen Jiabao purposely attempt to encourage the expression of opinions favoring political liberalization? Was he serving as an alibi for a regime that is as capable of encouraging a particular debate as it is of banning all others? Answers to these questions could explain the political history of the last decade, the history of the Hu Jintao-Wen Jiabao tandem. Their rise to power in November 2002 had rekindled hopes among many liberals for renewed influence by reformers among the party leadership.

THE ENIGMA OF THE HU-WEN TANDEM

And those hopes were not without historical basis. Wen had accompanied Zhao Ziyang during his famous visit to the Tiananmen demonstrators in May 1989. Hu Jintao, a leader from the Communist Youth League, which had a more liberal reputation than the Party itself, spent ten years in exile during the Cultural Revolution in the impoverished province of Gansu, where he met Wen. When they rose to power, they criticized the growing imbalance between the coast and inland China. That criticism was also aimed at the "Shanghai faction," a group of leaders whose power base included the prosperous coastal economy. The leading member of the faction was Jiang Zemin, who owed his rise to national prominence to the Tiananmen crisis and the purge of Zhao Ziyang. One Chinese-American analyst, Cheng Li, has built his reputation on the divide he sees between two groups: one is the Shanghai group, which lobbies for large state enterprises and is responsible for regional inequality. It has in effect merged with the "princeling" group from the families of the leadership. The other faction is represented by the Youth League group, which is less elitist, and is concerned about the social divide and regional disparities.[9]

That was only a step away from seeing the enigmatic Hu as a future Chinese Gorbachev. After all, Mikhail Gorbachev hardly stood out as an original thinker before he finally rose to power. The opposition between two factions with widely different options also revived the "struggle between the two lines" of the Party in the Maoist era. There was a "left" linked to powerful sectors of the socialist economy in opposition to a "right" that was both more populist in its concern for the inland regions, and more liberal owing to its relationship with its sponsors. These included Hu Yaobang, who had also been the head of the Communist Youth League during the Hundred Flowers in 1956. This theory also had the advantage of being rational. It was actually close to Chinese political culture, which values human qualities over formal institutions. This traditionally extols the struggle of upright men (*haoren*) against all vices, a line that also lent itself to adapting for China the philosophy of the Enlightenment. But as rational and attractive as it was, did those qualities make it real?

Nothing is less certain. After ten years in power, the Hu-Wen tandem left behind a feeling of unease despite the economic triumph of their policies. Wen in his role as premier came across as being empathetic with the weak or the victims of Chinese society, such as coal miners, the population of Sichuan struck by a deadly earthquake, or even travelers held up by a snow storm on the eve of the Chinese New Year. Like the appearance of the leaders on the social networks, this new image demonstrated the extent to which they took public opinion into account as well as the importance of managing it. Hence the issue was not the sincerity of "grandfather Wen," but his inability to follow through on his words. In his defense, Wen was denigrated in campaigns waged by the apparatus itself, which often circulated rumors of a split with Hu. This was already the case, for example, on the eve of the Seventeenth Congress in November 2007. In 2012 these denigrations and rumors were transferred to the second member of the tandem apparently in line for the November 2012 succession, Li Keqiang, who often appeared in Wen's wake. He was rumored to be lacking in economic experience and was likely to the replaced as premier by Wang Qishan, the deputy premier then in charge of economic and financial affairs. The unreliability of Wen's words on political reform, as demonstrated by the actual course of events, pointed to a major division within the top leadership.

Hu Jintao himself remained ambiguous as ever on political reform in the broad sense, including broader legal issues. His rise to power in 2002 and the subsequent renewal of his mandate at the 2007 CCP Congress were preceded by rumors that political liberalization was in the works. In fact, in 2004–2005, Hu set about strengthening the party. This involved a thorough investigation of each of its members. After 2007, it was the selection procedures within the party, including by election, that were reformed. Again in January 2012, his speech at a plenary session of the Central Committee was a perfect balancing act. In it he denounced a Western plot to subvert the Chinese political system, but he also stressed the international weakness of China's public diplomacy and soft power. It is possible to interpret the speech in one direction or the other. Some people saw in it a call for intellectual emancipation, while others saw in it an obsession for law and order. His favorite topic of harmony (*hexie*) within Chinese society as well as in international relations could also pass for a resurgence of a moderate form of Confucianism. Yet the notion of an internal equilibrium of the Party-state could equally take precedence over a proposal to separate powers, preempting political reformers. Or it could serve to prevent ideological factional debate—thus countering conservative activists.

AMBIGUITY, A RECIPE FOR SURVIVAL

This ambiguity may be explained by the political fragility of the Hu-Wen tandem. They never received an automatic majority in the Standing Committee of the Politburo, unlike Deng Xiaoping after 1985, or Jiang Zemin, whom Deng had imposed as a direct successor. It had been rumored that Jiang's personal secretariat was closed down, and he was nearly given up for dead in the fall of

2010. Yet he was still there and remained influential to the Eighteenth Party Congress in the fall of 2012. So was Zeng Qinghong, his initial preference for the 2002 succession, who had formally retired in the spring of 2010, and former premier Zhu Rongji, who had nurtured a formidable cadre of economic state administrators. They were part of the collective leadership when it came to matters of political succession, and the private criticism they leveled at the Hu-Wen tandem sometimes made the rounds in Beijing.

A second factor is that Hu pursued the objective set by Deng after the end of the Cultural Revolution, which was to ensure a stable core of leaders at the top, away from the interplay of factions and ideological grandstanding. The party remains an exceptional institution. Political succession at the top, and any appointments to a certain level below, are bargained among the leaders, with no independent or even outside process to legitimize them. Lasting examples of purely internal devolution of power are rare. The example of Singapore, which is often showcased by advocates of an authoritarian state of laws, is hard to view as a comparison point. Not only because of its much smaller size (a population of only five million), but also because the Lee family, from the founding patriarch Lee Kuan Yew to his son Lee Hsien Loong, has been in power since 1955 through the institutions of the PAP, the dominant political party. North Korea, a Communist autocracy, has become a dynastic monarchy, but can hardly be considered a model for others.

China's feat—perpetuating a government held *intuitu personae* with a high degree of institutionalization—remains extremely rare for temporal power. Only the former Republic of Venice and its doges (an official oligarchy until the eighteenth century) and contemporary Vietnam, also run by a Communist party, are comparable. Some people in China even bring up the model of the Vatican and its Curia of cardinals, who elect the pope and eventually defeat his intentions. It is quite an art to balance ambitions and prevent the formation of factions engaging in demagogy: in other words, to prevent a return of Maoist-like political struggle.

In his final years in power, Hu Jintao was commonly denounced by liberals for his failure to act decisively and for the stagnation of political reform that marked his terms in office. There is even a pun on his first name, making it sound like the word "trap," an allusion to the political gridlock of his reign. But political conservatives have always remained powerful, with the weapon of nationalism ready for use. Their capacity for blackmail includes, for example, circulating lists of "traitors to the Chinese nation." Hu Jintao, in his balancing act, wouldn't or couldn't put an end to this.

NO SEPARATION OF POWERS, BUT A STATE OF RULES

In defense of the Hu-Wen tandem, even if they shunned any radical breakthrough, they have greatly expanded the reach of rules and regulations and enforced them concretely. No drastic changes were made to the dogma, but the concrete operation of society and its relationship with the state changed profoundly, as illustrated by the following two examples.

The first was the increase in the number of official procedures. The Hu-Wen era saw a revival of procedural reforms, internal controls within the party-state, an increase in the resources and the technical capability of think tanks, and expertise in general, both within and outside of government. Hence China has moved to a consultative government governed by rules, with a corresponding process inside the party. Local party members' general meetings must take place, and not only when a new leadership is put in place every five years. The election of local party cadres, for which the number of candidates is greater than the number of seats, has been surrounded by more guarantees than elections of village and local district assemblies, which are the first step in the indirect election process for the National People's Congress. In 2007, at the Seventeenth Party Congress, there were 8 percent more candidates than there were positions to be filled. The Congress introduced multiple-candidate experiments within the party in two provinces. Under Hu Jintao, as under Zhao Ziyang from 1987 to 1989, the meetings of the Politburo were no longer held in secret. The meetings of his Standing Committee, which are much more frequent, continued to be held without any announcement.

Nothing illustrates better the emphasis on procedural and technical improvement than the reforms affecting the party's famous Organization Department and its job-appointment capacity—up to and including the principal leaders themselves. In the Chinese Nomenklatura, which is based on the Soviet system, appointments are dependent on the top echelon; many of the posts are subject to party membership and to veto by the party. [10] Exceptions are rare, like the case of the minister of science and technology, Wan Gang, who spent eighteen years in Germany working with Volkswagen, and is formally a member of a small United Front party, the "Chinese Public Interest Party" (*Zhongguo zhigongdang*). The requirement for membership of the Communist Party is not easily waived. Thus, a Westerner who ended up as vice president of a Chinese regional bank in which his own bank owned a share was surprised to find his name in the local directory of the cadres who are members of the party, for the simple reason that it is a requirement for jobs at that level.

Over the past ten years, these procedures have been reinforced, and they are now much more meticulous. Appointments of cadres by the Organization Department at each level are subject to control not only by the first echelon in the hierarchy immediately above but also the second echelon. This is to reduce the impact of direct personal relationships. The standard is also applied to a number of organizations—state enterprises, the media, and universities. In addition there is a rating system based on a certain number of performance criteria for all jobs, whether within the party, the state, or in major corporations. For example, if a grade is given for environmental performance and not solely for economic growth, local cadres receive an incentive to implement the "green" economy. The party's seat of power, which since the outset has held the famous *dangan*, information files that follow all members throughout their lives, is now engaged in human resources management.

The second institutional transformation involves the rise in opportunities for litigation by citizens. Some of these are age-old practices dating back to the Empire. This is the case of the right to petition by letter or visit (*xinfang*[11]), which allows any citizen to appeal by petitioning the upper echelons of the state or the party. It is now so institutionalized (in various forms) that a government agency exists to oversee the courts and the processing of those appeals, according to a procedure set in 2005. Evidently the arrangement also makes up for a lack of control by the central government of its widely dispersed local bureaucracy.

The legal and judicial system itself has also expanded considerably, including with the creation of a fund to aid low-income plaintiffs—both individuals and groups. Between 1998 and 2010, the legal aid budget increased thirty-five times, reaching the still modest amount of one billion yuan.[12] In 2010, the legal aid budget was supplemented by subsidies to private legal aid associations. There are more than 17,000 law firms and 200,000 attorneys.[13] That boils down to only 1.5 attorneys for 10,000 people, a proportion that remains below India's (probably a little more than 8 per 10,000 people in 2010) and in France (8.4 per 10,000 in 2010), not to mention Anglo-Saxon societies that live by litigation. All these changes, taken together with a wider reach of the rules and the possibilities for appeal to the government are creating more of a litigation culture, as well as a state that can be challenged. Yet these are the underpinnings of a legal edifice that is missing a vital part—a separation of powers and a check on constitutionality.

NO RULE BY VOTE FOR CHINA

The limit of this accountability is that holding elections remains impossible. Yet voting is formally everywhere, the advocates for the system might well say.

The People's Republic has had four constitutions since 1949. The last one, which was adopted in 1982, has already lasted for thirty years. At every stage of the political process, elections are theoretically essential, from voting for local and then provincial assemblies ultimately to the People's National Congress, up to and including the election by the legislature of the premier and his government, as well as the president of the People's Republic. The same principle prevails within the party, from the bottom up: everyone is elected. This invites irony, of course.

One significant example will suffice. The Central Military Commission, which is the nexus of party and army, was duplicated from the party within the state in 1982, to draw a distinction between the two jurisdictions. But there is not one iota of difference between the two commissions. Although its members are "elected" by the Central Committee in one case and by the National Assembly in the other case, the two processes miraculously coincide. The Commission(s) remain(s) the seat of power of last resort. The party commands the military, in other words the People's Liberation Army, and it can count on the army in the event of a major problem. That was true during the civil war, and Mao's takeover dates back to the time he became the head of the commission during the Long March. It was true of Deng, who relied on the commission to enforce martial law in 1989. The limits to individual power set by the collective leadership and by the remaining influence of former leaders are reflected in a waiting period that was imposed on Hu Jintao himself. He had become the party's number one in November 2002, but could only succeed his predecessor Jiang Zemin as the head of the commission one and a half years later. In the spring of 2003, he received only 92.4 percent of the votes in the People's

National Congress to obtain his position, while thirty-six deputies (1.2 percent) voted for Jiang Zemin to go on. This reflects above all a degree of factional struggle, but it is also making real—albeit in minuscule doses!—what was hitherto a pro forma electoral process.

Overall, the notion that the members of China's ruling bodies are elected is still a fiction, of course. China's high-level party entities choose the candidates, eventually with the Organization Department of the CCP. Three different justifications are heard in China for this.

LAW WITHOUT ELECTIONS

First of all, there are people who deny the very principle of elections. Not all of them are Confucianists behind the times. One of the chief representatives of a rule of law without elections was Pan Wei, who holds a PhD from the University of California at Berkeley, where the free speech movement was born in 1961. Pan Wei has an office at the prestigious Peking University (Beida) that is decorated with prints of decadent Rome, the Rome of the eighteenth century with its neglected monuments and streets. His arguments are not so much founded on a Chinese cultural exception (Confucianism or the bureaucratic tradition) as on an internal criticism of Western models and a nostalgia for the "mass line."

Pan speaks of "democratic superstition." For him, democracy can be summed up as a belief in the electoral process as a system of selection and decision making, thereby confusing elections with efficiency. However, on occasion, he also uses the argument that where there is insufficient socioeconomic development, democracy cannot be allowed. Pan contrasts this with the development of a rule by law, returning to the classical philosophy of the Chinese Legists from the fourth century BCE. The fact that he is both conservative and quite a nationalist does not prevent Pan Wei from attacking the party when it fails to meet his expectations. In so doing he invokes Chinese popular opinion, which would like nothing better than to lash out and sweep away all Western trends and their advocates. So his view of the people is close to that of the Maoist "mass line," rather than being rooted in democratic legitimacy. Nevertheless, he defends a constitutional process by law, with control by independent bodies within the government itself. In some respect, Pan Wei is not that far from those who wish to substitute technocratic rule for the give-and-take of electoral competition. He also recommends "a consultative rule of law" (*zi xing xun fazhi*), citing Hong Kong and Singapore as models.

THE MODELS OF SINGAPORE AND HONG KONG

The reference to Singapore has also been made by the party's Central School, which studied and promoted the Singaporean political model in 2007 and 2008.[14] Like Singapore, China has already implemented a system whereby "one party exercises the monopoly of the government over the long term, and a number of parties coexist." But China has yet to put in place a true "government by the elite" (*jingying zhiguo zhidu*) as seen in Singapore. The party school would be more circumspect today about praising the Singaporean example. Singapore does have much more freedom of information and freedom of speech, as well as several political opposition parties. Long restricted by district gerrymandering and government patronage, electoral competition is becoming more of a reality. In the 2011 legislative elections, the dominant party received only 60 percent of the votes even though the electoral system allowed it to retain eighty-one seats out of eighty-seven. A well-known government minister, formerly in charge of culture and information and then foreign policy, lost his seat in that election and left political life. Some quarters in the CCP would like to see Singapore as a role model, with its system dominated by one party and a $50,000 per capita income in 2011. Yet even this small city-state, trading emporium, and offshore haven is departing from Syracuse, Plato's ideal model for a benevolent tyranny, and is inching closer to elective democracies. Singapore has electoral provisions that favor the dominant party, such as a proportional remainder, under which several seats are reserved for the heads of losing lists in the majority vote, and others are reserved for "independents" who are appointed by the government. These rules indicate that Singapore still intends to mitigate election results and uncertainty.

In Hong Kong, handed over as a special administrative region to the People's Republic in 1997, the system negotiated by China with the British provides for both a chief executive and deputies to the Legco (Legislative Council), the local assembly, half of whom are elected on a territorial basis while the other half are elected by so-called "functional" trade associations. The pro-democracy opposition received 57 percent of the votes in 2008, but voting for the "functional" seats ensured a majority supporting the Hong Kong chief executive chosen by China. The relative proportionality of these seats has been a subject of incessant debate since the negotiations between China and Britain began. For the first time, the central government agreed in 2010 to assign five of the thirty-five "functional" seats to territorial districts. It has promised election of the chief executive for 2017, and direct voting for all seats by 2020, albeit with a committee entrusted with screening candidates.

Hence the theories developed by Pan Wei do not hold up for the two chief examples of limited or managed democracy in Asia—Hong Kong and Singapore. Of course, it would be even more impossible today to cite the examples of Korea and Taiwan to back up the same theories. They are electoral democracies without restrictions; and each has seen changeovers of political power between parties. In all these cases, a gradual change that started as a tactical concession, sometimes prolonging an authoritarian government for several decades, clearly resulted in a complete transformation.

TOWARD THE RULE OF LAW?

The fact remains that Pan Wei has identified a political trend in post-Communist China when he referred to a "consultative rule of law." Others refer to "consultative Leninism"[15] or a practice of "authoritarian deliberation."[16] This latter term may come as a shock. Our political imagination was conditioned by Athenian "deliberative democracy" as practiced by the orators on the Pnyx and the Agora in Athens. We are accustomed to following Karl Popper, who compared Socrates the democrat to Plato the authoritarian, without fully realizing that it was Plato who placed Socrates on the stage and somehow deliberated with himself through Socrates.[17] Socrates himself recognized the authority of superiors who possessed particularly strong ties to the divine and the authority of moral experts, which he deemed preferable by far to the judgment of the multitude.[18] There is in fact no need to refer to a hypothetical traditional Chinese governance, to Confucianism, or to the "mass line" in order to justify single-party rule tempered by mechanisms of self-control and consultation. Doubts, instability, and the counter-performance of democratic societies may suffice as a justification. That was the case in the early 1930s at the height of the Great Depression. It has been the case for some since the 2008 recession.

It is also possible to rationalize the gap between constitutional theory and the reality of political monopoly by explaining that all constitutions have their interpretative biases. Hence much of a constitutional order is not explicitly contained in the text itself, but subject to further rulings. That "second constitution," whether virtual, customary, or judicial, can be established by means of the courts (most frequently in the Anglo-Saxon world) or by parliamentary means (most frequently in France). Viewed from this perspective, China would just be an especially striking case of a regulatory rule of law outside the Constitution and the electoral process.[19] This would not necessarily rule out supervision and criticism (among different branches of the governmental system) and could even claim precedents in the imperial administration. In fact, control and supervision are a Chinese tradition, to wit the censorship function in the imperial period or the Control Yuan (Chamber) of Republican China, which still functions in Taiwan and holds supervisory power over the lawmakers and the government. However, as influential as bureaucratic institutions (a secretariat or traditional censorship system that could act as a brake on the emperor himself) and practices such as submitting memos and protests to the emperor might have been, they definitely did not cancel out the personal power of the emperor. To the contrary, in Taiwan the Control Yuan has become a constitutional organ, albeit less influential than the elected legislative assembly. It is no longer the secular arm of a political party. In China, the only corresponding institution is the party's Commission for Discipline Inspection, definitely subordinate to the party itself.

SEPARATING THE JUDICIAL SYSTEM FROM THE PARTY

A second interpretation is based on the idea that legal rule could chip away at arbitrary power. That can be an official trend, in response to the most publicized abuses. The highly publicized case in 2003 regarding Sun Zhigang, an unregistered immigrant in Guangdong, who was beaten to death in a temporary detention center, had significant consequences. A 1955 government regulation stipulating the detention of "drifters and beggars" was then abolished by the government, after several petitions to the National Assembly denounced the regulation as noncompliant with the 1982 Constitution. In this specific case, the decision was made by the government, and not by a judicial or parliamentary body. Another decision in this case reflected another tradition, that of a life for a life: one of the men who had beaten up the young Sun was condemned to death and executed.

But in 1999 when a court decision made in Shandong was referred to the Supreme People's Court, the Court declared it to be unconstitutional.[20] Sporadically such a constitutionality control can occur, at least over decisions by the courts themselves, if not over the actions of the government or the administration. This is akin to the mandatory review of death penalty cases by the Supreme Court. It is an important decision for yet another reason: in China the different levels of the judicial system and hence the courts can scarcely be considered hierarchical, and there are no rules for bringing a case before a particular court, or in fact in any particular location. To wit, Bo Xilai, whose alleged crimes were committed in Shenyang (Liaoning) or in Chongqing, was tried finally in Jinan (Shandong) in August 2013. It is also not the importance of the crime that determines which level of court, but rather the relative importance of the person accused. With this situation, local judges are much more prone to corruption.

In May 2012, the issue of the independence of the law came up again, this time in another direction. After the violent Chongqing anti-mafia campaign, which was often supported by the local courts, came the case of Chen Guancheng, the blind anti-abortion lawyer, held under house arrest by the security services in the province of Shandong, who succeeded in evading his guardians and seeking refuge at the US embassy in Beijing. This led to a movement to sever the dependence between the party and the "organs" (the police, judges, and public procurator). A former leader inched out in 1998 by Jiang Zemin, Qiao Shi, revealed that the party's Commission for Political and Legal Affairs (*Zhengfawei*), which became prominent first during the 1957 anti-rightist campaign, was placed again on the front burner after the 1989 Tiananmen crackdown. Moreover the head of the commission became a member of the Politburo in 1993. Qiao Shi suggested breaking off the ties between the party and the judicial apparatus.

This suggestion also had a bearing on the 2012 political succession. Zhou Yongkang, who held that position, and who was a member of the Standing Committee of the Politburo, had been weakened because of his close relationship with Bo Xilai and because of embarrassing affairs such as the one involving the blind attorney Chen Guancheng. It is hard not to point out that of the two successors of Hu and Wen after the Eighteenth Congress, Li Keqiang, deemed reformist and liberal, is one of the few political leaders to have received legal training. Wang Shengjun, the current president of the Supreme People's Court, China's highest court, never studied law or held any position in the judicial system before taking this position, which he owes entirely to his career in the *Zhengfawei*. However, his predecessor Xiao Yang, who was instrumental in increasing the control of the Supreme Court over the lower courts, and who also introduced the systematic review of death penalty cases, had a law degree and was a former minister of justice.

In the absence of elections, and in the absence of a political revolution, only Communist Party reformers can undo the control exerted by the party over institutions and over economic life. The paradox of reform is that even if it is supported from below, it must be pushed from the higher echelons of the party in order to succeed.

NOTES

1. Glenn D. Tiffert, "Chinese Constitutionalism in the 1950s," in *Building Constitutionalism in China*, ed. Stéphanie Balme and Michael W. Dowdle (New York: Palgrave Macmillan, 2009), 61.

2. Deng Xiaoping, "On the Reform of the System of Party and State Leadership," in *Selected Works of Deng Xiaoping*, vol. 2 (1975–1982) (Beijing: Foreign Languages Press, 1995), 319–42.

3. *People's Daily*, October 8, 2004, p. 2.

4. The Chinese version of this tribute in the form of a memory of a trip with Hu Yaobang in the wake of the famous "Trip to the South," by Deng on New Year's 1992, was published in the *People's Daily* of April 15, 2010. See http://news.sina.com.cn/c/2010-04-15/052420076846.shtml.

5. Zheng Qingyuan, "Moving in a Correct Direction to Reliably Advance Political Reform," *People's Daily*, October 27, 2010, reported on http://news. xinhuanet.com/politics/2010-10/26/c_12704266.htm .

6. *Beijing Chenbao* [Beijing morning], November 2, 2010. The article, which quickly disappeared from the website, was translated by the China Media Project of Hong Kong: David Bandurski, "Who Is Zheng Qingyuan?" November 5, 2010, http://cmp.hku.hk/2010/11/05/8592/.

7. Wen-Hsuan Tsai and Peng-Hsiang Kao, "Secret Codes of Political Propaganda: The Unknown System of Writing Teams," *China Quarterly* 214 (June 2013): 404.

8. *Fenshukengru.*

9. Cheng Li, *China's Leaders: The New Generation* (Lanham, MD: Rowman & Littlefield, 2001).

10. Kjeld Erik Brødsgaard, "Institutional Reform and the *Bianzhi* System in China," *China Quarterly* 170 (September 2002): 361–86.

11. Illustrated in 1992 by the first film by Zhang Yimou, *Qiuju, a Chinese Woman.*

12. "China's Legal Aid Funds Surge in 2010," *Xinhua*, February 2, 2011, http://en.people.cn/90001/90776/90882/7279101.html.

13. According to Yu Ning, president of the Chinese Lawyers' Association, quoted by *Xinhua*, December 25, 2001, http://www.chinadaily.com.cn/china/2011-12/25/content_14324123.html.

14. According to the Research Group of the Party's School, "The System of Political Parties in Singapore," *Xuexi Shibao* [Review of the Party's Central School] 420 (January 14, 2008), quoted by Mathieu Duchatel, "Singapore or Governance without Democracy," *China Analysis* 17 (January–February 2008): 7.

15. Steve Tsang, "Consultative Leninism: China's New Political Framework," *Journal of Contemporary China* 18, no. 62 (2009).

16. He Baogang and Mark E. Warren, "Authoritarian Deliberation: The Deliberative Turn in Chinese Political Development," *Perspectives on Politics* 9 no. 2 (2011): 269–89.

17. Karl Popper, *The Open Society and Its Enemies*, vol. 1 (1945, reprint Princeton, NJ: Princeton University Press, 2013).

18. Antony Hatzistavrou, "Socrates' Deliberative Authoritarianism," *Oxford Studies in Ancient Philosophy* 29 (Winter 2005): 75–114.

19. Stéphanie Balme and Michael W. Dowdle, "Introduction: Exploring for Constitutionalism in 21st Century China," in *Building Constitutionalism in China*, ed. S. Balme and M. W. Dowdle (New York: Palgrave Macmillan, 2009), 6.

20. Yu Xingzhong, "Western Constitutional Ideas and Constitutional Discourse in China, 1978–2005," in *Building Constitutionalism in China*, ed. S. Balme and M. W. Dowdle (New York: Palgrave Macmillan, 2009), 119–20.

Chapter Seven

Wukan, or the Possibility of an Election

In 2011–2012, a local revolt by farmers in Southern China against officials they had supposedly voted in office electrified China, and became part of the national debate about political change. Hopes for this change also lie with pressure from the grassroots level. The CCP has placed a lock at the top, which the reformers within the party seem unable to release. Conversely, there have been many developments in village elections at the local level.

Local self-government (*zizhi*) is a community tradition in China. In the imperial past this tradition was carried on by the educated gentry and the landowners. The CCP also relied on self-governing community bodies under its overall control in the "liberated" zones during the Sino-Japanese war. In 1987, direct elections with multiple candidates were introduced in Chinese villages. A temporary law was upheld in 1998 and amended in 2009 to allow the voters to vote out corrupt local officials. Elections are supervised in principle by district governments, which is the next administrative level up, where the first rung of elections inside the party and for the National People's Congress is also located. Village elections are nonetheless conducted under the watchful eye of the local party. The village leaders are "guided" (*zhidao*) if not directed by the district heads. Having locally elected leaders serves several functions for the government. It helps to have reliable local cadres supported by the people to fulfill its own objectives—from overseeing birth control to payment of the harvest tax (finally abolished in 2006). The elections provide direct representation for the villagers, but also a line of communication to administration. It remains extremely difficult to determine the degree to which they are really implemented, especially given the existence of a wide variety of different electoral procedures. The freedom to stand for office varies greatly, as does the role played by the party in elections. There are numerous conflicts between villagers and cadres, who tend to overstay their welcome in office and to deter competitors from challenging them. The studies done from local examples even yield very different figures for the number of villages in China. The least informed still quote a figure over a million. Those who use official data from the 1990s cite a figure between seven hundred thousand and nine hundred thousand. In reality, since 2005, the number of villages has fallen below five hundred thousand.[1] In any event, the figure is too large for a comprehensive study.

WUKAN, A MEDIA BLITZ

At the end of 2011, a conflict between villagers and local cadres in the village of Wukan (Guangdong) caught the attention of the international press. The villagers clashed with the local government over the confiscation of their land and proclaimed their desire for self-government after violent actions by the police. The authorities then started a blockade of the village. The villagers were probably saved by two factors: first the international media coverage, making it more difficult to crack down on a highly united population. The second factor has to do with the political situation in Guangdong. That province was run by Wang Yang, who made a name for himself in 2011 by announcing his support for further legal reforms and a role for private associations. Although initially he stayed in the background in the crisis, Wang Yang went on to resolve the issue in an exemplary manner by accepting the principle of new elections and letting the principal local leader, Lin Zulian, stand for election. Lin, a member of the party, had made it clear during the crisis that the revolt had backing from some higher quarters inside the party. In early 2012, the international media were predicting the advent of a local electoral democracy, and touting Wukan as a model that would undoubtedly be followed by other villages.

These comments overlook the fact that village elections already exist. On the one hand, the Wukan villagers simply managed to obtain the implementation of laws that have often been disregarded as elected power holders cling to their offices. In the weeks following the Wukan affair, other villagers revolted against their lawmakers. Some protests were suppressed; others made themselves heard with less fanfare. The "election campaign" in Wukan in March 2012 was exemplary (with official slogans referring to "democratic harmony," "obeying the law," engaging in "civilized discourse," and even "fighting like gentlemen"[2]). In the end, the spokesman for the revolt, Lin Zulian, won the election. Three years later, however, it seems that not much of the land seized has been returned or compensated for. One leader elected in 2011 has been arrested for bribery before new elections at the end of 2014, another had fled to the United States,[3] and another former activist gives a gloomy assessment.[4] Lin Zulian, however, was reelected in December 2014 during a closely guarded vote.

The Wukan situation may have served as an effective symbol within the party itself. Wukan belongs to the former district of Haifeng, a clan area (there are only seven different extended families in Wukan itself). The districts of Haifeng and Lufeng were the sites of the first land insurrections by peasants, before the CCP organized these. Their 1922 revolt against landowners was led by Peng Pai. He was a precursor to Mao in the peasant insurrection (and long dismissed by official history for that very reason). The peasant soviets of Hailufeng have been kept out of the limelight by the People's Republic, yet the symbol remains a powerful one. At a distance of 130 kilometers from Hong Kong and Shenzhen (the most developed region in all of China), a violent outcome covered by the media would have been a communication disaster for the government.

A SLEEPING BEAUTY: THE NATIONAL PEOPLE'S CONGRESS

A turning point in terms of elections could also occur at the most improbable and yet the most obvious place for China's institutions. The National People's Congress (NPC) is indisputably a product of poorly run elections. There are many limits on its independence, to say the least: several levels of indirect suffrage to designate delegates, an election process that is even more closed than theoretically allowed in the villages and within the party, and a single annual plenary session, traditionally set for the month of March. These restrictions nullify the immense power that is vested in theory with the NPC. It designates all top positions in the executive branch of the government.

The filter of indirect elections and a nomination process overseen by the party have actually ensured an astounding overrepresentation of a new group: Chinese billionaires. This is the perverse effect of an ideological innovation by former president Jiang Zemin, the "theory of three representations." By expanding political representation beyond the workers' and peasants' proletariat and fellow travelers of the United Front, he has opened the door for business owners. The richest among them in 2012 was Zong Qinghou, chairman of Wahaha, worth $7 billion.[5] He was topped in 2014 by Robin Lin, founder of the Baidu search engine, at $14.7 billion.

Furthermore, with one major exception, the presidents placed at the head of the NPC since 1978 have been leaders in retirement, more conservative than the party-state's number one, but just as anxious to wield their own influence through the National People's Congress. Although little publicized, the NPC's 175-member Standing Committee, its specialized committees, including the Legislative Commission, play a major role in drafting laws and regulations. The members of the Standing Committee are permanently in session, while the delegates to the NPC come to sit once a year and have no opportunity for intersession activities. Groups, factions, and clubs are unknown.

Yet votes by the NPC are important in three directions. First for the legislative process, because some bills can be amended or delayed for a very long time when there is no consensus. Second, for the selection of high office holders, because there is a percentage of nay votes or abstentions that give an actual indication of the popularity of the individuals. And last through its public discussions, resulting in comments posted on the web. Appearances and press conferences by key delegates on the sidelines of the single session are a testing ground for communications with the press. In March 2011, Bo Xilai was the leader who received the most attention in the Chinese and international press. In March 2012 it was Wang Yang from Guangdong who stood out. He indicated some support for political reforms, if not in content then at least with proposals for less ritualistic respect toward leaders, and less formality in meetings.

The once-a-year session of the NPC gives delegates an opportunity to vent out some protests. Issues such as the single-child policy, the status of migrants, and real-estate speculation have been raised frequently in the past few years. In casting their votes, the delegates can express disagreements. These may reveal factional discussions within the party, or some leaning, whether liberal or conservative. The record for votes against a government figure

(722 votes against) goes to Li Tieying, chosen in 1993 to be a State Councilor. That former minister of education, said to be a child of Deng Xiaoping born out of wedlock, had led the fight against political liberalization and against Hu Yaobang in 1986. In the past few years, it is the relationship of the supreme judicial organs (the Supreme People's Court and the public procuratorate office) that have polarized opposition. This is undoubtedly because of rampant corruption in the courts, but perhaps also because of opposition by lawmakers to any campaigns cracking down on that very corruption.

The role played by the NPC in the legislative process is more significant. But it is not what one might expect. In practice, rather than a force generating legislative proposals, the Congress is a filter that weakens, slows down, and sometimes blocks substantially the adoption of new bills. This reality is closely tied to the role played by its Standing Committee, a genuine chamber of party leaders. At its head, the chairman of the NPC is often a conservative. Only Wan Li, before 1989, and Qiao Shi after him have pushed for reforms. Peng Zhen used legalism to curb the reforms by Deng Xiaoping after 1978. Li Peng, the premier who shouldered the public responsibility for the Tiananmen crackdown, succeeded Qiao Shi. Then came Wu Bangguo, a close associate of former president Jiang Zemin, formerly in charge of agriculture. Since 2013, another former associate of Jiang Zemin, Zhang Dejiang, has taken over. Long-awaited reforms have been blocked in the NPC. This was true of China's company law and its enterprise bankruptcy law, its law on supervision of officials, and the law on private property.

In 2010 a reform by the NPC passed unnoticed. It involves measures to establish an even representation between the rural and the urban districts. Just as the urban population exceeds 50 percent of the total population for the first time in history, this measure, which has long been demanded by a sociologist from the Left, Hu Angang,[6] is finally being implemented. If direct elections were to play a greater role in the selection of "delegates" (who are not members of a parliament in the full sense of the word), this redistricting would guarantee more representation for regions with the most disadvantaged part of the population. Despite the symbolic inclusion of three delegates who supposedly represent the migrant population, the lack of social representation in the National People's Congress is its second Achilles' heel, second only to the lack of a clear electoral process. However, the urban elites are playing such a role in the transformation of China that one cannot help thinking that this measure in favor of the countryside would play out initially in a more conservative direction.

RETIREES IN CONTROL

Other customary practices remain in the party-state. An unwritten age limit forces the members of the Party to resign their positions at age seventy, and even in practice at age sixty-eight. Thus in 2012, seven of the nine principal leaders (members of the Standing Committee of the Politburo), and six of the other sixteen members stepped down at the Eighteenth Party Congress. Five of the seven new members of the Standing Committee of the Politburo, China's seat of power, are one-term office holders because of their age. Yet the committee in charge of selecting leaders includes not only outgoing officials but also retirees, with no age limit. This limits the power of those in office, who remain under the scrutiny of old comrades. Neither President Hu Jintao nor his colleagues had full authority to designate their successors, as they shared this decision with a wider group that is responsible for reproducing the core leadership. This is where the analogy with the Roman Curia of the Holy See takes on its full meaning.

In some sense, this has long been the case. In the early 1990s, there was talk of the power of the "Eight Immortals," the major survivors of the first generation and their influence running up to

Congresses. Crisis meetings resulting in the dismissal of a major leader were nearly always "enlarged" meetings of the ruling bodies, with elder leaders joining. This was the case from the fall of Peng Dehuai in August 1959 until the dismissal of Hu Yaobang in January 1987. Zhao Ziyang, CCP General Secretary before 1989, has revealed in his memoirs[7] that he was dismissed by an "enlarged" meeting of the Politburo held on June 19 and 21, 1989. He also explained that the meeting was not made public in China until 2004.[8] Three of the four speeches made against him (not including Li Peng, who was selected to chair the meeting) were made by retired leaders (Li Xiannian, Wang Zhen, and Chen Yun). According to Zhao, Deng himself spoke, and in a departure from written regulations but not necessarily from custom, he urged retired members to participate in the vote. In this regard, however, nothing surpasses the famous meeting of the Central Committee held by Mao in August 1966 to approve the launch of the Cultural Revolution. Some of the members were prevented from participating, while the addition of Peoples' Liberation Army (PLA) soldiers definitely "enlarged" the meeting. In any country other than China, this event would have been considered a military coup.

Yet circumstances were becoming quite different in 2009–2012. On the one hand, as Wen Jiabao had pointed out in his Shenzhen speech, the Chinese revolution was over, for better or worse. Although the official dogma does not recognize it, the Communist ideology underpinning the regime was becoming increasingly remote and hard to define. No individual leader had the power or influence of the regime's founder. In 1976 the issue had been one of returning from autocracy to collective leadership. At the end of the Hu-Wen decade, the problem became giving the leaders an actual mandate to govern. With the balance within the collective leadership at the top of the party, initiative was limited. This was more favorable to a consensus against new reforms rather than for them.

The reversal of a reform process into a conservative bias did not happen overnight. Initially, hostility toward the promoters of the Cultural Revolution had created a reformist dynamic and alliance. Yet as early as April 1979, Deng stated to his colleagues that, although he did not agree personally, he would follow their advice and put an end to the first Beijing Spring—this was the first break inside a makeshift coalition that had included activists for democracy. In 1986, he began to distance himself from his two reformist lieutenants, Hu Yaobang and Zhao Ziyang. This made him shift to a conservative coalition. And yet at times Deng resisted, dismissing his alter ego Yang Shangkun, along with his half-brother Yang Baibing,[9] an embarrassing symbol of the Tiananmen crackdown, and relaunching the opening up of the economy with his "trip to the South" (*nanxun*). However, the taboo on 1989 remained, in part because Deng himself was responsible for the repression.

Deng Xiaoping left his official position at the Thirteenth Party Congress in 1987. At the time, it was agreed that he would continue to play a leading role and in particular that he would retain control over the Military Affairs Commission, which he chaired until September 1989. A suggestion that he retire, made in a Guangdong province party publication, caused the fall of his main lieutenant, Hu Yaobang. During Mikhail Gorbachev's trip to Beijing in May 1989, the actual general secretary of the party, Zhao Ziyang, revealed to Gorbachev that Deng was still playing a role in "important decisions." He was then accused of betraying a "state secret."

Did Deng feel any belated remorse? As early as 1980, he had denounced the practice of lifetime positions for cadres. When he reintroduced reform during his journey to the South in January 1992, he referred again in one of his speeches to the need for leaders to retire. It was Jiang Zemin after him who made retirement a standard requirement. He may well have had an ulterior motive: one of the first leaders to whom the rule applied was his rival, Qiao Shi, who ranked number three in the party and was considered more reformist than Jiang. Qiao Shi had to give up his chairman-ship of the NPC in favor of Li Peng.

Jiang Zemin's term in office seemed more free from the con-straints of the collective leadership and the party elders. Jiang had nothing to fear from the conservatives, who felt certain he would continue the coalition of silence regarding 1989. His past, particu-larly his role as Shanghai's leader, was in sync with China's bu-reaucratic industrial complex. With these reassuring certainties at the top, it was actually under Jiang that many legal and regulatory innovations were adopted. Premier Zhu Rongji enthusiastically continued the economic opening, with China's accession to the WTO and the restructuring of the state economy. None of this constituted political reform, but the pressure on outside critics and activists did let up, with the exception of Falun Gong, the Buddhist sect.

REFORMING THE PARTY, CONTROLLING THE COUNTRY

The advent of Hu Jintao and Wen Jiabao in 2002 led to a misunder-standing. They sought initially a limit to the economic focus on coastal regions, which perhaps not coincidentally had been the power base for Jiang Zemin and his "Shanghai faction." In so do-ing, they raised the issue of a Chinese-style social divide and grow-ing inequity or income gap. However, their emphasis on control and supervision, and even on democratization, ultimately involved only the party, which was reformed in 2004 and 2005. Outside the party, democratization had come to a standstill and even retreated. The tremendous growth of the social media has also led to equally powerful instruments in order to keep them under check.

A more thorough reshaping of the conservative coalition took place in Hu's second term, starting in 2007. Foreign policy events may have played a role. Successive international campaigns (against the genocide in Sudan and China's support for Khartoum, and about Tibet) cast a cloud over the 2008 celebration of the Beijing Olympic Games. Other causes for concern were the election of Barack Obama with an emphasis on soft power, a renewed popularity of the United States in Asia, the feeling that the quagmire in Iraq was coming to an end, and the sudden rise of the Internet in China, including American portals such as Google. At the same time, the 2008 financial crisis in the West reduced the influence of liberal democracies as a model, at least from an economic standpoint. But the crisis also represented a threat to China's growth, which was too heavily predicated on exports. At the end of 2010, with nationalist fervor on the rise again in China, an increasingly hard-line domestic policy returned to center stage. The decision to award the Nobel peace prize to the jailed dissident writer Liu Xiaobo was interpreted by Chinese leaders as the result of an American plot. In early 2011, the outbreak of the "Jasmine Revolutions" in Tunisia and Egypt and the ensuing "Arab Spring" caused a furor among China's leaders. During a hastily called meeting of the Politburo after the fall of Hosni Mubarak,[10] they decided to block any news or analysis on the subject and to eliminate any "unhealthy trends" in the virtual media. The live TV feed from Cairo's Tahrir Square on television, showing Egyptian soldiers descending from their tanks to fraternize with the demonstrators was a genuine red flag for China's leaders, reminding them of the Tiananmen crisis. They started a counteroffensive that far exceeded the actual influence of the Middle East events on the Chinese public.

THE END OF THE CHINESE REVOLUTION

The political tension in the regime eventually burst open in the spring of 2012. For the first time since 1989, the arguments were not merely confined to the periphery of the government and civil society, in other words to think tanks and the web-based forums, which are patrolled by hired activists for the "maintenance of stability," or the so-called "50 cent party" (*wumao dang*[11]) in reference to their pay.

But they did start there, and of course, the unauthorized voices were the boldest. In the Chinese edition of the *Financial Times*, Ma Guochuan,[12] an economist and a veteran of reforms, went global with his criticism, challenging both state capitalism and also crony capitalism, or the capitalism of connivance, based on "ties of blood, marriage, or secret alliances." The criticism was not only economic. He denounced the populism that leads to crony capitalism because "an ambitious person can use the power of the people to build his own power." He attacked "statism," which was still very influential in China, and discussed the negative examples of pre-1945 German and Japanese militarism.

One of the fathers of Chinese reforms, the economist Wu Jinglian, also explained that China had reached a crossroads. He condemned the primacy of the statist model and called for expanding Deng Xiaoping's "1992 model" of reform and opening up to include political reform. According to Wu, the vested interests in what remains a command economy were using the threat of populism and nationalism against reform. They claimed that problems arose from reform itself. Instead, Wu contended, China's main problem stemmed from the incomplete reform and the absence of rule of law. Even more political and more iconoclastic, Hu Deping, the son of the deposed reformer Hu Yaobang, voiced his criticism more and more publicly. After causing a public stir with his comments on the Chongqing "model" and on Wukan, on February 26, 2012, Hu Deping posted a furious tweet on "the corruption of 96 percent of the cadres."[13] On March 5, Ai Weiwei, the artist who designed the general outlines of Beijing's famous bird's nest Olympic stadium, said he regretted contributing to the project and denounced the "moral bankruptcy" of the regime.[14] Ai Weiwei was taking a risk. The authorities had ended his secret detention in June 2011 and sentenced him to house arrest only on the condition that he would refrain from speaking out in public. But in the spring of 2012 that risk had apparently become acceptable.

REFORM TRAVELS NORTH

The debate on China's fundamental choices also came to light in the official national press. One need only compare this situation with the stony silence that had greeted Wen Jiabao's earlier speech in Shenzhen in October 2010, or with the chiding anonymous editorials signed as Zheng Qingyuan. Between the time when a current for political reform had been started in Guangdong and the moment when the Bo Xilai affair broke in Chongqing, another shift had occurred at the top of the Communist Party.

Because China is China, rooted in Confucian ritual and the symbolism of party-line struggles, a coded slogan was coined for this shift. In implicit opposition to the old slogan *moshi guohe*, a new theme was proposed—the theme of "top-down design" and "overall planning of reform." The expression had appeared in October 2010, the very month of Wen's speech in Shenzhen, in the official document for China's twelfth Five-Year Plan. Since then, it had been circulating in the official media and in discussions on reform. On February 16, the first page of the *People's Daily* featured a criticism of the taste of some provinces and some cadres for "bubble" growth at the expense of reality. Better yet, a vigorous defense of reforms and a criticism of the cadres who raise "structural obstacles" to preserve vested interests appeared in the same paper. "Better have imperfect reforms than to have a crisis resulting from the lack of reforms."[15] This was the first time the general failure to act and the clampdown on reforms were recognized and criticized.

Where was China going? At no time since 1989 had the terms of the debate been posed so explicitly as in 2012. Moreover, the de-

bate was often associated with the same location—Guangdong—
and expressed in the same terms used by Wen Jiabao in October
2010. The contrast some saw between that province and the Chongqing "model" ultimately led to the reformist revival. Wen Jiabao's
choice of setting for his speech, the Wukan (Guangdong) revolt for
renewing the local election process, made historical sense. Sun
Yatsen founded his first reformist government in Canton, his native
city. Hong Kong's influence—in economic terms but also through
media and frequent travel—is paramount in coastal Guangdong.
Zhao Ziyang was its party secretary during the Cultural Revolution;
at that time he had protected a rare pro-democracy species of the
Red Guards—and would later start the first experiments of reform
in Sichuan after Mao's death. Deng Xiaoping himself, when purged
by the ultra-Maoists in April 1976, found refuge in Canton under
the protection of Xu Shiyou, the commander of the military region.
In 1989, the authorities south of the Yangtze clearly did not fully
enforce the repressive guidelines from Beijing. Many Tiananmen
Square activists were sheltered in Canton before they could leave
for other countries. It was also logical for this region, which is the
most economically advanced in China, to play again a forward role
in the reform process. In 2006 and 2007, on the eve of the previous
(Seventeenth) Communist Party Congress, the region had already
served as a model for the "liberation of thought," and Wang Yang
was already developing there the idea of "devolution of powers"
(*fangquan*) to nongovernmental organizations. The idea was picked
up again in 2011[16] and in May 2012 it resulted in a move to liberalize registration formalities for NGOs. The flagship province has
often been "one step ahead in China,"[17] while displaying much
ambiguity. For example, Guangdong NGOs are looked on favor-
ably because of their ability to perform social welfare functions
more efficiently than the administration, rather than as an encouragement to civil society.

TOP-DOWN REFORM RESUMES

Dissidents and liberals were no longer the only voices claiming that reform was being blocked by vested interests, nor were they the only ones advocating the principle of a legality that would be binding on everyone, and hence on the party. The idea of an end to the Chinese Revolution[18] was also synonymous with an end to the Communist Party's exceptional status above the law. Nor were they the only voices espousing the need to resume the reform process. There was recognition that part of the leadership had blocked the reform process. In March and April 2012, these views had also spread inside the party-state.

Since 1989, when Communist systems were shaken to the core, and after the challenge of Tiananmen Square, the regime had placed under wraps any policy debate at the top. It also made a distinction between economic reforms and political debate, allowing the former and limiting the latter to changes of the legal system and governance. The separation of politics from economics has certainly been a success, given the high growth of the past quarter of a century. But the ban on political change has led to mounting tensions and increasingly placed the leaders and their rites in splendid isolation.

The regime's reaction to the Arab Spring showed again how much it dreads the notion of a revolution from the bottom up. It is well aware of the corruption eating away within its ranks. However the notion of another revolution doesn't make sense: even with galloping inequality, on the whole, overall progress remains enormous. A Chinese middle class has been created, or more accurately an upper-middle class. As critical or even as cynical as it often is, this new stratum benefits from the status quo and is opposed to risk taking. The idea of reform from the bottom up—in other words the gradual influence on the regime of a semi–market economy and more open society—meets with limits. These are the immense powers wielded by central authorities. They are endowed with unprecedented financial and technology resources, and they have placed themselves in a situation where they are the only ones capable of holding the country together.

By default, the resumption of reform from the top down remained if not the most attractive, at least the most probable scenario for change. An entire generation had been held back after 1989 and Tiananmen. The bolt on reform was still in evidence not only in the political realm, but also in China's economy. Regardless of who won out in the economic debate, the advocates of economic liberalism or those with a focus on the public sector and social issues, both of these choices required a reformed state. Without independent control and without a political system capable of enforcing the proper legal notions, such a change would not take place.

NOTES

1. See the various editions of the official *China Statistical Yearbook*. The average population of a Chinese village is between one thousand and fifteen hundred.

2. *"Minzhu hexie," "guifan schoufa," "wenming yanjiang," "junzi zhi zheng,"* from a photo in the town hall, published in *Libération*, March 3, 2012, p. 9.

3. Dan Levin, "Years after Revolt, Chinese Village Glumly Returns to Poll," *New York Times*, April 1, 2014.

4. "Wukan Youth: Zhang Jianxing," *China Digital Times*, June 19, 2014, at http://chinadigitaltimes.net/2014/06/wukan-youth/

5. According to the data from the 2012 Hurun China Rich List, available at http://www.hurun.net/EN/HuList.aspx?nid=14 .

6. Author in 1995 with Wang Shaoguang of a report on regional disparities in China.

7. Zhao Ziyang, *Prisoner of the State* (New York: Simon & Schuster, 2009), 39–42.

8. Lyman Miller, "More Already on Politburo Procedures under Hu Jintao," *China Leadership Monitor* 17 (January 2006): 12.

9. Yang Shangkun, president of the Republic (a largely honorary position), but first and foremost vice chairman of the Military Affairs Commission in 1989, and his half-brother Yang Baibing implemented martial law and the crackdown in June 1989.

10. Perry Link, "The Secret Politburo Meeting Behind China's New Democracy Crackdown," *New York Review of Books*, February 21, 2012.

11. An expression designating web commentators paid by the government for their postings in discussion forums.

12. Ma Guochuan, "Shenmoyang de daolu Zhongguo buhai zou?" [What are the roads that China must avoid?], *Financial Times* (Chinese edition), March 7, 2010, http:///www.ftchinese.com/story/001043534?=2.

13. Tweet reposted on YouTube at http://www.youtube.com/watch?v=0w9b4axgbN0.

14. Interview in *Yomiuri Shimbun*, March 5, 2012, http://www.yomiuri.co.jp/dy/world/T120303003904.htm.

15. "Tan huanjie zhengde," editorial in the *People's Daily*, February 16, 2012, available on http://news.qq.com/a/20120216/000153.htm.

16. Jérôme Doyon, "The Guangdong Model: Towards Genuine NGOs," *China Analysis* 38 (November–December 2011): 30–34.

17. Ezra Vogel, *One Step Ahead in China: Guangdong under Reform* (Cambridge, MA: Harvard University Press, 1989).

18. Wang Hui, a populist conservative, also published a well-known book, Wang Hui, *The End of the Revolution: China and the Limits of Modernity* (London: Verso, 2009). Wang blames the liberalism of the 1980s for the ideological decline and the accession to liberal globalization in China. His theory is attracting postmodern criticism the world over but it thinly masks an apology for the indefensible—Mao and his mass movements.

Chapter Eight

2009 — The Turning Point

The year 2009 was a turning point in China's foreign policy. China's previous relations with its partners had not been a bed of roses. But since Mao's death, it had followed a principle of elementary caution that can easily be summed up: never enter confrontation with more than one partner at a time. Worry about Western sanctions after 1989, the fear of being strategically encircled and ideologically isolated, had prompted China to develop a good-neighbor policy with Asia.

That did not automatically make it a very cooperative government in international terms. In numerous cases, particularly at the United Nations, China has found for itself a niche as the core element of a rejectionist coalition against new international norms and intervention. Thanks to this, much more often than Western countries, it has been in the majority at the UN General Assembly. In the Security Council on the other hand, it has resorted only rarely to the veto, and much less often than the United States, for example.

When it becomes a member of an international organization, China applies a high priority to national sovereignty and may therefore act as a brake on that organization. Conservative in general and hostile to what it terms "interference in domestic affairs," and also to sanctions or any new and legally binding standard, Chinese diplomacy in general is hardly a force bringing renewal to global governance. From 2006 to 2008, China was placed on the defensive by two events: the genocide in Sudan, where for a long time it blocked intervention by the UN; and the March 2008 turmoil in Tibet, which exposed China to international criticism in the Olympic year.

A DISPLAY OF MILITARY POWER

There is therefore nothing new about the contrast between the global dynamism of the Chinese economy and a defensive and fairly unconvincing diplomacy. But China's conservatism had also dictated caution in the management of its international claims and conflicts inherited from the past. A turning point in that last respect came in 2009. Perhaps the first inkling surfaced in December 2008—when two Chinese government vessels entered for the first time the waters of the Senkaku/Diaoyu islands, claimed by China but controlled by Japan. In March 2009, the government actually announced for the first time in more than a decade, a slowdown in the increase in military spending to a mere 7.5 percent. For China, this was the first departure from over 10 percent yearly increases for the PLA since 1998. In the middle of the global financial crisis, had China become aware that it was less likely than ever to be surrounded by enemies? Had it began shifting its priorities to the recovery of the domestic economy and to social as opposed to military expenditures? In any event, this unusual slowdown (which has not occurred since) seems to have had the opposite effect a few months later. There was an unprecedented level of praise for the PLA with the parade celebrating the sixtieth anniversary of the People's Republic in October 2009. This was an occasion for a gigantic display of Chinese military might in the heart of Beijing, with a media outpouring glorifying the army.

MOUNTING TERRITORIAL INCIDENTS

The sixtieth anniversary of the PRC was followed by a turning point in China's relations with its neighbors. In the space of a year, incidents occurred in the South China Sea with the Philippines and Vietnam, and in the East China Sea with Japan. In September 2010, a particular incident raised the level of tension between China and Japan. The captain of a Chinese trawler, sighted in the vicinity of the Senkaku, chose to ram twice the Japanese coast guard vessel that had intercepted it. The incident was filmed, and the captain, described as drunk, was detained for two weeks in Okinawa. This led to an uproar and demonstrations in China until the Japanese government overrode the local prosecutor office and freed the captain. Chinese public opinion was totally unaware of the fact that the Chinese maritime administration, the military equivalent of the Japanese coast guard, had been detaining hundreds of Vietnamese and Filipino fishermen, arrested in waters claimed by China as an exclusive economic zone. Moreover, less than a month after the great tsunami and the Fukushima nuclear disaster, in March 2011, a Chinese military helicopter buzzed another Japanese coast guard vessel.

In 2010, China also stepped up territorial pressure on India, claiming that it considered Indian officials born in the state of Arunachal Pradesh as Chinese citizens. This surge of activism also targeted the US Navy directly. A "civilian" fleet harassed the USS *Impeccable*, an electronic surveillance vessel, in China's exclusive economic zone near the Island of Hainan, and attempted to steal its top-secret towed antenna.

Since October 2009, China has stepped up these shows of force amid a xenophobic burst of enthusiasm in public opinion. However, it has stopped short of any military action that could lead to an involuntary confrontation and escalation. The strategy seems designed to assert power by creating tension, but it is also reversible and without much risk taking in the short term. Was this truly a turning point in China's international relations or a momentary deviation, and if it was a turning point, why? Was it due to decisions made at the top, or did the leaders lose control over some parts of their own bureaucracy, which was in effect acting as a nationalist lobby? Were China's leaders feeling growing pressure from the grassroots level, civil society, and the media because of nationalist activists, and had that pressure reached the top echelons of the regime? Or were we getting a first look at the conclusions drawn by China's leaders from their astounding economic success and from the recession plaguing the old developed capitalist economies? These questions have remained vexing ones for foreign governments, because no definite answer has been found. Within the US government, for example, President Obama conferred with many experts in the fall and winter of 2010 and 2011 before revising his China policy. A meeting of officials at the highest level reportedly resulted in as many opinions as there were participants regarding China's true strategic objectives.[1]

TACTICAL OR STRATEGIC RETREAT?

The incidents gradually subsided from November 2010 until July 2011. The pause was undeniably flagged by Dai Bingguo,[2] then the most senior foreign policy official in China, outranking the foreign minister. Some incidents persisted in the South China Sea in the first half of 2011, until a declaration made with the Association of Southeast Asian Nations (ASEAN) in July, setting the "guidelines" for settling maritime disputes. Chinese diplomacy seemed to have made the mistake of endorsing the most extreme interpretations, which held that the entire South China Sea was a Chinese territorial area. But the Foreign Ministry (Waijiaobu) spokesman now made a distinction between issues related to the exclusive economic zone and navigation and fishing rights, on the one hand, in which China plays an active role, and issues affecting territorial sovereignty on the other hand. According to the Waijiaobu spokesman, disputes over territorial sovereignty apply only to "some of the Nansha Islands and the demarcation dispute over part of the waters of the South China Sea. What should be pointed out is that neither China nor any other country lays claim to the entire South China Sea."[3]

Could this distinction hold in the climate of domestic political tensions against a backdrop of mounting stakes? First of all, the economic stakes involved in the development of maritime zones alone are tremendous. When China issued an international tender to develop oil fields in the same area where Vietnam had already granted a permit to Exxon, it was obviously upping the ante. In March 2012, while Wen Jiabao discussed the need to maintain good relations between China and its neighbors, several members of the National People's Congress, including representatives of the army and the State Oceanic Administration, raised the issue of allocating further resources to defend China's rights over what they called "three million square kilometers of ocean territory." A few weeks later, another round of incidents and claims ensued with Japan and Southeast Asia. A tense confrontation occurred with the Philippines in May over an atoll known as Scarborough Shoal. After the Philippines brought a Navy ship to the area and after objections by the United States, the Chinese ships withdrew from the reef. However, by standing guard around it, they effectively denied any access to Filipino fishermen: one PLA officer has publicly termed the tactics a "Chinese cabbage," whereby the atoll is surrounded by several strata of Chinese ships.

These contradictory events came at a time of extreme political tension. They suggest that territorial boundaries had also become an issue in domestic debates. Moreover, from 2009 to 2012, moves toward hard-line domestic policies seemed to alternate with phases of international tension, as if a conservative offensive within the Chinese leadership was moving from one area to another, never fully abating.

Post-2012 developments—under president Xi's far less disputed leadership—lend credence to the notion that there was previously great tension within the leadership. In effect, president Xi's rule has enforced both an inflexible political line on domestic dissent and debate, and a tough attitude toward neighbors. The proclamation of an Air Defense Identification Zone (ADIZ) covering disputed areas of the East China Sea, and the deployment in the spring of 2014 of an exploration oil rig in waters claimed by Vietnam with the resulting incidents, demonstrate that the 2009–2012 trend was no fluke.

Nonetheless, China's policy remains shifting and unpredictable in the short term. A new cycle began occurring in late 2014. On the occasion of the APEC summit in Beijing in November, China and the United States reached an agreement on the prevention of military incidents at sea; a meeting between President Xi Jinping and Prime Minister Shinzo Abe has resulted in a communiqué whose ambiguous wording nonetheless states different views between China and Japan on their island dispute and mentions progress toward maritime crisis management. Skeptics—and they abound—point out that maritime incidents that have occurred have never involved Chinese military vessels—but only paramilitary or civilian boats, not covered by the China-US agreement.

Ironically, the breakthrough followed by only two months another deterioration in Sino-Indian relations. A visit to India by President Xi Jinping in September 2014 coincided with the dispatch of Chinese soldiers to an area of disputed control between the two countries. Starting on the eve of the visit and prolonged after it ended, the incident brought a sharp retort from India's prime minister, Narendra Modi. Clearly, China retains the capacity to intensify or tone down incidents at will.

Is there the potential for a nationalist offensive likely to challenge the country's growing integration and its compromises? It may seem simplistic to consider China's international relations in light of tiny islands, empty maritime space, or zones for developing maritime resources. However, such issues are of considerable symbolic and strategic importance. They involve all of China's maritime neighbors. They may one day also include enormous energy resources. It may be a good thing for regional peace that so far such resources have been proven only in the vicinity of Japan and very near the Vietnamese coast. But offshore exploration techniques have considerably improved, making it increasingly likely that deep-water resources can be uncovered.

Maritime disputes also involve the strategic balance between China and the United States, regarding the control of the most crowded navigation lanes in the world. Because they are part of history, such disputes reflect China's identity and international positioning. Finally, they occur within an Asia lacking any collective security arrangement other than a series of defense agreements with the United States. This is leading to the sharpest increase in military expenditures in the world—in China of course, but also in India as well as in several Southeast Asian countries.

THE NORTH KOREAN MIRROR

The turning point in foreign policy did not stop there. The year 2010 saw the imminent succession of North Korean leader Kim Jong-il, who was weakened by a cerebral hemorrhage. The appointment of his youngest son, twenty-eight-year-old Kim Jong-un, and the need for the North Korean regime to remain a credible threat, led to military incidents with South Korea not seen since 1968. China's increasingly high-profile behavior on maritime issues may have encouraged the North Korean leaders to emulate it. In order to justify North Korea's nuclear program, the North Koreans have also explained to their Chinese counterparts that they were merely following China's example vis-à-vis the United States in the 1960s.[4] In February 2010, the South Korean frigate *Cheonan* sank with forty-six sailors aboard following an explosion, which the investigation later determined was caused by a torpedo. Through a process of elimination, investigators concluded that it could only have come from North Korea. However, China flatly refused to condemn North Korea at the United Nations Security Council, denying the findings of the investigation and merely demanding "moderation by all parties concerned." On July 9, the Security Council condemned the action, but without naming the perpetrator. That resolution was immediately described by North Korea as a "great victory."

It therefore came as no surprise that North Korea started up again a few months later. During a South Korean military exercise in the Yellow Sea, in waters near the armistice line that are controlled by Seoul but nevertheless disputed by North Korea, the North Korean army shelled the civilian population of Yeonpyeong Island. This was the most serious violation of the cease-fire agreement since the 1953 armistice. Yet once again China took a protective stance toward the North Korean regime. Meanwhile the entire membership of the Standing Committee of the Chinese Politburo[5] had hosted Kim Jong-il and his son in Beijing in May 2010. President Hu Jintao then traveled to Changchun in northeast China for a second meeting in August. China was switching from a role as an intermediary (as the United States had been hoping for a decade) to acting as a sponsor, shielding Pyongyang's ruling dynasty and also consolidating its own economic hold on North Korea's foreign trade.

These incidents unleashed the anger of South Korean public opinion against China. But the anger also reflected South Korean president Lee Myung-bak's inability to influence either China or Pyongyang. The South Korean government threatened Pyongyang with the worst if it ever resorted to the same behavior, but received neither apologies nor concessions. Shortly thereafter, China made a considerable investment in the North Korean economy. This took the form of mining or industrial renovation agreements, the transshipment of goods and merchandise through Chinese ports, and a flood of imports on North Korea's parallel markets. Beijing has so little fear of a military conflict that it has built a highway along the North Korean border. Extending this highway to the North Korean port of Rason, which abuts both China and Russia, will give China its northernmost access to the sea.

China has been able to increase its influence over North Korea because of that country's isolation coupled with international sanctions. Has this led to the creation of what is sometimes called Northeastern China's "fourth province"? North Korea has a strong desire for independence. In the spring of 2012, the North Korean navy did not hesitate to detain scores of Chinese fishermen venturing into North Korean waters, doing to China what China had done to the Philippines, Malaysia, and Vietnam! Still, in 2010–2012 ties between Beijing and Pyongyang had become closer than ever since the end of the Korean War.

BEIJING SCRAPS ITS PUBLIC DIPLOMACY

The new image of an assertive or even aggressive China was not only due to incidents on the ground. It also stemmed from a reversal of public diplomacy, with intransigent positions appearing to take center stage.

In May 2010, the first "strategic and economic dialogue" (or SED as it is called) between China and the United States in Beijing provided an opportunity for a diatribe by a senior PLA officer in front of the other participants at the meeting. Did he mention the South China Sea among China's "core interests"? There are no sources other than US media on this. Yet the Chinese government has never denied the assertion. In truth, for the Chinese government to clearly state that the South China Sea is *not* a "core interest" might be seen as downgrading its own claims.

In the spring of 2009, during the G20 summit in London following the global financial crisis, Chinese public diplomacy succeeded brilliantly in depicting its country as the savior of the global economy. China contributed a substantial amount (although less than Japan) of loans that could be made available by the IMF. It agreed to cooperate on the issue of off-shore tax havens, participating in a surveillance mechanism for that purpose. Yet by the end of the same year, the impact of this international cooperation was negated by China's role in deadlocking the Copenhagen Climate conference.

In Copenhagen, China made a show of intransigence. Not only did it reject a binding agreement, but also the aloofness of Premier Wen Jiabao, while Chinese negotiators like Deputy Minister He Yafei were blocking discussions among heads of state, gave the impression of disorganization and perhaps of internal disagreement. In truth, the United States was no more ready than China for a legally binding emissions reduction agreement. China had earlier lobbied other emerging economies, starting with India, to prevent such an eventuality. But President Obama made a last-minute suggestion—a plan to verify actual greenhouse gas emissions with measurement stations installed in each country. Such a plan was sure to ruffle China's feathers: with its insistence on sovereignty, it has little tolerance for intrusive verifications. Thus in the end, the United States left it to China to play the role of naysayer.

The damage caused by the maritime incidents with neighboring Asian countries has been much greater. One skeptical Chinese expert has explained this with a tongue-in-cheek reference to a statement by Bismarck: "If you have five neighbors, it is a good policy to get along with at least three of them."[6] The reference is not insignificant given the obvious comparisons between China's rise and Germany's rise under Kaiser Wilhelm II. At the end of 2010, China's foremost geopolitical journal would write that in that year

China had improved its relations only with Europe and North Korea.

OBAMA CHANGES HIS CHINA POLICY

China also appears not to have responded to earlier overtures made by some of its major partners. In the United States, an incoming Obama put together a team that had long been in favor of good relations with China. His adviser for Asia, Jeff Bader, had even carried the Olympic torch during its passage in Sichuan province in August 2008. Barack Obama, who, unlike his rival John McCain, did not meet the Dalai Lama during his campaign, proposed a "strategic partnership"[7] on the eve of his first official trip to China. His predecessors had never made such a proposal to China. In a joint US-China statement wrapping up the trip, he repeated the expression "core interests" (*hexin liyi*) first mentioned by China. These "core Chinese interests" are very vaguely defined, at times covering Chinese sovereignty over Taiwan and Tibet in a narrow sense and at other times covering all its territorial interests or even broader national interests as well. President Obama received little in return. Some of his public comments during his trip were censored in the local press.

Since the outbreak of the global financial crisis in the summer of 2007, the Chinese media and Chinese experts often portray the United States as being on the decline, stressing US fiscal problems. In November 2008 China ended its policy of slowly revaluing its currency. The yuan was to move with the dollar—that is, it would be devalued until June 2010, during two years of global recession. China's exports and foreign exchange reserves have continued to balloon ever since, as does the US trade deficit with China. With China's support for North Korea, the United States faced the challenge of enforcing its anti-proliferation policy. Chinese experts lent little credence to overtures by the Obama administration, often emphasizing instead the soft power trap embodied by US supremacy over the Internet and social networks.[8] Moreover, the Chinese government started to display increasing confidence in asserting itself. On the very day of a meeting between Secretary of Defense Robert Gates and President Hu Jintao in January 2011, the Chinese media were full of reports on the first trial of a Chinese stealth fighter plane, the J-20. In August 2011, when Vice President Joe Biden attempted to prolong a public statement in Beijing by a dialogue with the press, he was interrupted off-handedly by his hosts, who motioned to the audience to move toward the exit.

Barack Obama did not acknowledge publicly that his overture to China had failed. However, he was to adjust his strategy accordingly. The United States began paying more attention to India and to Southeast Asia, where Secretary of State Clinton announced that "the United States is back." Those words were meant less for Asia as a whole than for a subregion very neglected by the Bush administration. In fact, Chinese diplomats had become accustomed to stressing to their neighbors that China "was there to stay," implying this was perhaps not the case of the United States.

Above all, for the first time, the United States reacted publicly to the maritime incidents between China and Southeast Asia. At the ASEAN Regional Forum, in July 2010, China's foreign minister Yang Jiechi was criticized by twelve governments of the region, emboldened by US support. Caught unaware, Yang Jiechi retorted that "China is a large country, and the other countries are small countries." This lesson in realism did not go down well in the region.

In short, China handed the United States an opportunity on a silver platter to renew ties with its worried Asian neighbors. Those countries were not all former allies and friends. In October 2009, the United States began reversing its hard-line position with regard to Burma. The sanctions imposed to protest the dictatorship and human rights violations were still in place. However, in September

2009, fearing the possibility that Burma might become a nuclear power with the assistance of North Korea, the United States attempted a policy of "positive engagement" with the Burmese junta. Meanwhile China had turned international sanctions to its own economic advantage. But it also stirred Burmese national prickliness, especially with the construction of upstream dams on Burmese rivers, designed to generate electricity that was then sold to China. In October 2010, unrest flared up in the ethnic regions near the Chinese border. The Chinese army responded by entering Burmese territory to support its local allies. These incidents and the reaction against China's overbearing presence undoubtedly proved to be a major incentive for the Burmese junta. After the lengthy rule of General Than Shwe, it moved to liberalize the country and open up to the outside world.

Vietnam, which was concerned about the repeated military incidents around the Paracel Islands in the South China Sea, also drew closer to the United States. At the end of 2011, President Obama, on a trip to Australia and Japan, was able to announce the creation of a marine rapid reaction force in Port Darwin, Australia. He reinvigorated a seemingly commercial coalition allying free trade with converging strategic interests. The Trans-Pacific Partnership, first established with midsize Asian economies (including Vietnam), has been designed with the ultimate aim of attracting two Asian economic heavyweights, Japan and South Korea, thus counterbalancing China's influence through trade.

As his campaign for a second term drew nearer, Barack Obama adopted a tougher policy toward China. It was now out of the question for him to appear soft. Statements by the United States reflected this tougher policy. For example, during a trip to Manila in November 2011, Hillary Clinton referred to the "Western Philippine Sea," echoing local sentiment as well.

EXPLAINING THE TURNING POINT IN
FOREIGN POLICY

Observers have been intrigued by the tougher line taken by China toward its neighbors. They have attempted to find an explanation within China itself. Pekinology has one thing in common with fortune-telling: it is based on the interpretation of very tenuous signs. In truth, no one has had access in at least ten years to the decision-making process of China's leadership, which has become a black box.[9] Perhaps for that reason, Pekinology is highly vulnerable to any oral confidence, whether true or false, made to foreigners who are then convinced they are penetrating the inner sanctum of government. Compared with boring written accounts in the press and Chinese journals constrained by censorship and stilted language, nothing is more credible than "secrets" learned around a dinner table. In addition, observers can have their own bias. US diplomats and analysts, who are by far the most numerous and the best equipped to observe China, also have a patriotic instinct that sometimes causes them to deny their country's possible loss of influence. Some of the Chinese with whom they liaise are also in charge of maintaining relations with the United States, and they tone down official Chinese statements. Lastly, the celestial bureaucracy in its complexity lends itself well to functional analyses of internal rivalries, without assigning them an intentional and political significance. This approach leads to assumptions regarding the process of policy making itself rather than strategic debates within the leadership.

THE HYPOTHESIS OF
BUREAUCRATIC FRAGMENTATION

A certain number of "truths" therefore led to a consensus at the end of 2010. First of all, according to this consensus, President Hu Jintao was a lame duck because of the upcoming Party Congress and November succession. Furthermore, according to the same consensus, Hu, who in any event had never based his leadership on foreign policy, had a hesitant and indecisive style. Chinese diplomacy was no longer represented within the Politburo. Its flag-bearer until November 2012, former diplomat Dai Bingguo, has been described as a Chinese Metternich because of his cleverness and malleability. Yet Dai did not have the political stature of his predecessors, such as Deputy Premier Qian Qichen, not to mention the memory of Zhou Enlai, the legendary chief of Chinese diplomacy after the civil war. His successor, former foreign minister Yang Jiechi, has even less political authority. Below them, the Chinese Foreign Ministry has been said to be falling behind, undermined by the rise of more dynamic state actors, ranging from the PLA and its General Staff (rather than the minister of defense, which is merely a cog in the machine), to its General Logistics Department, at the head of an arms procurement lobby. Along with the Ministry of Foreign Trade—the "Mister No" of international trade talks—major state enterprises and the more technical agencies also carry weight. There is also the issue of the autonomy and the ability of the State Oceanic Administration to stir up trouble. That entity has resources at sea rivaling those of the military, but it has the advantage of not committing the People's Liberation Army or its navy directly. The agency is only one of China's five agencies involved in maritime affairs. They have expanded more rapidly than the Chinese navy itself.

This explained the risk of fragmentation for decision making, or of increased autonomy on the margins of those multiple actors. Such fragmentation could also encourage ideological or policy discrepancies. Thus the PLA or one of its arms could try and create the conditions for obtaining power projection assets, particularly an aircraft carrier and its battle group, a sign of formal membership into the club of the major powers. China's new economic clout, which is giving rise to new actors and giving traditional actors more resources, also leads to fragmentation. Such a wide array of economic or military decision-making centers could swamp central government control. At the top, defense has been vested almost exclusively with China's number one leader. Until November 2013, no national security commission existed to bridge over various entities, and even when it has been created, it seems to deal as much or more with internal security issues as with international strategy.

A RUNAWAY PLA?

At the nexus between the party and the army lies the influential Military Affairs Commission. The commission is duplicated in the party and the state. Whoever runs it is actually the country's leader of last resort. This has been the case since Mao. Hu Jintao, who did not start off in a position of personal strength over the PLA, has reportedly ended up placing that sector off limits to the other members of the Standing Committee of the Politburo. He had little patience for the generals, even those he appointed himself. Hence the commission began to meet less and less frequently, and only two of its members, Xu Caihou and Guo Boxiong, the two military members of the Politburo, really called the shots, as President Hu himself did not attend all the sessions.[10] Yet the commission is the only link between the top level of the party-state and the PLA. The army's refusal to take direct orders from Premier Wen Jiabao during the May 2008 earthquake in Sichuan shows that aside from the party chief himself, ties between the political and the military can be tenuous indeed. Suggestions by experts from Beijing think tanks that a National Security Council be created have long been dismissed: Why create and develop a new stratum of decision making when the power game is completely political and personal?

Furthermore, the leaders can in any case bring together all the experts they want and enlist the support of research institutions to draft reports for them. All the same, the lack of intermediation between the party's top leader and the army creates the risk that things will get out of hand. Foreign analysts stress over and over the phenomenon of "silos" for Chinese government agencies, referring to the poor interdepartmental or interagency coordination among the ministries, and, in the case of the army, with civilian authorities. The incidents that occurred in 2010 might be explained by this hiatus. Hu's theoretical monopoly at the top would have resulted in practice in insufficient control and communications mechanisms among the different "silos" over which he ruled.

In this view, Chinese bureaucracy is unintentional. Its functional processes, including local deviations, take precedence over a global strategic view. China's recent inability to control external policy could be ascribed to the ignorance of an emperor too far removed from his army, and absorbed by domestic policy making.

But does this theory hold up under examination? The same argument has been used in two compelling cases. The first is the unexpected test of an antisatellite weapon in January 2007, which was reportedly conducted without the knowledge of either the Foreign Ministry, whose spokesman was unprepared for the embarrassing questions from the international press, or the top civilian leaders. The other occasion was the test of a major new weapon, the J-20 stealth fighter plane, at the very moment when the US secretary of defense met Hu Jintao in January 2011. Robert Gates made the first trip to China by a US secretary of defense in six years. In both cases, we are given the same explanation: China's top leader must have been unaware of the tests. In a slightly more sophisticated variation, one source adds that the J-20 test, delayed by bad weather, was reset by the PLA's General Logistics Department of the Army without referring to higher echelons. The explanation is hardly credible given that several members of the Politburo, including presumptive successor Xi Jinping and Wu Bangguo, are known to have witnessed the flight in Chengdu, 1,500 kilometers from

Beijing. It is possible but unlikely that President Hu could have been unaware of the coincidence involving the date of a test postponed because of bad weather, or even that he might have underestimated the amount of official publicity that would surround the event. But the idea that Hu could be unaware of the agenda of his main colleagues is inconceivable in a system of collective leadership and mutual control.

THE MILITARY LOBBY HYPOTHESIS

These episodes did suggest the possibility of a tactic of "plausible denial" by China's former top leader, president Hu Jintao. Since coming to power in 2002, Hu Jintao had involved himself visibly very little in controversial decisions, preferring instead the protective shadow of the collective leadership. His fingerprints were therefore hard to find, if not for some trademark catchwords. The disadvantage was that this left the field open to a variety of influences, including by elements that may hope to force the hand of the top leader. Along with the theory of the fragmentation of decision-making centers, the influence of nationalist groups cannot be dismissed, particularly in the army. Some higher officers, admittedly retired, publicly espoused an extremely firm nationalist line in 2009 and 2010 and again in March 2012. Appeals for loyalty to the party by the army increased after those latter episodes. One such appeal in the official organ of the PLA clearly raises the issue of "internal loyalties" in the army, calling for "being constantly mindful in one's thoughts and actions of the primacy of the Party, the Military Affairs Commission and President Hu Jintao."[11] In China's system, this should have gone without saying.

The more signals have accumulated around the "black box" of decisions at the top, the harder it became to draw definite conclusions. The constant rapid rise in China's military expenses is of course a fact—one that makes China the second ranking military spender in the world. As a result, goals once thought to be out of reach are now coming within grasp, and will be even more attainable in the next few years. To rescind these goals now would look like failing patriotic duty. Still, aren't the mounting numbers of incidents and nationalist agitation signs of a deliberate strategy rather than the product of a slow drift?

There have been three theories. One is the above-mentioned increase in the number of decision-making centers defending their budgets and their role, with inadequate control from above. But hasn't the CCP and central government always fought against such phenomena? The second theory holds that there is an actual nationalist and militaristic wing pressuring civilian leaders and perhaps acting in conjunction with conservatives in the party. The financial crisis in the West and resulting interpretations regarding the decline of the West would seem to help these groups. Lastly, we cannot dismiss the highly concentrated and hence limited control over the army under the person of Hu Jintao, who often avoided clear choices, preferring a strategy of ambiguity.

This ambiguous approach backfired as China's actual capacities continued to grow. Aspirations that once appeared totally out of reach had become credible, with practical consequences that caused unrest in the Asia-Pacific region. President Xi Jinping, Hu Jintao's successor, has taken a much more forthright approach and essentially ended the speculation about unintentional drift, but he has also sharpened the edges of confrontation between China, its neighbors, and the United States.

NOTES

1. Interviews in Washington, April 2011.
2. Dai Bingguo, "Stick to the Path of Peaceful Development," New China News Agency, December 6, 2010. The article was immediately reproduced on the Foreign Ministry website and by various major official media.

3. Statement by Hong Lei, spokesman of the Waijiaobu, February 29, 2012, http://www.fmprc.gov.cn/mfa_eng/xwfw_665399/s2510_665401/2511_665403/t910855.shtml.

4. Interview at the China Institute of International Strategic Studies (CIISS), Beijing, April 2012.

5. According to a researcher of an official Chinese institute, the reason for the presence of the entire membership was simply a provision in the 1957 treaty between China and North Korea stipulating that North Korea may ask to be hosted by China's governing bodies.

6. Interview in Beijing, September 2012.

7. Radio interview of President Obama on the eve of his departure, later described by the White House as "an off-the-cuff remark" with no particular significance (interview in Washington, June 2009).

8. Anne-Marie Slaughter, "America's Edge: Power in the Networked Century," *Foreign Affairs* 88, no. 1 (January–February 2009).

9. For an approach by numerous actors who are (perhaps) involved, see Linda Jacobson and Dean Knox, "New Foreign Policy Actors in China," SIPRI, Policy Paper 26, September 2010, Stockholm.

10. We are indebted to Kim Tae-ho (Hallym University, Seoul, March 2011) and to Charles Freeman and Bonnie Glaser (CISS, Washington, April 2011) for this information and these converging analyses.

11. "Budui ganbu 'ye chongzheng'xianxiang bingbu xianjian" [A propos of the phenomenon of the 'internal loyalty' of the military cadres], *Jiefang Qunbao* [Liberation Army daily], June 17, 2012, as reported on http://news.ifeng.com/mainland/detail_2012_06/17/15356890_0.shtml.

Chapter Nine

Nationalism: An Alibi for Great Power Realism

The tougher line taken by China's foreign policy, the rise in military expenditures, and the propensity for incidents involving issues of sovereignty may not be merely a strategy conceived at the top. For a regime that was first crafted during the Sino-Japanese war, nationalism is the first basis for legitimacy. Hence Chinese public opinion also plays a role. But does it act like the choir in the classical tragedies of ancient Greece, simply repeating and amplifying the decisions made at the top? Or has it become an independent variable, with both more open access to international news *and* heated debates on Chinese social networks? If so, could this force the leaders to take a harder stand on national issues, and could it stigmatize moderation as tantamount to compromise?

In China, political demonstrations and advocacy of political democracy are still banned, yet nationalist sentiments have been allowed to appear front stage. Protests have broken out repeatedly against foreign partners—the United States, Japan, and even France in 2008. Nationalist anger has been on display in Internet forums and social networks, and also in street demonstrations and with statements by high military officers who are technically retired but still enjoy widespread public visibility.

These spurts of activism also reflect a system of education and propaganda that has indoctrinated public opinion, particularly the young generations after 1989.[1] There are signs of conscious manipulation. The Chinese government can authorize a protest whenever it needs to support its international claims, and it also has the ability to suppress unwanted expressions. China's government is accustomed to manipulating emotions as a way of sending a message to its partners. It often presents itself to other countries as both a messenger and a moderating influence on a patriotic public that is easily provoked. Nationalist rhetoric also serves to keep at bay more liberal expressions, including by those who want a democratic transition in China.

THE FOREIGNER, A SOURCE OF CURIOSITY

This touches on the more general issue of the relationships of the authoritarian state with society. Chinese society has certainly been emboldened by the market economy and consumerist individualism. Foreign policy in a broad sense (including defense), as the area where control is tightest over information and indoctrination, remains a special case. Nevertheless, it also attracts a tremendous amount of public curiosity, and it is rife with value judgments. Those judgments may stem from patriotic activism, or, to the contrary, from a desire to point out the flaws in Chinese culture. The irony is obvious.

Foreigners have long been a forbidden and yet prestigious source of information. The party's internal newsletter, *Cankao Xiaoxi* (News of reference) the circulation of which was once tightly restricted because of its more revealing content, was based largely on dispatches from foreign press agencies. *Global Times* (*Huangqiu Shibao*), the party's new press agency, in its English or Chinese version, which is now more widely read than the *People's Daily*, focuses largely on international analysis and commentary.

There is nothing new about this penchant for international affairs. It reflects the long-standing Chinese curiosity about the world at large, and the belief that foreigners know more about it. This author learned first about it from an incident in July 1982. In a departure lounge at the Xiamen (Fujian) airport, which was still very provincial at the time, a child of around twelve sent over by his parents after a whispered conversation, suddenly came to ask "Why was Gromyko dismissed?" As a matter of fact, the famous Soviet foreign minister had just resigned, and this author was at a loss to explain why.

The information revolution has done the rest, even though its reach toward the entire population is often exaggerated. The information revolution has more of an impact in the area of international affairs because of the countless foreign websites that can be accessed within China. Someone who strongly wants to get information can now do so, as the firewalls installed under official censorship are not 100 percent effective.

THE MEDIA, INTERNET, AND THE MOLDING OF PUBLIC OPINION

Nevertheless, a majority of web users are content to keep up with international news through forums and social networks, which release short and hence oversimplified news and analyses at lightning speed. So there is news from abroad, but at the same time that news is subject to a prodigious amount of disinformation.

The news is filtered by censorship, which uses key words to go after any sites deemed hostile or that contain sensitive information regarding domestic affairs as well as foreign policy. In a more general sense, directives are handed down in real time from the CCP's Propaganda Department, regarding news that may or may not be mentioned or that should be emphasized. Some of these directives are permanent and are now well known. One bans the reporting of too much bad news in periods leading up to sensitive holidays or anniversaries. These directives also apply to international relations: for example, the directives stipulating that the United States be presented in a critical light, or the ban on reporting foreign views deemed "hostile," or the directive to interpret international events with the aim of drawing the desired political lessons from them. [2]

Lastly, web activists who promote patriotic views are treated with indulgence. Criticism in the other direction is unlikely to remain online for long. One of China's renowned experts in international relations suddenly realized he could not e-mail to a relative one of his own articles published abroad. The key words contained in the article would cause his e-mail attachment to disappear.

Official mainstream media—national television, its news bulletins, and its American-style televised debates; the *Global Times*, referred to earlier; and Phoenix TV from Hong Kong—devote a huge amount of coverage to international news. For the sake of credibility they feature foreign journalists and experts on their shows. However, the topics and opinions are filtered (although less so in foreign-language broadcasts aimed at international audiences). This sometimes involves self-censorship by the participants. What could be more attractive than to reach out to the largest audience in the world, even if it involves a degree of self-censorship? On the other hand, particularly in publishing and the written press, there is more demand for radical domestic views, rather than for moderate but tedious explanations. Some Chinese experts have been the first to understand that a virulent form of nationalism could attract a wider audience at no risk. This is the case of the long-standing best-selling book in China's economic publishing market, *The Currency War*.[3] The first volume explained financial history through plots largely hatched by the Rothschilds, Morgan, and others. Ironically, the author, Song Hongbin, earlier worked in the United States on so-called structured financial products, but has failed to identify these as a cause of financial crises. In his third installment, Song Hongbin predicts a single world currency, resulting from an American plot in 2024. His publisher, CITIC Press, is an establishment outlet.

SOCIAL FRUSTRATION AND NATIONALISM

Is the Chinese public more nationalistic and easily provoked than the government? Chinese diplomats and experts often make the assertion. It is sometimes supported by opinion polls, particularly conducted at regular intervals by the Communist Youth League and its daily paper. These lend credence to the notion of a turning point since 1989 that is for the most part anti-liberal, anti-West, and nationalistic, particularly among the youth. [4]

Nothing is less certain. These polls usually consist of voluntary responses to published questionnaires—in other words, with no guarantee of anonymity, a serious drawback in China.

Another example contradicts these highly controlled polls—one conducted on a more scientific basis surveying the urban population of Beijing between 1998 and 2002. That period was marked by tension in response to the bombing of the Chinese embassy in Belgrade by the United States, the EP-3 plane incident near Hainan, and deteriorating relations with Japan. According to that survey, the public in general and China's middle class to an even greater degree (80 versus 70 percent) was convinced of the benefits of international interdependence with nearly 55 percent in favor of friendship with the United States. Opinions were divided over the principle of nationalism, right or wrong; they were divided over the elimination of tariff barriers, and a strong minority was opposed to increasing military expenditures. [5]

In fact, isn't nationalism particularly widespread among college students and recent graduates in urban areas? Doesn't it serve as an outlet for young people who are unable to find a job, or are underpaid, sometimes described as "ant tribes" (*yizu*) because of their difficulty in finding housing as well as jobs? Moreover, nationalist demonstrations offer an opportunity for more spontaneous and sometimes incongruous calls for action. Thus in Wuhan, during a demonstration against France in front of a Carrefour store in 2008, one protester held up a sign on which he had written, "Is this really your only reason for demonstrating?" before being promptly removed from the crowd.[6]

Just as hostility to globalization in the developed countries reflects other frustrations, the rise of nationalism in China is becoming an outlet for a young and educated middle class to express its frustration at being held back by the lack of jobs for high-skilled workers and the sudden rise in urban real estate prices. There were in the past even more strange correlations. In 1986 and in 1988 some anti-African racist incidents broke out on college campuses on the eve of pro-democracy demonstrations. In both cases, the catalyst proved to be resentment by Chinese students of the benefits enjoyed by African students on scholarships from the Chinese government.

Hence there exists in Chinese society a category of young, educated people frustrated in their aspirations by mounting inequalities, whose attitudes are confined to neo-nationalism. That same category is also the most likely to turn its discontent against the party-state. It is far from embodying the middle class as a whole, not to mention workers and peasants, except when there are strikes in foreign companies (the most uncompromising were held in Korean firms). There seems to be little participation by the Chinese *laobaixing* (ordinary people) in nationalist demonstrations, and oddly few people aged over forty.

WESTERN MODELS CENSORED

Extreme nationalist opinions are usually tolerated and are very rarely rejected by Chinese leaders. They represent a safety valve for discontent and frustration and also a disincentive for anyone too eager to recommend imported political reforms. Although there are a handful of leaders who, like Wen Jiabao, have played at liberal self-criticism, there are no longer any who openly back foreign models or call for emulating an open global culture. That approach was banned in 1989 with the Tiananmen events. The last trace of any leader calling for foreign political and economic models dates back before May 1989 to the publication encouraged by the secretary-general of the party, Hu Yaobang, of a Shanghai magazine, the *World Economic Herald*.[7] The *Herald* was accused of propagating those models and was shut down in April 1989 by Jiang Zemin. That move in fact earned him his stripes with Deng as a national leader.

Similarly, a made-for-TV documentary series that created a stir all over China, *River Elegy*,[8] contrasted "yellow" China—that is, continental, agrarian, bureaucratic, and chauvinistic—with "blue" China—that is, maritime, mercantile, liberal, and open to other countries. The series was blamed for the events of 1989, and could not have been produced thereafter.

However, proponents of nationalism are easy to find in influential institutions. In 1999 after the bombing of the Chinese embassy in Belgrade, the *People's Daily* simply launched its own nationalist forum: *Qiangguo Luntan* (Forum for a strong nation[9]), which is a bellwether for testing official actions against one target or another. In 2005, at the prestigious Tsinghua University, an extremely nationalistic journal was published, *China and World Affairs*. The managing editor was Justin Lin Yifu (later to become the chief economist of the World Bank), and its contributors included well-known advocates of nationalism or conservatism like Pan Wei or Yan Xuetong. However, only six issues of the journal were published—in 2005 and 2006.[10] The case resembles that of another journal, *Zhanlue yu Guanli* (Strategy and management, affectionately referred to as "S&M" by its readers in Washington), which was shut down in September 2004. Although the journal was a masterpiece of geopolitical intransigence, it was terminated because of an article critical of North Korea.

One website, which was both Maoist and nationalistic, attracted attention until it was shut down on April 6, 2012, as a reaction to the Bo Xilai scandal. Utopia,[11] which claimed to be one of the six hundred most visited sites in China, and which is attached to a Beijing bookstore, was known for turning out a large number of virulent nationalist articles. In February 2012 the site launched a contest prompted to designate the "ten biggest traitors in China" from a list of eighteen names thrown into the hat.[12]

Nationalism is never viewed as a sin warranting a prison sentence or dismissal from one's job, nor does it usually result in an official or public rebuke. There are many nationalist activists, but there is no dissident nationalist movement because the regime does not see any adversary on that front. The exceptional era of the 1980s seems remote indeed. Then, people promoting reforms also supported the notion of introducing Western ideas. By contrast, in a January 2012 speech, Hu Jintao denounced "the increasing intensity of the Western plot to divide and weaken Chinese culture and ideology."[13] There is nothing new in such a speech except for the fact that Hu expressed regret (quite well placed in fact) over the weakness of China's soft power in the world. These same arguments were used by Mao nearly all the time, and by Deng whenever necessary for political purposes, capping any political debates on the future of the system.

So the foreign policy debate does exist, in public opinion and among the experts. But the terms of the debate are just as biased as in the field of domestic policy. Like a yo-yo, the regime can give free rein to nationalism and its inferiority-superiority complex, with talk of a China humiliated and surrounded by arrogant adversaries. It can also point to the geopolitical strength of a new China that imposes its will on waning, divided, or just smaller nations. There is further evidence of control by the party-state. Nationalist movements appear and vanish, sometimes as a result of a single order or even without any apparent order at all. If the unrest continues, then the reason must lie in internal divisions at the top echelons of power.

A CASE STUDY: SINO-JAPANESE RELATIONS

There is no better example to illustrate this control than the example of Sino-Japanese relations throughout the history of the People's Republic. This is indeed the one area where emotional reactions can safely be predicted. Japanese aggression and occupation have left deep wounds. The West, and Europe in particular, misconstrues or fails to understand the ins and outs of China's relations with Japan. China's reactions are based both on the feeling that revisionism is the prevailing attitude in Japan and on the long-standing legitimacy of anti-Japanese feeling in China.

Yet the Chinese government controlled and even prevented the expression of anti-Japanese feeling from 1954 until the early 1980s. When hosting Japanese lawmakers in 1954, Zhou Enlai placed "sixty years of strained relations" back in the context of a "history and a friendship stretching back several thousand years." Those were exactly the same terms that were to be used in 2006, when the Chinese government curbed anti-Japanese protest movements. In October 1955, Mao was hosting a group of traditional Kabuki theater actors from Tokyo. He told them "there is no reason for us to ask you to account for your past debts. You have already apologized. You cannot continue to apologize every day, can you? It is not good for a country to sit around whining. That is something well understood here in China." The following year, a public trial for war crimes of a thousand Japanese soldiers was to end in the acquittal of 95 percent of them. Many of them had made terrifying confessions about their crimes, which they never recanted after returning to Tokyo. Those confessions were buried in the archives, only to be released half a century later in 2005 in the midst of a dispute between China and Japan![14] Until 1982, literature, films, and even war memorials avoided accusing Japan. In the 1960s, some historians from Nanjing were even accused "of inciting national hatred and vengeance" when they described the massacre committed in their city by Japanese troops.[15]

When diplomatic relations were reestablished in 1972, China waived all claims to reparations. In an effort to avoid incriminating Japan as a whole, history manuals and official sources stressed that the war had involved "a handful of Japanese militarists." Both sides were counting on the fact that it would be forgotten. Propaganda in the Maoist era never capitalized on the existence of extreme right-wing movements in Japan or on visits by Japanese politicians to the Yasukuni Shrine, the nationalistic war memorial in Tokyo. When the ashes of fourteen class-A war criminals found guilty in the Tokyo trial (including Admiral Tojo) were transferred to this shrine in 1978, it did not set off any official reaction by China. In the same year, the two countries signed their peace treaty and agreed to set aside their territorial differences. Japan began providing economic assistance to China and played a major role in the first phase of Chinese reforms, through loans and investments. Even this was not a complete departure from the 1950s or the 1960s. Starting in 1950, despite the Korean War and US sanctions, the Japanese Diet had passed a law allowing Japanese companies to trade with China through intermediaries, known as "suitcase companies," often located in Hong Kong. In the early 1960s, when China emerged from the Great Leap Forward, its first foreign financing was provided by Japan for a fishing fleet.[16] The Japanese agreed to a "deferred payment," since foreign loans were banned under the Maoist doctrine of self-sufficiency.

JAPAN: A DOMESTIC POLICY CHALLENGE

The attempt to confine the war to the dustbin of history first hit a snag in 1982, when the official Chinese media launched a brief attack against Japanese school textbooks, in response to demonstrations held throughout Asia but not in China. In subsequent years, the reformers in power in Beijing, Hu Yaobang and Zhao Ziyang, were to forge deeper ties with Japan while publicly boasting of the Sino-Japanese entente. Hu Yaobang even held a friendship festival and invited three thousand Japanese youth to Tiananmen Square. Japanese prime minister Nakasone's official visit to the Yasukuni Shrine on August 15, 1985, did not change the rules of the game. The Chinese reacted with restraint, but student demonstrations broke out a month later. The *People's Daily* did little to encourage them, alluding to the specter of the Red Guards during the Cultural Revolution. Hu Yaobang was to continue his policy of friendship with Japan, going so far as to embrace Yasuhiro Nakasone during his visit in November 1986. Any demands were confined to the economy; Japan had become by far China's main partner.

But political conditions then changed completely in China at the level of the party's top leadership. The conservatives soon launched a vicious attack against Hu Yaobang's vague references to political reform. In that context, and according to a direct account by Zhao Ziyang in his memoirs, Hu's attempts to reach out to Japan were among the charges leading to his dismissal in 1987.[17] His conservative adversaries saw a political advantage in stirring up anti-Japanese demonstrations, which were in fact directed against the party's general-secretary, who was seen as too liberal.

In conclusion, in its totalitarian phase, Maoist China after 1954 prevented the expression of anti-Japanese feelings. In the most intense period of political liberalization (between 1978 and 1986), those feelings began to come out belatedly, but they were held in check by the party apparatus. However, it was the internal struggle within the top leadership of the party over all kinds of other issues that caused those feelings to explode in full force. Two years later, when corruption was a dominant theme of the Tiananmen protests, anti-Japanese feeling was almost completely absent. To the contrary, it was the death of Hu Yaobang, who was both a reformist leader and a scapegoat of the nationalist conservatives, that sparked the protests.

PATRIOTIC EDUCATION

So what has changed with respect to Japan since 1989? In the very short term, officially nothing. Concerned about international sanctions after Tiananmen, the regime resumed its good relations with Japan, whose Western partners in the G7 excepted it from the international sanctions on China as early as July 1990. But over the longer term, a complete reversal occurred in terms of propaganda. This reversal did not target Japan, but it was to have serious consequences for Sino-Japanese relations. After burying the liberal decade from 1979 to 1989, the party took back control over education and propaganda directed at public opinion, especially the youth. As foreign news sources dried up, a major patriotic education campaign was rolled out. The youth of the 1980s knew practically nothing about the Sino-Japanese War. Reviving the memory of that war was to form a staple of China's educational campaign. Crimes by the Japanese army, particularly in Nanjing; revisionism in some Japanese media; territorial problems; and also the behavior of the Japanese in China were to become easy targets of public emotions. Anything could be targeted, not only historical or geopolitical themes. Topics such as manufacturing defects in Japanese cars or the sight of nude Japanese students on a theater stage at a year-end celebration in a Chinese university became sources of incidents and protests.

Of course, some real skeletons came out of the closets. The Nanjing massacre has been officially memorialized, and a generation of activist historians has waged an international campaign. In 2003 an accident suffered by some workers digging up Japanese chemical shells left over since the war (an operation subsidized by the Japanese government) became the theme of another campaign. Incidents and protests often happened on the eve of the meetings of the official Japanese commission that sets the amount of development aid for China, and would serve to push for more aid.

In November 1998, President Jiang Zemin's trip to Japan proved to be a key event. Two disagreements became public. The first disagreement (over Japan's refusal to formally exclude Taiwan and its vicinity from possible Japanese-American military cooperation) proved to be much more important strategically than the second one: Jiang Zemin failed to obtain for China the apologies in writing for the war that Japan had made to South Korean President Kim Daejong two months earlier. However, it was the second reason combined with the general theme of Japanese apologies that was to serve for eight long years as the official reason for the breakdown of government relations between the two countries. Some point to the alleged anti-Japanese feelings of Jiang Zemin, who was reportedly beaten at the age of fourteen by Japanese soldiers. Yet those feelings had not surfaced during his first years in power.

From 1998 to 2006, Sino-Japanese relations underwent a crisis, at its most intense in the spring of 2005. The visits to the Yasukuni Shrine by Japanese prime minister Junichiro Koizumi are usually cited as the official reason. China chose its battle wisely. International public opinion could hardly sympathize with such a gesture at a site that includes the war criminals found guilty in 1946 by the Tokyo Tribunal, even if the shrine honors millions of dead from all wars. The tablets in their names are hard to remove, owing to the nongovernmental nature of the shrine. Thirteen of the fourteen families of the condemned soldiers nevertheless agreed to transfer them, but not the family of Admiral Tojo, who was Japan's commander in the Pacific. Protests broke out in China and were especially vociferous in 2005, at a time when the popularity of Prime Minister Koizumi was at a low point in Japan.

Again in September 2010, the incident of the Chinese captain arrested by the Japanese coast guard suddenly sparked protests in five major Chinese cities, including Chongqing and Chengdu. The protests in Chongqing saw a massive turnout, and they were perfectly organized. Even though the region, which was the seat of the Republican government during the war, was bombed by the Japanese air force, it was never occupied. Didn't local party leader Bo Xilai, who had ties with some people in the army and in the top leadership, seem unusually enthusiastic in stirring up nationalist sentiment?

However, during the same period, the Chinese government also made a number of pragmatic arrangements with Japan. Cooperation over old buried chemical weapons led to an official agreement. The Chinese authorities supported the patriotic demonstrations on the Senkaku/Diaoyu Islands; however they made no changes whatsoever in their actual attitude regarding sovereignty. They adjusted to the reduction and then the disappearance of economic assistance from Japan. High-ranking Chinese visitors regularly celebrated two thousand years of friendship between the two peoples.

In reality, the authorities wanted to play both ends against the middle in their relations with Japan.[18] Giving the appearance of a reconciliation while shoving the major problems in the relationship under the rug has led to a "cold peace" (*lenghe*)—an allusion to the Cold War. The authorities believed they could continue pragmatic relations. On both sides, the experts pointed out the constant increase in trade, making China Japan's leading market, ahead of the United States. However, either in order to pressure the Japanese government or because nationalism became both a means of control and an outlet for Chinese public opinion, China allowed those protests to continue, although not visibly nor clearly directed by the party's mass organizations.

THE ROLE PLAYED BY PUBLIC OPINION IN FOREIGN POLICY

The encouragement of nationalist sentiment has resurfaced several times since the anti-American demonstrations of 1999 (after the bombing of the Chinese embassy in Belgrade). These were followed by demonstrations against Japan, notably in the spring of 2005 and in October 2010, and against France during the events in Tibet after March 2008. Those demonstrations were frequently well organized and often provided with banners and slogans that cannot have been developed or manufactured far from the eyes and ears of the party and state security. In 2008, this form of control was expanded to cover demonstrations abroad by Chinese residents, generally students.

The fact that these demonstrations were tolerated, managed, or encouraged does not mean that spontaneous feeling did not play a part. The bombing of the Chinese embassy in Belgrade by a B2 stealth fighter plane flying all the way from Missouri had major repercussions in 1999. Once it became news, Prime Minister Koizumi's stubborn determination to visit the Yasukuni Shrine was disparaged all over Asia. His behavior showed a lack of understanding of what is at stake in public diplomacy. Masahiko Komura, a Japanese lawmaker who has twice served as foreign minister, and who is in favor of closer relations with China, explained in private[19] that Koizumi acted not so much out of his beliefs but because he wanted to maintain a level playing field with China and did not want to appear as giving in. This contrasts with Yasuhiro Nakasone, who was infinitely more nationalistic and convinced of the right to visit the shrine, but who, for the sake of relations with China, did not visit it a second time during his term of office.

In the case of the anti-French demonstrations in 2008, it is hard to see how France could attract the hostility of the public in China, as the sacking of the Summer Palace dates back more than a century.[20] The anti-French flare-up was a reaction to protests targeting the Olympic torch in Paris after the Lhasa crackdown of the previous spring. The feelings stirred up by China's policy in Tibet were not limited to France. However in Paris, one demonstrator tried to grab the torch from the arms of a disabled Chinese athlete. The incident received nonstop coverage in China, where, understandably, it aroused indignation. The best performances are based on real emotions, and this image indeed played a powerful role.

Inevitably, the demonstrations sometimes went further than intended by their sponsors or by those who encouraged the development of nationalist thinking. The nationalist activists who were also anti-Japanese joined with other anti-Western movements and with ideologues and publicists who persisted in condemning the betrayal of China by elites "selling out to the West." At that point, the government had to sound a retreat, and so it sent messages throughout its communications channels indicating that the demonstrations had to stop. Just like street demonstrations, excesses by web users can also be ended in the blink of an eye, but not without an order issued off the record. In the spring of 2005, it had been the former ambassador to France, Wu Jianmin, a diplomat, who had become the president of the Beijing Diplomatic University, who made the rounds of the universities to recommend toning things down about Japan. Westerners generally pay more attention to the ascending phase of nationalist campaigns than to their unwinding, which is much less of a media event. Interestingly, in August 2014, it is the same tireless tool of China's public diplomacy that recommends moderation toward Japan.

In the regime's political repertory, mass movements are a frequent tool. In 2008, this approach was even extended to other countries, where several Chinese embassies lent their support to the slogans used by Chinese residents demonstrating against their host country's policy, seen as favoring the Dalai Lama. This was undoubtedly a first since the Cultural Revolution, when the Red Guard movement boiled over in Hong Kong, changing briefly into a riot against the British colonial administration; or in 1969, when the regime stirred up incidents sparked by "volunteers" with the Soviet border guards on the Ussuri River. Never turning violent (except in Korea) and as a response to the pro-Tibet demonstrations, these 2008 overseas demonstrations nonetheless illustrate the long arm of Chinese authorities over their citizens.

But the same tradition of encouraging mass movements, a characteristic of the Maoist system of government, also includes the ability to end them. In judging the degree of control the system has over public opinion, one need only consider how quickly and uniform are changes in the public expression of opinions. That speed and uniformity differ according to the topics involved—and foreign relations is one area where synchronization is the most striking.

NOTES

1. One author has done an especially good job of tracing this indoctrination through trends in the official cartography: William A. Callahan, "The Cartography of National Humiliation and the Emergence of China's Geobody," *Public Culture* 21, no. 1 (2009): 141–73.

2. The resurgence of propaganda, generally in a form that is not directly ideological, is very well described by Anne-Marie Brady, "Guiding Hand: The Role of the CCP Central Propaganda Department in the Current Era," *Westminster Papers in Communication and Culture* 3, no. 1 (March 2006): 58–77.

3. Song Hongbin, *Huobi Zhanzheng*, vol. 1 (Beijing: CITIC Press, 1997).

4. Polls taken in 1987, 1995, and 2003. Cf. François Godement, "Un manifeste nationaliste," *China Analysis* 3 (January–February 2006): 23–24.

5. Alastair Iain Johnston, "Chinese Middle Class Attitudes Towards International Affairs: Nascent Liberalization?" *China Quarterly* 179 (September 2004): 603–28.

6. Local account, May 2008.

7. The *Shijie jingji baodao* was published in Shanghai from 1980 to April 1989.

8. *Heshang*, a documentary based on the history and path of the Yellow River, was broadcast in China and abroad in June 1988 before it was withdrawn in September 1988. Its fate paralleled exactly the fate of Zhao Ziyang, who was subjected to an initial self-criticism at the Beidahe Party meeting in late August 1988.

9. Accessible at http://bbs.1.people.com.cn/boardList.do?action=postList& boardId=1.

10. *Zhongguo yu Shijie Guancha* [China and world affairs]; see François Godement, "Un manifeste nationaliste."

11. http://www.wyzxsx.com, an address that is now blocked.

12. Danwei, an Australian site for research on the Chinese Internet, published an interview with the founder of Utopia after it was shut down: http://www.danwei.com/interview-before-a-gagging-order-fan-jinggang-of-utopia/.

13. Published in *Qiushi*, a theoretical journal of the CCP in 2012. A translation is available at http://chinacopyrightandmedia.wordpress.com/2012/01/04/hu-jintaos-article-in-qiushi-magazine-translated/.

14. Justin Jacobs, "Preparing the People for Mass Clemency: The 1956 Japanese War Crimes Trials in Shenyang and Taiyuan," *China Quarterly* 205 (March 2011): 152–53 and 158–59.

15. Daqing Yang, "Convergence or Divergence? Recent Historical Writings on the Rape of Nanking," *American Historical Review* 104, no. 3 (June 1999): 58, quoted by James Reilly, *Strong Society, Smart State: The Rise of Public Opinion in China's Japan Policy* (New York: Columbia University Press, 2011), 59.

16. Yoshihide Soeya, *Japan's Economic Diplomacy with China, 1945–1978* (Oxford: Clarendon Press, 1998).

17. Zhao Ziyang, *Prisoner of the State* (New York: Simon & Schuster, 2009), 167.

18. François Godement, "Deux tigres peuvent-ils cohabiter sur la même montagne? Une table ronde sur les relations sino-japonaises," *China Analysis* nos. 6–7 (July–August 2006): 12–18.

19. Interview in Tokyo, October 2004.

20. Thibaud Voita, "'A bas la France!' Account of Anti-French Movements in the Spring of 2008," *China Analysis* no. 18 (May–June): 10–13.

Chapter Ten

A Faulty Diagnosis

At home and abroad, China's ability to tone down its actions and end public displays appears to be intact. In 2010–2011, orders for moderation proved effective in two areas: verbal claims concerning the South China Sea (but not with Japan) starting in August 2010, and relations with the United States from December 2010. In 2014, a serious rise in tension with Japan, and with Vietnam where PRC nationals were physically harmed and had to flee the country did not cause any demonstration in China: proof, if need be, that these outbursts can be controlled, and perhaps even turned on and off at will.

This control over foreign policy as a whole begs the question of what lay behind the leaders' decision to act as they did. One term has been at the heart of the successive reversals: "core interests." What these interests are has become a subject of debate. They usually include Taiwan and Tibet, defining an area where China has no intention of backing down on its sovereignty claims and where it reserves the right to use force. The term was used for the first time in the official press in February 2002[1] —before Hu Jintao came to power at the time of the Sixteenth Party Congress. More-over, that term was not coined in the writings of a nationalist acti-vist, but in those of one of China's most moderate geostrategic experts, Wang Jisi, whose access at the time to President Hu Jintao has been common knowledge. President Obama agreed to use the term in the joint Sino-American statement at the end of his first official trip to China. Starting in 2009, the term was used occasionally in the official Chinese press to include the South China Sea. This was not done by chance. The United Nations had set a deadline in May 2009 for the countries sharing its continental shelf to submit their claims. China immediately abandoned the idea of multilateral negotiations, switching back to bilateral negotiations. This put generally weaker and divided Southeast Asian countries in a situation of inferiority. Thereupon Malaysia and Vietnam took the initiative to stake major claims. This led China in turn to file with the United Nations a "verbal memorandum" that included for the first time in an international claim a map with the infamous "nine-dash line"—a dotted line around the South China Sea. This was an indication that China might lay claim to the region's entire maritime zone.[2] Hence, ironically, it is the prospect of an international legal arbitration provided by UNCLOS, the Law of the Sea, that has ratcheted up tension in the region.

SINO-AMERICAN CLASH

Until the spring of 2010, the three components of China's claim to the South China Sea remained disconnected. Naval flare-ups occurred, mainly involving Vietnam and the Philippines, which are the countries closest to China and also diplomatically or militarily the weakest. In addition, direct and indirect challenges were made to the presence of the US Navy in Chinese EEZs (Exclusive Economic Zones). Lastly, at times the official press blew the claim out of proportion by extending the notion of core interests to the whole South China Sea. Nevertheless, no connection had been established among these three components.

It was an initiative by the United States in the spring of 2010 that caused those elements to merge. The US press reported that during a preparatory meeting held in Beijing in March for the Sino-American SED (Strategic and Economic Dialogue), one of the Chinese speakers included the South China Sea in China's "core interests."[3] Indirect accounts also reported that one Chinese official got up and left during the dialogue itself. After those leaks in the press, a certain number of Southeast Asian governments seized the opportunity of the ASEAN Regional Forum to challenge China's attitude. The response was blunt and tactless. Chinese Foreign Minister Yang Jiechi explained that "China is a large country and the other countries are small countries; that's a fact." In the fall of 2010, two Chinese high officers, who were technically retired, but who were still highly active in Beijing's think tanks, General Luo Yan and Admiral Yang Yi, attempted to outdo each other with their anti-American rhetoric. Other voices chimed in, this time official, criticizing the way the United States was handling its public debt problem. For the first time, China openly raised the issue as a worried creditor. But such talk evidently fed into comments on the decline of the United States and the superiority of the Chinese economic model.

A debate definitely opened up, at least among Chinese institutes, think tanks, and geopolitical experts. It focused on the reality of the US decline and even of a historic crisis for capitalism, and on China's international strategy. In 2010, China's foremost geostrategic institute devoted a panel discussion to it, and an overview of the discussion was published.[4] The most radical position within the institute was held by a researcher from a military institution. The moderate position, which predominated in the conclusions, came from CICIR researchers. There was no difference between them when it came to an overall prognosis pointing to China as the world's leading country by 2025. But the most radical viewpoint held that capitalism would suffer from a financial crisis as deep as the 1930s crash, casting further doubt on the liberal economy as a whole. The moderates stressed that the United States would continue to enjoy military preeminence for some time. Some of them believed that China should go along with the inevitable decline of the United States rather than confronting it head-on. The debate also focused on China's military program. The moderates were critical of the emphasis on one or more aircraft carriers, which they saw as less effective than space weapons or cyber warfare.

This was an exceedingly realistic debate between two opposing sides. One side believed firmly that China's economic advantage was undeniable. They pointed out that in Asia "the flesh is stronger than the spirit," in other words China's attractiveness to its region in terms of trade would prevail over any ideological or geopolitical reluctance. Others felt that in order to be attractive, China had to do its part toward global governance and contribute to international public goods. The panel criticized the Foreign Ministry as "weak." But its findings also reflected a more moderate view that there is real competition with the United States, but it is "rational and measured."

THE HAWKS COME HOME TO ROOST

A relatively arcane publication was the first sign of a reversal, or rather a change of views at the top. On December 6, 2010, Dai Bingguo, China's most senior foreign policy official, published a new document.[5] In it he reaffirmed China's plans for "peaceful development" and international cooperation. He discussed foreign policy in the legacy "of modesty and prudence" followed by Deng Xiaoping. He defined China's core interests in an ambiguous and restrictive fashion. Or, perhaps, in a restrictive yet ambiguous way: this was his "personal understanding" of those core interests, rather than a firm commitment. Only Taiwan was explicitly cited as a territorial issue. But three very broad areas were also defined as core interests: the political system, including the leading role of the party, and socialism; "sovereignty, territorial integrity and national unity"—which were left without boundaries; and the "guarantee of sustainable social and economic development."

This was two months before President Hu's state visit to the United States—an important date and a good reason for China to tone down its rhetoric. The document by Dai Bingguo could lead one to conclude that China had returned to prudence with regard to its core interests, since he made no mention of the South China Sea. But then he did not mention Tibet or Xinjiang either: only a few months earlier, these were on the usual list of "core interests." Dai's attempt to sound reassuring was in fact a return to ambiguity, Deng Xiaoping's trademark in foreign policy. Even after his analysis there is nothing to prevent all of China's territorial claims from being brought up again as "core interests."

The ambiguity applies to long-term strategy rather than to one man or one moment in history. The events in 2011 attest to this. On the one hand, nationalistic outbursts and anti-Western vindictiveness were toned down. More moderate voices suddenly spoke out in the press and even abroad. Wang Jisi published an article[6] in *Foreign Affairs* in which he gave an optimistic version of Sino-American relations. Having become something of a Chinese Raymond Aron because of his clear-headedness and moderate views, Wang is sometimes torn between the rationale of a policy he knows is fraught with conflicting goals, and a yearning for a more decidedly liberal and cooperative foreign policy. There are serious indications that Dai Bingguo drew some inspiration from Wang in drafting his own document. Yet Wang went further. Writing in Chinese shortly after the *Foreign Affairs* article, he stated that China's ambiguity regarding its future intentions was keeping it from an international perspective. Deng's favorite maxim, "Hiding one's talents and biding one's time," raised doubts and questions about the future.[7] Wang wanted an addition to the famous maxim in order

to reflect modesty and humility. This was a stand in favor of regional integration and cooperation and against international confrontation.

At the same time, the two nationalist officers Luo Yan and Yang
Yi traveled to Washington to repeat from meeting to meeting that
their positions reflected only their personal views and not those of
the Chinese government. Hu Jintao's official visit went well, although he did not change out of his gray business suit and don a
black coat for the state dinner at the White House.

ON THE GROUND, A TENUOUS LULL

Thus China modified its foreign policy statements to make them
consistent with a return to moderation. But what did this change? In
the first six months of 2011, Chinese maritime entities again
stepped up the number of incidents with the Philippines and Vietnam in the South China Sea.[8] In July there were signs of a respite.
China got the ASEAN countries to acknowledge in writing that
they would deal with it as separate countries, hence bilaterally, and
not as a common organization. This division among the Southeast
Asian partners is worth noting. In January 2012, for the first time,
the *People's Daily* cited the Diaoyu islands among China's "core
interests," accusing Japan of openly challenging them. In March
2012, incidents with Filipino and Vietnamese fishermen resumed;
at the same time a warning was issued to Japanese coast guard
vessels. In the spring of 2014, a massive oil rig for deep-sea drill-
ing—a $1 billion-plus piece of equipment—was set up in areas
usually controlled by Vietnam, 130 miles from its shore. A pitched
battle involving fishermen, sailors, and frogmen with PLA vessels
standing at the ready ensued, with casualties among the Vietnamese. The incident triggered Vietnam's most violent anti-Chinese
riots since 1979. In July 2014, a typhoon led to the departure of the
Chinese oil rig. In late August 2014, barely a month before a

planned state visit by Xi Jinping to New Delhi, the PLA staged another incursion into Indian controlled Ladakh.

Other issues in this strange sequence of events are worth mentioning. First, there is no question that China has control over the way the incidents have unfolded. The most spectacular events always involved fishing flotillas, or in the above case oil companies that do not commit the Chinese state itself. Arrests of foreign fishermen were made by the Chinese maritime administration, which has armed vessels of the appropriate size, but the PLA navy itself stayed mostly out of the action: it has deployed solely against Vietnam, which is not covered by any defense treaty. Challenges to the US Seventh Fleet came from submarines that popped up where they were least expected. China intends to keep up a strategy of annoyances, rather than letting itself be dragged into an escalation, which could occur, for example, if there was an overreaction to any of China's major naval units. Yet it toys with the red line: in incidents with Japan, a Chinese destroyer has "lit up" a Japanese navy ship with its homing radar, and Chinese jetfighters have flown as close as thirty yards from Japanese self-defense planes.

ECONOMIC INTEGRATION: A COUNTERWEIGHT

Far from the South China Sea, China's foreign policy is bound by other powerful economic interests stemming from the country's integration into the global economy. The dollar is China's main reserve currency, helping to keep the renminbi low by converting the massive gains from foreign trade. This obviously creates a synergy with the United States, even though it is not very popular in China. The stakes go far beyond the country's foreign policy, with many more concrete repercussions such as never before seen in a Communist regime. At a different level, the growing taste of Chinese elites, including the families of leaders, for American society cannot be denied. It would have been inconceivable to imagine the

families of Soviet leaders, let alone the children of a Moscow chief
of military intelligence, residing in the United States (which has
happened for his Chinese equivalent). Hu Jintao's daughter can
marry a new computer entrepreneur who spent his professional life
in Silicon Valley in the United States. Wen Jiabao's daughter
worked for Credit Suisse-First Boston. As we pointed out, the
daughter of Xi Jinping, the presumed successor, studies at Harvard,
and so did Bo Xilai's son. The United States is not the only country
concerned. Since the early nineties, the son of Qiao Shi, then a
member of the Standing Committee of the Politburo and the head
of the Public Security Supervision Committee, has been employed
by the BBC's international service in London. The son of Zeng
Qinghong, another member of the Standing Committee and vice
president of the Republic until 2008, bought a luxurious villa on the
Sydney harbor in Australia albeit after his father's official retirement. Obviously, China's new urban classes are not the only people
influenced by globalization and entertaining a newfound proximity
with the West.

This porosity of Chinese society and even of the leadership has
often been identified as the Achilles' heel of Chinese foreign policy. Do merging financial interests lead to convergence, assimilation, and ultimately the loss of independence? In any event, in
China they raise widespread cynicism regarding corruption at the
highest levels of the party-state. However, these phenomena affect
mainly domestic policy and the conduct of economic affairs rather
than foreign policy.

The global reach of major Chinese companies has also contributed to the theory of China's dependence. Rivalry among them is
said to be behind China's economic breakthrough in many cases; at
the same time their interests are said to be taking China's foreign
policy in risky areas. Sinopec and CNOOC, the two oil industry
giants, are in competition in Sudan and Nigeria. Huawei and ZTE,
two companies officially considered private but which enjoy strong

support from the government, are fighting over international tele-communications markets. Huawei in particular, a company that was founded by a former officer and that is chaired by a former state security cadre, has an opaque shareholder base, with stock allegedly held by some of its own employees. Yet it was given a line of credit of more than $30 billion by the China Development Bank. That bank is known to be the envy of other Chinese banks, partly because it has a better track record in China itself, partly because of the influence of its founder, Chen Yuan, the son of a prominent Mao-era leader,[9] and also because it has managed to present itself as a commercial investment bank, although it is obviously state owned and policy oriented.

According to a well-informed Chinese source on Iran, a nation whose first economic partner is now China, representatives of Chinese firms are critical of China's official diplomacy, which they claim is too sensitive to Western pressure over sanctions. After the sudden loss of $18 billion in contracts in Libya with the fall of Gaddafi, the major Chinese companies and the army, furious at having to improvise an evacuation of Chinese citizens, lashed out at the Chinese Foreign Ministry. At the UN during a weekend of lively discussions in the Security Council, the Chinese representatives had let Resolution 1973 pass, authorizing the use of force in Libya to prevent a massacre of the civilian population.

But does anyone really believe that the Chinese ambassador to the UN or even the foreign minister had the power to decide in that situation? Did they make the decision in 2002 and 2003, when China chose not to veto a US invasion against the Iraq of Saddam Hussein? To the contrary, the example shows that in some cases the Chinese government can weigh its strategic interests against the economic interests of its corporations. In the case of China's support for North Korea, the two happen to coincide to some extent, but it is strategy that prevails. Are China's commercial interests in North Korea, as real as they may be, sufficient to explain the strategic protection granted to that regime? In 2011, China's trade with North Korea amounted to $6 billion. For Pyongyang that is huge— an estimated 70 percent of North Korea's foreign trade and one-fourth of its gross domestic product. But the same amount represents only one-sixtieth of China's trade with South Korea, less than two-thousandths of China's foreign trade as a whole. It would be in fact much easier to justify a more favorable policy toward South Korea because of economic imperatives.

A FAULTY STRATEGIC DIAGNOSIS

The theory of deep divisions in Chinese foreign policy has long held true with regard to decisions in the most important areas: relations with Asia, a natural stronghold and a focus of China's claims, as well as with the United States, China's main partner and strategic rival. China's actions abroad are sometimes clouded by scattered efforts, bureaucratic divisions, trends in public opinion, and special interests. However, China is never crippled by these factors for any length of time, nor is it ever forced to veer off in an unexpected direction because of them.

What is striking about China's approach to foreign policy is the fact that it is both tenacious and meticulous. It can boast of abundant and increasingly skilled human resources. Chinese diplomacy excels in what is known in political jargon as "bilateral relations," meaning country-to-country relations. The foundation of its foreign policy lies in the timeworn tradition of saving face at all costs. The numerous trips abroad by Chinese leaders and the quality of the official welcome, extended for example to the smallest of the European Union's twenty-eight member countries, attest to this. However, this is also evident in the furious response to symbolic affronts like demonstrations by opponents abroad, or intentional incidents. For example, when China was in full crisis mode with the United Kingdom over the political regime in Hong Kong on the eve of the handover in 1997, Christopher Patten, the last governor of Hong Kong, was once forced to go on foot to meet his official interlocutors from Beijing because his official vehicle had a flat tire. When US vice president Walter Mondale made the first official visit in 1979 after the diplomatic recognition of the People's Republic, he was of course welcomed at the airport with all the official honors. However, to meet Deng Xiaoping, he had to climb a tall stairway at the National People's Assembly, at the top of which China's president,[10] who was barely five feet two inches tall, leaned down toward him. There are countless stories attesting to China's attention and sensitivity to matters of face.

Of course it is impossible to tell what China's ultimate intentions are. Its leaders discuss them only in vague ideological terms. They are believable when they claim that their priority is domestic development and stability, in other words national interests and the interest of the regime. But to believe that their ability to act and to mobilize support and their capacity for self-restraint and compromise, on the other hand, is altered by trends in public opinion or by Chinese financial lobbies is turning on its head the hierarchy between the party-state and society.

To the contrary, the consistency of events with long-held predictions and ambitions is striking. Thus the maritime incidents of 2010 and 2011 are a direct application of the February 1992 law on territorial sovereignty and sovereignty over adjacent zones, which permits the use of force throughout all those areas.[11] At that time there was already talk of the tussle between the PLA navy and the Foreign Ministry, which was more concerned with good neighborly relations. But the growth of the navy has been the most tangible aspect of China's defense policy since 1982. The man who took over at the helm of the Military Affairs Commission in 1992, Liu Huaqing (rear admiral in 1955, promoted to general and placed in charge of the Chinese navy in 1982) was extremely close to Deng Xiaoping. In light of these facts, pointing out any sign of hesitation in China's foreign policy is a secondary matter. The only real difference between the 1990s and 2010–2011 is that China long made only short hops from one uninhabited island to the next, avoiding confrontations or targeting only one country at a time (more often than not, the Philippines or Vietnam). China has broken with this restraint in 2009. To believe that the sudden polarization of conflicts is due to bureaucratic disorganization is to underestimate the system as a whole. It is far more likely that the intensity of the international crises occurring in 2008–2009 led to a sudden decision based on an optimistic risk assessment. The advent of the global financial crisis on top of the American quagmire in Afghanistan, the weakening of Japan, and the divisions among Southeast Asian countries had all come together at the right time.

One fundamental factor remains: the only true blackmail practiced within the collective leadership stems from the imperative to defend the regime and the territory as defined by the PRC. This imperative holds true for Taiwan, but it can be expanded. This is competitive peer pressure within the political system. Blackmail means that as a political succession approaches, potential rivals will not risk opening up internationally: Hu Yaobang attempted to do so with Japan in 1986 and suffered the consequences. But even that mutual blackmail did not rule out realism whenever China was in a weak position overall. The PRC has engaged in compromise and settled a certain number of territorial conflicts when it was isolated internationally and vulnerable.[12]

Like in other areas, the system applies "fuzzy logic" in that interests and debates do exist, and blunders do occur, just like competition among government agencies and major companies. Here Hu Jintao also illustrated his principal political talent—after ten years in power, no one was capable of saying what his personal opinions were.

Yet an evasive presentation does not imply a lack of strategy. There are areas, particularly economics, where "muddling through" with experimentation is the main resource. Not so in foreign policy. The assertiveness and even aggressiveness demonstrated by China since 2008 are based on a faulty diagnosis pointing to a definite weakening of the world around it—from its Asian neighbors to its great rival, the United States. Scratching surface descriptions of a multipolar world, one easily discerns predictions of an unmanageable international era of "warlords" (in reference to the most chaotic period in the history of contemporary China, the 1920s). Realism, Charles Darwin's legacy that has left a deep mark on Chinese geopolitics, is combined with China's strategic tradition and art of war. Strength analysis and the belief in power struggles are basic tenets. After all, the CCP itself has lived through a long history of struggles, from the civil war to clashes among factions and rival political views.

REDISCOVERING CHINA'S STRATEGIC HERITAGE

There is also a continuity between the events of 2010–2011 and strategic notions developed earlier: in the early 1990s, a full-scale anti-Western reaction after Tiananmen; in the 1980s, a return to classics of Chinese strategy. Two American researchers with vastly different backgrounds have closely studied the body of Chinese texts on strategy, both in classical history and through the debates of the 1990s. Alastair Iain Johnston, who is quoted above, published a historical study that is prophetic.[13] He sees in China's strategic tradition two opposing schools of thought. One is an accommodating culture that associates norms of behavior with conciliation, and is based on the tradition of Confucius and Mencius. The other is a warlike culture based on a strategy of realism, embodied by Sun Tzu in particular. It is this latter approach that has often been extolled in discussions of strategy in China. It was first glorified by Mao, who undoubtedly identified more with Sun Tzu than with Lenin or Clausewitz. The issue raised by A. I. Johnston (at a time when these topics were still off-limits to Chinese academics) has inspired differing attempts to create a Chinese school of international relations, from Wang Yizhou (University of Beijing) to Yan Xuetong (Tsinghua University). The two threads that Johnston sees running through the classics have appeared during various phases throughout Chinese history, and they still do to this day. Michael Pillsbury took an even closer look at the present. He translated and interpreted a vast body of strategic texts and discussions from the 1990s.[14] He made himself unpopular with most of the community of China scholars in the United States, because his conclusions went against predominant interpretations. Working against him was the fact that he was one of the influential actors in the Office of Net Assessment of the Pentagon, long managed by Andrew Marshall to promote America's "revolution in military affairs"—in other words the technological escalation that became the agenda of George W. Bush and Donald Rumsfeld in 2001. But should the messenger bearing bad news be killed? The texts uncovered by Pillsbury and their predictions made almost a generation ago, are supported by recent facts. As early as 1987, some strategic researchers in China believed the Chinese economy would surpass the US economy before 2025. They cited the coming decline of the United States and a multipolar world sometimes verging on anarchy. In the early 1990s, they predicted that China would have several carrier battle groups by 2010, as well as a manned space station. Both plans are now underway. More debatable are the prediction of a conflict over the reunification of Taiwan by 2010, and also the obsessive interest Pillsbury saw for asymmetrical conflicts and "magic weapons" that were supposed to make up for China's military inferiority. Still, certain recent developments do reflect these views, such as the emphasis on cyber warfare and the development of antisatellite weapons, pointing to the possibility of a "war of debris" in space. The fact that China has developed a long-range (more than two thousand kilometers) anti-ship ballistic missile, nicknamed the "carrier killer" (*hangmu shashou*) now has the strategic community in an uproar.[15]

These conclusions can be viewed in perspective. In every army there are scenarios that are sometimes extremely improbable or quite simply incorrect. But it is undeniable that the field of strategic analysis in China is still far from espousing theories of joining a globalized world. Rather, it reflects a warlike tradition that is bolstered again by China's economic rise.

NOTES

1. *People's Daily*, February 28, 2002, quoted by Michael D. Swaine, "China's Assertive Behavior—Part I, Core Interests," *China Leadership Monitor* 34 (February 22, 2011), http://media.hoover.org/sites/default/files/documents/CLM34MS.pdf.

2. The note can be viewed on http://www.un.org/Depts/los/clcs_new/submissions_files/mysvnm33_09/chn_2009re_mys_vnm_e.pdf.

3. Edward Wong, "Chinese Military Seeks to Extend Its Naval Power," *New York Times*, April 23, 2010.

4. See *Xiandai Guoji Guanxi*, journal of the CICIR (China Institutes of Contemporary International Relations) (November 2010): 1–24; and analysis by François Godement, "La stratégie chinoise en débat," *China Analysis* no. 32 (March 2011): 41–48.

5. Dai Bingguo, "Zhongguo guojia weiyuan Dai Bingguo: jianchi zou heping fazhan zhi lu" [State Councilor Dai Bingguo: Adhere to the path of peaceful development], *Waijiaobu Wangzhan*, December 6, 2010.

6. Wang Jisi, "China's Search for a Grand Strategy: A Rising Power Finds Its Way," *Foreign Affairs* 90, no. 2, March–April 2011.

7. Wang Jisi, "The question of China's international position and the strategy maxim 'Hide your talents and wait for the right time while participating'" (in Chinese), *Guoji wenti yanjiu* no. 5 (2011).

8. Carlyle A. Thayer, "Chinese Assertiveness in the South China Sea and Southeast Asian Responses," *Journal of Current Southeast Asian Affairs* 30, no. 2 (2011): 77–104.

9. Chen Yun, the person who coined the phrase, "crossing the river by feeling for the stones."

10. Interview with Michel Oksenberg, former national security adviser for Asia.

11. The law is filed with the United Nations: Law on the Territorial Sea and the Contiguous Zone of 25 February 1992, http://www.un.org/depts/los/LEGISLATIONANDTREATIES/PDFFILES/CHN_1992_Law.pdf.

12. Taylor M. Fravel, "Regime Insecurity and International Cooperation: Explaining China's Compromises in Territorial Disputes," *International Security* 30, no. 2 (Fall 2005): 46–83.

13. Alastair Iain Johnston, *Cultural Realism: Strategic Culture and Grand Strategy in Chinese History* (Princeton, NJ: Princeton University Press, 1998).

14. Michael Pillsbury, *China Debates the Future Security Environment* (Washington, DC: National Defense University Press, January 2000), posted on http://au.af.mil/au/awc/awcgate/ndu/chindebate/pills2.htm.

15. Mathieu Duchatel and Alexandre Sheldon-Dupleix, "Missile anti-navires: La nouvelle arme magique," *China Analysis* no. 31 (Spring 2011): 38–41.

Chapter Eleven

Integration vs. Sovereignty: The Strategy Debate

During the great decade of reform (1978–1988), the illusion that the party-state would automatically dissolve into the new market economy raised hopes of a political transition. Then, during another decade (1997–2008), between the death of Deng Xiaoping and the Olympic Games, when China reached its peak on the international stage, a new hope replaced the old one: the hope that China would convert to the rules and standards of international governance and to a set of multilateral objectives that had been consolidated since the end of the Cold War. That hope was not without justification. China was entering the global trading system and was signing on to several arms limitation treaties. Its representatives were extremely knowledgeable regarding all the legal aspects of sovereignty and the global system; they had excellent negotiating ability. They were also becoming involved in new areas like human rights, workers' rights, and the environment.

China's growing involvement in international governance obviously raised hopes that this would influence not only its own experts but also ultimately its leaders. China's experts, whether in arms control, the environment, international trade, financial management, or law, are a sieve through which innovations and ideas

enter the country. The elites are increasingly influenced by international education and values, and they are also looking for legal
safety, which is not assured in China. Through these successive
layers of international socialization, one might hope that Chinese
leaders themselves would be induced to give up their realist views
inherited from the nineteenth century. Those views had been based
on the primacy of state sovereignty and on strategic rivalry. Instead
of playing those zero-sum games, post–Cold War China would now
join the post-1945 liberal order, after becoming a member of its
institutions. Its economic and financial success would provide the
incentive to join a system of global rules.

Multipolar power competition would become relative and no
longer paramount. Market competition would decide it, more than
military might or a clash of ideologies.

Undeniably, there are Chinese experts who share these liberal-
internationalist views. For example, a group of Chinese academics
and bankers have drafted a report entitled *China in 2020*. The report states as an objective "joint integrated and multipolar governance," based on the growing convergence of values and the decline
of ideologies.[1] Even this kind of analysis is not exempt from pre-
suppositions rooted in realist doctrine, such as the postulate of lasting American military hegemony, and a Sino-American economic
duopoly that towers above all other economies.

Do these views really influence leaders and their long-term decisions? One would need to know to what extent China's leaders
have made theirs and internalized international norms, or whether
they are simply adapting to circumstances and what they view as
new outside constraints. Of course, this question applies to any
sovereign state, not just China. Answers often vary between the
short term (which tends toward realism) and the long term, which
can push toward integration. This will dictate a principle of cooperation, shared interests and values, whereas the old realist approach

is based on the axiom of competition and an underlying belief in the survival of the fittest.

THE HISTORICAL PRECEDENT OF JAPAN

China is not the only state to which these questions apply. Sovereignism and isolationism are not exclusive to China. The United States as a power is committed to universal values in the name of what it calls its "manifest destiny." Yet at the same time it often rejects the intrusion of international treaties in areas that might interfere with the national interest. Examples of this can be seen in the refusal by the United States to ratify the total ban on nuclear testing, its refusal to ratify the United Nations Convention on the Law of the Sea (in effect since 1994), its refusal to accept the jurisdiction of the International Criminal Court, and even its persistent support for a US-run system of web domain names. Because of its sheer size, China also has every chance of remaining a viable sovereign entity well into the twenty-first century, whereas European countries, for example, can envision their future only as members of a larger market and region. Contemporary Japan, which is facing a population decline, has been handicapped by its relative isolation within the Asia-Pacific region. Because of its problems in overcoming war legacies, and its long-standing reluctance to promote regional economic interdependence, it is not a regional leader, even for Asian democracies.

As an emerging power without any inherited guilt complex, China should not suffer from the same handicaps. Japan is nevertheless the most relevant historical precedent to approach China's rise. Back in the 1920s, Japan was that era's emerging power in the process of catching up with the industrialized countries. Like China today, it hesitated between the path of multilateral integration and that of a solitary rise to power. Japan had been a founding member of the League of Nations in 1919, pleading that racial equality be enshrined in its principles. It was President Woodrow Wilson, per-haps the original role model for liberal internationalism, who had turned down this request! A number of liberal Japanese diplomats and/or aristocrats remained committed to internationalist diploma-cy, but the caste of young officers, large economic groups seeking expansion abroad, as well as intellectuals who were both populist and nationalist drove Japan toward the conquest of Asia. They exploited discontent over the Diet, parties, and politicians. One key factor played into their hands. Japan's civilian government had only limited control over the army, whose commander-in-chief, however remote, was the emperor. Internationally minded diplo-mats and military proconsuls opposed each other at times, but also complemented each other. Japan practiced then what a historian has termed a "foreign policy without ideals."[2] It was based on a balance of power and was also justified by the example of Western coun-tries as colonial powers. In the words of one prominent Japanese diplomat in 1933, "the Western powers taught Japan the game of poker, but once they had accumulated most of the chips, they de-clared that game immoral and switched to the game of bridge."

In the 1920s, even before the worldwide depression that was to rip apart its society, Japan was already wavering between two value systems. One of those value systems was premised on the US "Open Door" principle in contrast to exclusive colonization by Eu-rope; it favored stabilization by negotiating the balance of power in the Pacific. The London Conference in 1920 set the ratios to be respected among the major naval forces and promised (without asking its opinion) that China would be opened up to everyone. The other value system involved zones of exclusive influence, the bal-ance of power, and also an ideology of revenge in the name of Asianism.

For a very long time relations between Japan, the Western pow-ers (essentially the United States and Great Britain), and even Re-publican China (as personified by Chiang Kai-shek after 1926) waxed and waned. Japan alternated provocation and conciliation while the Western powers also hovered between sanctions and "appeasement." The appeasement usually associated with Europe, the Munich Conference of Hitler, Neville Chamberlain, and Georges Bonnet was in fact derived from England's pragmatic attitude toward Japan after their era of friendship ended. Until 1936, China, itself the object of a rivalry between Japan and the West, strove on several occasions to reach a deal with Japan that would halt its advance into China.

Before 1929 and the Great Depression, it was impossible to foresee Imperial Japan's rush headlong into militarism. Moreover, the Japan of the Taisho era in the 1920s was very different from the China of today. Ironically, Japan had a multiparty system and more democratic institutions than the People's Republic. But its political culture reflected the notion of ethnic supremacy and the worship of strength. Milder versions of these traits have survived in twenty-first-century China.

THE TEMPTATION OF A SPHERE OF INFLUENCE

Nevertheless, what is striking is the analogy between ambivalent foreign policies, with one foot in international regulations and global trade, and another in regional hegemony. A comparison can also be made between the dilemma facing the Westerners of the 1920s, torn between accommodation and countermeasures as a response to Japan's ambitions, and the dilemma now facing the United States: whether to adapt to China's mounting power while at the same time gambling on the possibility that it will opt for integration, or to oppose it with the support of its partners in the international system. Domestic factors also converge on some key aspects: the ambiguous expressions of Japan's emperor, the autonomy acquired in his name by an army beyond the control of the civilian government, and in China the coincidence of a fragmented bureau-cracy with pressure or blackmail from strong nationalist currents.

One cannot help pointing out also that beyond the potential de-cline of the United States (which moderate Chinese experts dis-count and perceive more as a trap), they have seen in 2008–2009 similarities between the world after the 2008 recession and the rising perils of the 1930s. Two of the most popular Western geopol-iticians or philosophers in China are Alfred Thayer Mahan, who developed the strategy of British naval supremacy in the nineteenth century, and Carl Schmitt. Before siding with Nazism, Schmitt leg-itimized the idea that some states are more important than others. For that reason and by imposing their rules, they play a dominant role in their regional zone of influence. When applied to neighbor-ing regions, the notion of "core interests" is reminiscent of the spheres of influence, which Japan even convinced the United States to recognize for a short time in 1919. Today, a realistic Chinese attempt to define a stable compromise with the United States is likely to start with a "return to Yalta"—in other words to the Cairo conference of 1943, which guaranteed that China would recover Taiwan and territories annexed by force by Japan. To Roosevelt and Stalin, that also meant Okinawa, and therefore the Senkaku/Diaoyu islands. That would mean establishing a balance of power in the Pacific, where the Chinese navy is deployed beyond the "first chain" of islands (from Japan to Taiwan) toward the "second chain," the Philippines and Singapore.[3] This whole perspective is indeed a far cry from the globalized world; it is much closer to the era of the 1920s, when the United States and the United Kingdom attempted, and failed, to establish with Japan a maritime balance in the Pacific.

There is no clear regional precedent that dictates whether China will adopt a worldview based on common standards and coopera-tion or whether, to the contrary, it will adopt the notion of multipo-lar competition in a world turning its back on post-1945 Western institutions. Opinions abroad are as divided on this issue as they are in China. Outside China, since the 1990s, those among international relations specialists who are also sinologists have frequently subscribed to the first view. A number of studies have concluded from China's process of international trade or environmental negotiations that there was a genuine trend of acculturation and convergence.[4] Some, such as Bates Gill have even seen as a success China's soft power in Asia, and have seen a paradigm shift in Chinese defense as it deals with new transversal and transnational challenges.[5] In 2014, Bates Gill added a chapter to his book on the subject for the Japanese edition, where he reverses his perspective from recent events.

According to these views, there is a trend in China in favor of global norms and institutions, even though it remains concerned about the sovereignty issue.[6] Conversely, non-China experts who do not have direct access to Chinese sources often draw a more pessimistic conclusion, one that leads inevitably to a confrontation.[7]

There are exceptions within these two groups. Thus, drawing only on strategic writings by officers of the PLA, Michael Pillsbury inferred an apocalyptic vision of a looming confrontation as a result of China's rise.[8]

Conversely, some non-sinologists have seen a China that is definitely committed to international cooperation and multilateral standards, even losing sight of the fact that those standards became concrete only after the end of the Cold War in Europe.[9] The European Union's policy of positive engagement with China and, to some extent, the American China policy have been based on these premises. According to the European Union's first official report on China, published in 1995, the odds were in favor of reform, integration, and responsibility, with China playing a role in the new world order.[10] The US doctrine, exemplified by the suggestion made to China in 2005 that it become a "responsible stakeholder,"[11] is just as explicit: "Relationships built on shared interests and shared values are deep and lasting." Both Europe and the United States have chosen to trust the likelihood that Chinese society would change.

China's other partners are merely banking that it will play a much greater role in the future than it does today. Either they are adapting in advance by making concessions (through appeasement, thus allowing China to make effortless diplomatic gains, thanks to the shadow cast by its future influence) or else, while there is still time, they seek commitments from China for the future. This is the defensive and therefore more realist version of constructive engagement. There are no longer many voices for the third option of containment, because ensuring China's cooperation seems to be an overriding international objective. Yet it often cooperates only belatedly, and sometimes merely pays lip service to the notion of cooperation. For optimists, this is a glass half full rather than half empty. Realists emphasize instead that China makes ample use of all its positions inside global institutions without much positive contribution, and that it sticks to the protection of its sovereignty. In August 2011, Robert Zoellick, who had earlier coined officially the term "responsible stakeholder" as a goal for China, referred to it instead as a "reluctant stakeholder."[12]

INTEGRATION OR ADAPTATION?

Judgments also differ depending on whether they apply to the Chinese state or society. Change within China's multifaceted society is seen more confidently, given the explosive growth of media and the extent to which China has already opened up to the world. Judgments based on the policies of the party-state are more pessimistic. Between the two viewpoints lies a gray area that comes closer to the truth. For example, when China's arms control and antiproliferation policy is looked at for its integration of international standards or its realist adaptation to international constraints, it becomes clear that any changes made in the 1990s were dictated by realistic adaptation.[13] China sticks to its position in terms of sovereignty, and gets away with it by pointing back to the responsibilities of the other major powers. However, it is also sensitive to the risk of being isolated or surrounded; it is equally sensitive to the loss of international legitimacy, which can become a bigger problem over time.

Hence it is moving toward participation without contribution to international institutions or standards, while at the same time using them legally to protect its sovereignty. Over time, with increasing global interaction, this limited participation can nevertheless lead to a widening range of mutual interests. Neither the collapse of Western markets, nor global warming, nor a situation of global anarchy are in China's interests. Its interdependence is now much deeper than it was before the era of opening up and reform.

Sovereignty remains an absolute priority. No gains will persuade China to give it up. In a number of areas since 2008, China has either called a halt to, or even reversed the course of change. From human rights (where formal ratification of a United Nations covenant is still in question), to the World Trade Organization (where the 2001 agreement for membership now appears to be the ceiling rather than the floor for Chinese concessions), to disarmament (no significant change since the signing of the Comprehensive Nuclear Test Ban Treaty in 1996), and to the environment (where agreements after the Kyoto Conference of 1997 have long remained on hold), China has balked at more convergence.

Alastair Iain Johnston points out objectively that even for the United States, sovereignty takes precedence over international cooperation.[14] The parallel should be extended. In fact, in the twenty-first century, the United States and China are the only two countries whose sovereignty can withstand globalization. The United States because, as a world unto itself absorbing people, cultures, and global savings, it embodies globalization in its ascending phase. China, because in restoring its strategic heritage, its leaders have given it the means to integrate but also to resist globalization. It has one foot in the international system and one foot outside. It is combining the military tools of strategic realism with commercial diplomacy. It is combining a command economy with market competition. It controls society while allowing the individual to flourish. In short, China has a dual strategy.

GOING BACK IN HISTORY, BUT HOW FAR?

In China, the argument is made that if international standards and regulations were produced with or by China itself, in other words, if the world order were less "Western" and more "Chinese," China would make more of a contribution to the international system. This idea of a Chinese standard and a "Beijing consensus" or even a Chinese theory of international relations has taken the place of condemnations of an unjust imperialist order. Nearly all examples and advocacy for this are found in Chinese history—often in its imperial era and sometimes in ancient dynasties. In Beijing it is no longer even fashionable to quote the Qing (1644–1911, including the era of the clash with the West) or the Ming (1368–1644, the conquest of China's own West, Admiral Zheng He and his "non-colonization," the tributary system), or even the Song or the Tang. One has to go back to the Zhou, Han, and Qin dynasties more than two thousand years ago to find examples that are popular today in Chinese international relations circles. This was the period of the Warring Kingdoms followed by the unification of China, involving a combination of "international" competition and incorporation under a recognized authority. Hence the past consolidation and unification of China may serve as a model for designing an international strategy in the era of globalization. This is not the product of a new strategic culture, but the rediscovery and interpretation of ancient Chinese culture.

Geopolitics is in search of instant answers, for example, to evaluate the clash of interests and competing claims in the South China Sea, and it assesses the relative power of nations. But a sense of history helps. One cannot compare on the same scale a nation like the United States, which has always projected itself into the future, and a nation like China, which has always sought to find its identity in the past. One must also move beyond what was after 1945 a historical interval, when the Pacific turned into an "American lake" while China underwent a phase of international withdrawal.

China's foreign policy, more than that of any other country, is characterized by a conflict between notions of heritage, the interdependence stemming from foreign trade, and the anticipation of unprecedented power. Heritage sometimes serves as a fallback position for a diplomacy that shuns initiatives. In the short term, a conservative foreign policy is the best way to avoid risks, and first of all the risk of criticism within China itself. China's decision-making process vacillates between retrospection and anticipation. The "five principles of peaceful coexistence" model borrowed from India's Pandit Nehru after 1955 are always there. The most important of these principles remains non-interference in domestic affairs, a concept on which absolute sovereignty is based. But China's strategy, which once combined neighborhood diplomacy with hostility toward the US and Soviet "superpowers," has also adapted to expanding international interests. The protection of its citizens (giving it a new stake in the international order) and China's investments abroad (the behavior of its businesses in terms of labor and environment) are raising new questions. These issues can trump government-to-government relations.

Inherited principles also influence decisions, particularly through burgeoning public opinion spoon-fed on nationalism. Its underlying narrative successfully combines a complex of inferiority

and victimization on the one hand with a growing feeling of superiority on the other hand, based on decades of successful reforms
reinterpreted as the "Chinese model." Likewise, the nature of the
bureaucratic system and of the state economy favors rigidity in
foreign affairs.

The People's Liberation Army is a vertical command structure
that does not lend itself to communication or public diplomacy. Yet
in the modern world, both of these tools have become an indispens-
able complement to any projection of strength. Diplomacy avoids
risks and responsibilities and is not inclined toward innovation,
either institutional or individual. The major state enterprises, especially in their relations with authoritarian countries, can also wors-
en China's image, as one Chinese geopolitical expert points out
with regard to Burma. [15]

One thing is certain. When faced with a choice between principles and pragmatic interests, more often than not, the People's Republic has chosen pragmatic adaptation. In the early 1950s, despite
the fact that it was supporting the Communist underground through
the Chinese minority working on the rubber plantations of Malaysia, it went ahead and purchased from Malaysia a substantial portion of its rubber harvest, which it greatly needed for its economy.
As a major copper producer, Maoist China very quickly ousted the
ambassador from Allende's Chile, the world's largest copper producer, after the 1971 coup. National interest has always taken precedence over Third World ideology. The same realism can dictate
accommodation to the needs and values of others. So realism also
demands that China's partners examine, in any proposal they make,
what's in it for China. This, more than any vision of the future, can
get China to move away from its strategic heritage.

NATION-BUILDING AND TERRITORIAL CLAIMS

History informs China's international strategy. The very formation of the Chinese nation was a process of territorial expansion backed by a population boom and migration. The "march to the South" and to the West could not have taken place without a strong state. Early on, it determined the outer limits of the "national" territory, leading to attempts to justify present-day claims that may be episodic or permanent, as the case may be.

None of the claims made today have continuously been made in the past, not even regarding Taiwan, which Mao did not see before the Sino-Japanese war as belonging to China. Certainly there was no claim to the South China Sea, which was forgotten at the end of the Qing Empire and went unmentioned in the first years of the PRC, nor a claim to Tibet, which has been conquered and given up three times since the fourteenth century. On the other hand, Outer Mongolia, which was once part of the Soviet Union and is now an independent and democratic state, was long claimed by Republican China. Vast stretches of Siberia were claimed over Russia from 1969 to 1991, before Sino-Russian talks achieved success by focusing on the Ussuri River, with much less at stake. The former Korean kingdom of Kokuryo, straddling parts of today's Northeastern China and the Korean peninsula, is sometimes described as having been Chinese, which is a source of irritation to North and South Korea both. The Indian state of Arunachal Pradesh, which shares a border with Burma and Tibet, has been disputed by China since the British drew the McMahon Line (1914), separating India from Tibet. But that Chinese claim lay dormant until 2008, when the Dalai Lama declared the Tawang monastery at the border with Chinese Tibet to be part of India and hence under his control. In September of the same year, the UK's Gordon Brown reached out to China, repealing his country's doctrine of merely recognizing China's "suzerainty" (and not sovereignty) over Tibet. These two contradictory events—an annoying statement by the Dalai Lama, and a concession without compensation by the region's former colonial master—proved sufficient for China to break its silence: it has been consistently challenging India over Arunachal Pradesh ever since.

In short, the catalog of Chinese territorial claims is not immutable. China can dip into it or on the contrary reduce it at will, sometimes using it as an irritant or improving relations with a neighbor. In 1978 Deng Xiaoping postponed "for future generations" the issue of the dispute with Japan over the Senkaku/Diaoyu islands. Chinese diplomacy has signed a joint declaration with ASEAN in 2002 (albeit not legally binding) on the "conduct of the parties in the South China Sea." In 2015, it is opening talks with South Korea over their maritime borders and respective EEZs. These are positive examples of China's versatility. It can go in both directions.

THE TWO TERMS OF CHINA'S STRATEGIC CULTURE

But well before its nineteenth-century clashes with the West, China also created a system of relationships in which brute force played only a limited role compared with economic interests and a ritualized form of soft power. This was the tribute system, which peaked under the Ming, creating interdependent relationships with neighbors and distant partners. This system has been brought back into fashion by a Chinese school of international relations that emphasizes the "win-win" nature of that system, whereby tribute involves both gift and counter-gift. Indeed, the Chinese empire could sometimes give more than it received, for example, to subjugate the people located beyond the Himalayan pass of Karakorum, located in present-day northeastern Pakistan and Afghanistan—in other words, in places where China's military had no chance of prevailing by themselves. In short, the tribute system might be the ancestor of a form of free trade based on Chinese standards and rules.

Thus the Chinese empire wavered between two terms of its strategic culture. One was belligerence, based on the primacy of force and ruse enshrined by China's Machiavelli, Sun Tzu, and his *Art of War*. The other term, derived from Confucian rhetoric on the harmony of interests, inspired a policy of gradual assimilation based on mutual interests. The Qing in particular reintroduced and adapted to contemporary tastes the "Five Baits," defined by a memorialist for the Han emperor in the second century BCE.[16] They used trade to attract the peoples surrounding them. To that end, they created a system of controlled trade, under which a role was assigned to designated merchants. That is the system referred to by Westerners as the "Canton system." Thus a policy devised in Western China to attract and assimilate tribes and states within the Chinese empire was also applied locally to the British. Of course, "divide and conquer" was second nature to the Chinese state. It was a practice first honed when China came into contact with the vast medley of Central Asian people before it was applied, with less success, to the Western barbarians.

Empire building took precedence then over nationalism. In Central Asia in the mid-eighteenth century, the Qing also experimented with a mixed economy in the form of new institutions, in particular the system of "management by merchants, supervision by officials" (*guandu shangban*) applied to new companies in sectors targeted for modernization.[17] In the final third of the nineteenth century, this system would be at the heart of policies aimed at strengthening the dynasty in the face of the West's superior resources. Foreign policy, in this case toward contiguous Central Asia, thus led to the creation of an important economic institution within China. China's foreign policy grew out of the history of China and its strategic culture. But in turn, foreign policy could ricochet and inspire developments at home. This was the case with reforms designed to introduce Western thinking or innovations (such as the College of Interpreters, or China's Maritime Customs, which were controlled by the British as a result of the Unequal Treaties), but it could also inspire purely domestic changes.

This inevitably brings to mind the international growth not only of reformed Chinese state-owned companies subsidized by the government but also the growth of new companies (like Huawei or ZTE in communications and Haier in appliances), which are neither public in a formal sense nor completely private. The hybrid nature of Chinese capitalism is inherited from a form of management by delegation dating from the imperial era, rather than an offshoot of Soviet-style planning.

The Qing dynasty also pacified and assimilated Western China by using two contrasting approaches: first by establishing military outposts and settlements (an institution revived almost to the letter as the *bingtuan*, Xinjiang's Construction Corps, by Mao), and second by encouraging emigration beyond the Great Wall, especially emigration by the "naked branches" (*guang gun*, as poor and therefore bachelor male peasants were called). In other words, the Qing used the military to colonize neighboring regions, but they also used population movements and commerce as a means of bringing them into the fold. That movement continues today—in Xinjiang and in Tibet in particular, where the "new people" are recent immigrants, more often than not from the overpopulated Sichuan province. China's thrust into Africa from the late 1990s bears a striking resemblance to this "internal colonization" of the Qing dynasty. Along with embassies, political relations, and the rhetoric of "mutual benefit" from trade, which is generally controlled by the state and its enterprises, one finds also widespread emigration among the poor—contract workers or even prisoners under conditional release, shopkeeper families forming networks and putting both Lebanese tradesmen and Western import-export companies out of business.

No single theory—whether based on power politics or, on the contrary, on the creeping advance of the Chinese economy, Chinese society, and soft power—can explain China's international breakthrough, nor can it explain the direction of its foreign policy. Officially China has embarked on plans for an army capable of holding its own, if not with the United States, then at least with any other nation. But it has also started using terms like *free trade* and *win-win*, once the slogan of the Clinton administration coined for the purpose of opening the door to the Asia Pacific region. For China, *win-win*, like the tributary system before it, implies a form of allegiance to Chinese rules and values, if only because China has a command economy whose actors are governmental or quasi-governmental. However, the notion of win-win is based more on persuasion and interests than on pressure or the use of force.

Of course, between the era of geographic and demographic expansion via the tributary period and the rise of contemporary China toward a wider sphere of influence, two centuries intervened, during which the country's influence faded away. Despite its ideological pretensions and its capacity for mobilization, Maoism did not restore China's influence beyond its newfound independence. In foreign policy it was generally cautious in its actions, if not its words, while taking drastic turns when it came to domestic policy. It would be an exaggeration to say that Maoist China from 1949 to 1976 did not engage in any military ventures. Indeed, it took part in two major wars, the Korean War in 1950 and the three-week "war of the peaks" with India in 1962. The first was really a decision made by Stalin, and the second reflects Maoist China's propensity to assert its territorial claims by force. It did so over Taiwan, with the takeover of the small coastal islands in 1955, the bombing of Quemoy and Matsu in 1958, and over Tibet, where, after the People's Liberation Army entered the country in 1950, the Chinese government took over in 1959. In the middle of the Cultural Revolution, it initiated incidents, albeit limited, with the Soviet Union over the Ussuri. At the very beginning of the reform era in 1979, Deng Xiaoping supported a three-week military "lesson" in Vietnam. Afterward, even against the advice of some of his own generals, he asserted that the People's Liberation Army would be stationed in Hong Kong after the handover to China.

A CULTURE OF BELLIGERENCE HELD IN CHECK

But these actions are the exception rather than the rule. China reluctantly entered the Korean War in October 1950, urged on by Stalin, who had gotten involved in it to support Kim Il-sung, the North Korean dictator. Beijing issued repeated warnings to the United States against a US military advance up to the Yalu, the river forming the border with Korea. China's military actions against Taiwan from 1955 to 1958 were symbolic actions designed to demonstrate that China meant business in the longer term about reunifying Taiwan with the mainland. After 1958, shells loaded with tracts took the main role in bombings of Quemoy and Matsu and until 1996, China engaged in no further actual military operations in the Strait of Taiwan. In March 1996, China established air and sea exclusion zones for the purpose of conducting missile testing around the island, which hinted of a potential blockade. The arrival of two US aircraft carriers at the entrance of the Taiwan Strait (contrary to the rumors of the time, however, they did not sail through the strait) ended the challenge. China had placed a calling card, but without risking a conflict.

The offensive against India in 1962, like the one against Vietnam in 1979, comprised carefully controlled and time-limited operations, regardless of their military success, which in both cases is doubtful. After 1949, China has had territorial disputes with every one of its fourteen neighbors. But it has often backed off from these and has also entered into agreements, in direct contrast to the reputation of intransigence created by its own propaganda. As for its propensity to use force, this is more likely when there is an actual challenge to a Chinese population, especially the Han, China's major ethnic group. China is more inclined to compromise when it is in a position of weakness or when divisions within the country threaten it. A classic example is the ban issued by Mao in 1965 on any direct military involvement against the United States in Indochina, limiting China's support for North Vietnam to arms shipments and the supply of firemen, engineers, and construction workers to repair infrastructure bombed in Vietnam. By contrast, in 1954, the PLA, led by the future Marshal Chen Yi, had participated directly in the decisive siege against the French troops at Dien Bien Phu.[18] The restraint on the part of China in 1965 stemmed both from its cautious approach to the United States and from the fact that a political struggle was underway in China itself. Since the reform period in 1979, China has not been involved in any direct military conflicts, and initially (from 1979 to 1989), its military expenditures even stagnated. Neither the extremely limited skirmishes with Vietnam and the Philippines in the South China Sea, nor the military maneuvers around Taiwan in 1996 can be considered military offensives in the true sense.

China's post-Mao leadership has persistently chosen peace and has withdrawn its support for insurgencies around the world. This behavior contrasts with another long-term fact: since 1989 and the Tiananmen events, which caused the regime to increase again its reliance on the army, China's military expenditures have increased every single year by more than 10 percent—with the exception of 1998, the year of the Asian economic crisis, and 2009, owing possibly to repercussions from the global financial crisis. China's military budget, even as officially estimated at $141 billion in 2015, is the second-largest in the world after the United States. It is more than three times that of its closest Asian competitor, Japan.

Why hasn't the increase in military expenses from 1989 to 2009 had more of an effect on China's foreign policy? This is probably because nearly all of China's successes since 1978 have stemmed from global integration. This was not a break with China's heritage.

Reform and opening up, which were founding programs of the Deng Xiaoping era, echoed China's history since the nineteenth century. "Opening up" is a successor of the former "Western affairs movement" (*yangwu yundong*) of the nineteenth century, which also included the idea of a self-strengthening China. It was later encouraged by the "Open Door" diplomacy that the United States promoted toward China, as opposed to a narrow European colonial view and Japan's quest for exclusive control. Reform has been an overriding obsession of China's elites ever since they first came in contact with the West in the new Treaty Ports. Viewed from this perspective, China's "transition" is indeed a never-ending process. Then, the imperial bureaucracy and a Confucianist society were at stake. Now, the Leninist and Maoist underpinnings of China are in question, and with them the future of China's political culture and identity.

THE POROSITY OF CHINESE INSTITUTIONS AND SOCIETY

One of the paradoxes of sinology is that it is often Westerners who extol the uniqueness and singularity of Chinese culture from a body of classical writings. The more these sinologists specialize in literature and textual rather than contextual analysis, the less likely they are to take a broad approach. They are also more likely to interpret Chinese texts and institutions literally, making them seem inaccessible and exotic. This was by no means the case of a historian like Joseph Needham, whose monumental work on the history of science in China was at the same time an ode to exchanges among civilizations.

Indeed a clash occurred when a partly symbolic system of thought came into contact with the largely logical canons of Western culture. However, China's political culture and its institutions are no less porous than its curious individualistic society when it comes to outside influences. When it came into contact with the West, China based its relation to the outside world on the opposition of *ti* and *yong* (essence vs. usefulness), in other words, inner perseverance and assimilation. The appeal of foreign, and especially Western, models has been constant since the influence of the Jesuits under the Qing. When the Qing entered into a historic treaty with tsarist Russia in Nerchinsk (1689), the interpreters and intermediaries in the negotiations were Jesuits, and the treaty, which was first drafted in Latin, also bore the marks of their influence. Here we see that China, which at the time was "closed," in some sense recognized the usefulness of an international institution, the Church, and of an international language. From 1854 in the era of unequal treaties and open ports, the Qing entrusted a new Maritime Customs administration to foreigners, making it an essential pathway for Western-inspired models. Its most notable head would be a former British consulate employee, Robert Hart. He ran the administration for forty-eight years. It is hard to find the same kind of influence in Maoist China or even in contemporary China. But the Nobel Prize–winning economist Robert Mundell, whose work covers optimum currency areas, has a permanent residency permit in Beijing, and he has certainly had a major influence on China's monetary management. For example, he has largely inspired the fixed parity of the yuan with the dollar, which since 1994 has made China (more than Japan!) a member of an implicit dollar zone in Asia; then its "crawling peg," or limited flexibility; and lastly, a limited internationalization of the yuan without free convertibility.

The acceptance and use of foreign influences is not merely a pragmatic tool for "dealing with the barbarians." And Westerners are not the only foreigners to have exerted a major cultural influence on China. For two and a half centuries, the Chinese lived under the domination of a Manchu dynasty, the Qing, whose language, rules, and military system differed greatly from those of the Han culture. In the capital itself, Beijing, there were Manchu and

Chinese districts closed between each other at night, with hospitals reserved for the Manchu, who made up a third of the population. Although those who rejected the foreign Qing dynasty based their opposition on Han legitimism ("Down with the Qing, restore the Ming" was their motto), the fact remains that the founding dynasty of contemporary Chinese nationalism, the ruling dynasty that incorporated five different peoples in a national melting pot, was itself foreign. Foreigners tend to identify China's first "cultural revolution" with the movement of May 4, 1919, a nationalist movement directed against the Treaty of Versailles and foreign encroachments into China. However, that movement was critical of Chinese society as a whole and had a high regard for Westernization. At that time, it was Confucianism that was disparaged and blamed for all the failures of Chinese society.

Before Confucianism and until the eleventh century, Buddhism and through it Hinduism prospered in China. Hindu monks, mathematicians, and astronomers penetrated as far as the Chinese imperial court. One of them ran the astronomers' office in the eighth century, as Nobel Prize–winning economist Amartya Sen points out.[19] The spread of Buddhism by itinerant monks also encouraged the dissemination of written texts and free debate—two traits otherwise disparaged by the imperial bureaucracy.

The appeal of foreign models reached its purest form with the events of May and June 1989 on Tiananmen Square when students erected a cardboard replica of the Statue of Liberty, renamed the Goddess of Democracy. The global media was then able for weeks to report the events on live television until power was cut off for the final assault. The degree of openness of the decade of the 1980s is still amazing. But it was also based on pragmatism, which saw the relative gains to be derived from Western and capitalist models and solutions.

STRATEGIC DUALISM ALLOWS FOR REVERSIBILITY

Extraversion leads to versatility—the ability to seize upon models and adapt them to the situation in China, but also to change them by rejecting grafted additions that might have earlier be seen as adopted for eternity. In 1911, the Chinese cut off the pigtails imposed by the Manchu dynasty; in 1960, China rejected the Soviet model and all its advisers, turning its back on a decade of rich economic, cultural, and linguistic influences. The reforms made after 1978, the borrowing from Western capitalism (ideas and institutions rather than financial capital), and human exchanges with the outside world inevitably led to tension with the other facet of Chinese political culture, rooted in preservation and control. The difference between the Chinese regime and any other political system is that the party-state, operating above society with no constraint other than preserving a façade of legitimacy, can orchestrate policy reversals. The events of 1989 can be compared with the aborted reforms attempted during the Hundred Days of 1898, when the Empress Dowager Cixi did away with the supporters of the reformer prince Guangxu but spared his own life. But after 1898, the empire was virtually unable to bring about economic change, and any political reforms that resumed were quickly eclipsed by the revolution of 1911. After 1989 the party-state pushed through a political counterreform, yet also accelerated the country's economic development and integration with the global market.

In the period that opened up after Tiananmen, nationalism was encouraged in education and the media as a reaction to the West and to democratic influences.[20] The intelligentsia and those among the leaders who had embarked on the path of Westernization were denounced. Sanctioned by the G7 countries (including by Japan for only a year), China focused its diplomatic energy on its Asian neighbors, especially in Southeast Asia. Supported by the United States during the Cold War, countries like Indonesia, Singapore, and Brunei became alarmed when the United States changed course and began promoting democracy and human rights after the fall of the Soviet Union. They established (or reestablished in the case of Indonesia) diplomatic relations with China. This was the first time China was rewarded for its antidemocratic attitude—by three countries that were among the most closely involved in global trade. They agreed over political stability and soon over "Asian values" as opposed to the global values espoused by the West. In 2015, more than fifty countries, following the United Kingdom, jumped the gun on the United States and applied to join the China-led Asian Infrastructure Investment Bank (AIIB). The move validates China's strategy of mixing international integration with its own shadow organizations competing with the post–World War II Bretton-Woods international institutions.

In this way, opening up to the outside world came to be balanced by the concept of "national preservation"—*baoguo*—and the desire to control society, which was hardly a new policy. Both cases involved a swing of the pendulum. Nationalism, which is often portrayed as patriotism in China, is part of the country's historic legacy, as are tensions over its identity and a tendency to shut itself off from the outside world.

Control and limits on trading outlets with foreign countries, such as seen under the Qing dynasty and the attempt at autarky during the Mao era, is a recurring theme in Chinese history. So is the fear of foreign influence, such as in the explosion of xenophobia at the end of the nineteenth century and the convergence of anti-Western movements since 1989. As a result, nationalism is viewed as reactive and defensive, even in a context of unprecedented progress for the country. In October 2009, during the extraordinary military parade organized to mark the sixtieth anniversary of the People's Republic, the soldiers saluting the flag when it was raised on Tiananmen Square each took 169 steps, one for each year since China's defeat in the Opium War in 1840. Thus the recall of past humiliation is legitimizing the military and China's foreign policy.[21]

This can go in two very different directions. One is revenge, extolling naked strength and applying to the contemporary world the rules of nineteenth-century geopolitics. *Wolf Totem*, a Chinese novel that received rave reviews in 2004, glorifies the behavior of "wolves" in the Mongolian steppe in contrast to the naiveté of the Chinese "lambs."[22] The other direction relies on a soft power approach. It contrasts concepts and actions by China, past and present, with European crusades, conquests, and the "mission to civilize." This is the China whose navigators discovered Africa without really coming ashore (although it waged war on Sri Lanka), the China that supports developing countries and whose overriding objective is the "democratization of international relations" (Hu Jintao), a China that proclaims it has never engaged in aggression or colonization, and that never dictates to others—a China with clean hands. This latter direction is just as important as the geopolitics of force. It explains why, even though it has risen to become the second-largest power in the world, China has retained a foreign policy position based on innocence and surprised naiveté. It uses its inferiority complex as an asset on the international stage.

China's foreign policy cannot be separated from its political culture. Nor can it be separated from conflicts within that culture or from the sentiment of national identity. Praise for modernizing mandarins or criticism of their weakness with regard to foreigners, either celebration or denigration of Chinese culture—all this is part of the landscape, and these oppositions are not about to disappear. The official denunciation of Liu Xiaobo, a winner of the Nobel Peace Prize in 2010 and a political prisoner, is often based on the words he had used twenty-two years earlier in Hong Kong, discussing in jest the need for China to experience "three hundred years of colonization" so that in the end it could finally bring about a historic revolution. This anecdote reflects both the shift by Chinese elites to Westernization in the 1980s and the subsequent condemnation of Western ideas by nationalists. Even China's foreign policy experts and officials have gotten used to being the brunt of abuse and threats over the Internet. Some are sent calcium tablets in the mail that are supposed to give them a stiffer backbone in dealing with the West. In June 2012, Admiral Zhang Zhaozhong, a regular military commentator on national television, launched into a diatribe against "a million traitors"—diplomats, economists, and members of the military—who, "are working with the United States." Zhang is used to making outrageous statements. He has raised the possibility of a nuclear strike by China in response to any Western military action against Iran. The fact that he referred to a "million people" was disturbing because that figure is on a scale with the worst Maoist campaigns in the past. But his outburst also symbolizes the cultural divide among China's elites.

In the end, foreign policy cannot be insulated from the context of China's domestic politics or from the trends in Chinese society.

In theory, an authoritarian regime equipped with a centralized apparatus, subject to supervision by a Leninist party, has immense advantages in conducting its foreign policy. Discussions take place at the very top, and for the most part, China's foreign partners have no knowledge of them. The machinery of the state can be set in motion and operate away from public opinion. The government can make sudden shifts in foreign policy without fear of criticism, as with the 1959–1963 break with the Soviet Union, the normalization of relations with Japan in the midst of the Cultural Revolution, or the intensity of the strategic rapprochement with the United States in the first phase of the reform in 1978–1979. But is that always the case?

DEMOCRACY IS PART OF THE COMPETITION

The People's Republic tends to be forgetful when it comes to history, even the history of the Communist Party itself, the official version of which was banned during the Cultural Revolution. Even today, its worst totalitarian phases (the Great Leap Forward and the Cultural Revolution) are swept under the rug, especially in educating the young. But Chinese society has recovered its heritage and its strategic identity. Above and beyond the narrative of the "century of humiliation," classical culture still has universal appeal in China. The official ideology has retained from it the Confucian terms of harmony and benevolence, interpreted as a theory of mutual advantages, a Chinese version of the liberal notion of win-win. Foreign controversy regarding whether China has soft power misses the point. In practice, it is commercial diplomacy and the mutual benefit of partnership with China that embody the reality of Chinese soft power.

But China's legacy of strategic culture also includes Darwinian geopolitics. It draws its sources from Chinese strategic realism, including a focus on forward defense against neighbors. Preparing for war is recommended at the very least as a guarantee of peace, reproducing the old Latin adage, *si vis pacem, para bellum*. The extreme attention paid to appearances, to "face," and to devising scripts that limit China's partners to an entirely predictable course of action are also part of this tradition of forward defense. At the same time these rituals are the traits foreigners, especially Westerners, have come to expect from China's government, as they evoke images of the Middle Kingdom and the "Forbidden City." How strongly has that imagery pressed itself on Western envoys, and would Henry Kissinger's views on China be as much recognized without the image of the Great Wall of China?

Here we meet with a second risk in interpretation. The first one was a belief in the fairy tale of international convergence. China's regime and its system cannot be absorbed into the market economy.

But the second risk comes from taking literally myths about China's strategic identity, and imagining a culture clinging to its nationalistic, vengeful, and warlike legacy from the past. The imperial legacy is a script, the nationalist vulgate a narrative, and the intangible nature of borders a myth to which it lays claim. The regime draws on these at will but abandons them when it seems timely to do so. The staging of the past is all the more necessary because China's leaders have not much new on offer, nor do they have a grand design for the international system. If they had one, would they have missed the opportunity offered by the 2008–2010 financial downturn in the West to establish their influence? Would they have allowed their global strategy to be taken hostage by a return to territorial quarrels in Asia? Their attitude is one of adapting to the international system or resisting it, depending on the balance of power they perceive. After 2008, they inferred from the global financial crisis that this balance had shifted in their favor. The first button they pushed was the most traditional—asserting claims in what China believes to be its rightful space. Ironically, other more innovative initiatives such as taking on a greater role at the UN or in international financial institutions were actually considered more risky.

Two years later, China's instinctive push for sovereignty has resulted in a near coalition of its Asian neighbors—near, but not complete, a course of action well described by the word "hedging." Japan, which engaged in its separate trade with China during the Cold War, or South Korea, whose firms now depend on China as a market and as a producer, would like to keep the golden goose alive. Just as China's push outward grows out of historical instinct rather than from a clear strategy, Asia's guarded response is a precautionary principle, not an enthusiastic alliance with the United States.

China's de-escalation, signaled in December 2010 by Dai Bingguo, is a return to ambiguity, rather than a change of direction.

Mutually beneficial and bilateral commercial diplomacy, with the appearance of a monetary zone around the Chinese currency, could conceivably balance the more warlike image of China's maritime push. What would truly be astonishing would be for China to put an end to this dualism.

Some Chinese experts and ideologists see the cost, in terms of lost international influence, that is the result of a balancing act between economic integration and imperial temptation. They are looking for a new Chinese paradigm in international relations, and they draw it from history. The most noteworthy example of this, if not the example the most likely to persuade democratic public opinion, is provided by Yan Xuetong.[23] Disdainful of current international institutions, which reflect the past power imbalance in favor of the West, Yan seeks his model for international relations from the era of the Warring Kingdoms. The most influential of these, the kingdom of Zhou, overpowered the others through its "humane authority"[24] and not through conquest or hegemony in the strict sense. Yan recommends the same model for twenty-first century China. But Yan does not frown upon the most simplified realism: to be considered a global power a country must have a population "of at least 200 million people." He also believes in finding signs of the humane authority of the Zhou in the Chinese Communist Party's United Front policy. But to use that very domestic model for international relations is the sign of an authoritarian approach. The party's United Front has actually been a tactical instrument designed to gain power, a decoy that today still manages eight totally unknown small "democratic" parties.

Yet when Yan traces the contemporary outline of "humane authority," in the most unpredictable way he rediscovers a program of political reform that seems to be inspired by the China of 1989. Today's humane authority, he writes, is the universal law of democratic elections, of responsible leaders, particularly in terms of corruption, freedom to travel, and freedom of thought. Admittedly,

Yan does appear to reserve these rights for the prince's advisors—think tanks and their experts!

Yan Xuetong is often labeled as a Chinese neoconservative because of his geopolitical realism and his anti-Americanism. He is also a talented public intellectual for international affairs. His plunge into classical strategic thought has made him aware of a major obstacle to an innovative Chinese foreign policy: the failure of the political system to transform itself. As president Hu Jintao did in January 2012, he laments the ineffectiveness of China's soft power. But Yan also understands that the competition among models, on which his view of international relations is based, implies a thorough political reform by China. Yan analyzes with cold realism the fact that Western hegemony has reached its limits on the global stage. But the essence of China's political system also keeps its foreign policy in check and limits the impact of a dazzling economic success. After an all-out effort to find the roots of China's strategic future in its historical identity, Yan finally discovers one small prerequisite to its influence—applying democracy to politics. "The electoral system has become the universal political standard these days. . . . China must see to it that the moral principle of democracy is a principle promoted by it."[25]

A democrat perhaps in spite of himself, Yan Xuetong joins Hu Yaobang, Zhao Ziyang, and Wen Jiabao among a long list of Chinese reformers who finally came to advocate China's vital need for democracy.

NOTES

1. "Integrated and Multipolar Governance: Looking at China's International Standing in 2020" (in Chinese), *Caijing*, October 19, 2011.

2. *Mushiso* or "policy without ideals," according to Akira Iriye, quoted by Thomas W. Burkman, *Japan and the League of Nations: Empire and World Order, 1914–1938* (Honolulu: University of Hawaii Press, 2008), 11.

3. Shang Wenmu, "Back to Yalta: A Roadmap for Sino-US Relations," *China Security* 19 (March 2012): 49–56.

4. Michel Oksenberg and Elizabeth Economy, *China Joins the World—Process and Prospects* (New York, Council on Foreign Economic Relations, 1999).

5. Bates Gill, *Rising Star: China's New Security Diplomacy* (Washington, DC: Brookings Institution Press, 2007).

6. Rosemary Foot, *Rights beyond Borders: The Global Community and the Struggle over Human Rights in China* (Oxford: Oxford University Press, 2000); and Rosemary Foot and Andrew Walter, *China, the United States and the Global Order* (Cambridge: Cambridge University Press, 2011).

7. Aaron Friedberg, "Will Europe's Past Be Asia's Future?" *Survival* 42, no. 3 (Fall 2000): 147–59; and Aaron Friedberg, "The Future of U.S.-China Relations: Is Conflict Inevitable?" *International Security* 30, no. 2 (Fall 2005): 7–45.

8. Michael Pillsbury, *The Hundred-Year Marathon: China's Secret Strategy to Replace America as the Global Superpower* (New York: Henry Holt, 2015).

9. Charles Grant and Katinka Barysch, *Can Europe and China Shape a New World Order?* (London: Centre for European Reform, 2008). Charles Grant returned to his theory in 2010: Charles Grant, "China's Peaceful Rise Turns Prickly," Centre for European Reform, January 22, 2010, http://centreforeuropeanreform.blogspot.com/2010/01/chinas-peaceful-rise-turns-prickly.html.

10. European Union External Action Service, Communication of the Commission, "A Long Term Policy for China-Europe Relations," Brussels, June 5, 1995, http://eeas.europa.eu/china/docs/index_en.htm.

11. Robert B. Zoellick, "Whither China: From Membership to Responsibility?" National Committee on US-China Relations, New York, September 21, 2005, available on http://2001-2009.state.gov/s/d/former/zoellick/rem/53682.htm.

12. Robert Zoellick, "China 'Reluctant Stake-Holder' in World Economic Woes," remarks to the Asia Society, August 14, 2011, http://asiasociety.org/business/economic-trends/robert-zoellick-china-reluctant-stakeholder-world-economic-woes.

13. Alastair I. Johnston, "Learning Versus Adaptation: Explaining Change in Chinese Arms Control Policy," *China Journal* 35 (January 1996).

14. Ibid., p. 61.

15. Zha Daojiong, "All Roads to Myanmar," *Pacnet* no. 6A (January 25, 2012), http://www.csis.org/files/publication/Pac1206-A.pdf.

16. The "Five Baits" defined by the memorialist Jia Yi are: elegant clothing and carriages, fine food, music and female companions, palatial homes, and imperial favors and receptions.

17. Peter C. Perdue, *China Marches West: The Qing Conquest of Central Eurasia* (Cambridge, MA: Harvard University Press, 2005), 263.

18. François Joyaux, *La Chine et le règlement du premier conflit d'Indochine—Genève 1954* (Paris: Publications de la Sorbonne, 1979), 66.

19. Amartya Sen, "Passage to China," *New York Review of Books*, December 2, 2004.

20. Zhao Suisheng, *A Nation-State by Construction: Dynamics of Modern Chinese Nationalism* (Stanford, CA: Stanford University Press, 2004).

21.   *Wu wang guo chi* [Never forget the national humiliation] (Beijing: Zhongguo huaqiao chubanshe [Overseas Chinese Editions], 1992).

22.   Jiang Rong, *Le totem du loup* (Paris: François Bourin, 2007).

23.   Yan Xuetong, *Ancient Chinese Thought, Modern Chinese Power* (Princeton, NJ: Princeton University Press, 2011).

24.   A term inferred by Yan Xuetong from the Chinese character for *wang*, meaning both "monarch" and "rule."

25.   Yan Xuetong, *Ancient Chinese Thought, Modern Chinese Power*, 219.

Conclusion

Xi Jinping Resets China

The window has closed. In October 2012, Xi Jinping took over the three functions of party general secretary, president of the PRC, and head of the Military Affairs Commission. Since then, it has become evident that Xi has accumulated more power and more personal authority than any Chinese leader since Mao Zedong. In 2009–2012, there had been open debate in China about political reform and about economic and foreign policy, and almost as open defiance of the outgoing leadership's authority over the party-state. But this expectant and dramatic atmosphere has vanished as Xi has taken control of China. Defying predictions, he has re-established the primacy of the party over the state. He is reinstating personal leadership instead of the "collective leadership" that was thought in the past decade to be the new norm in China.

Xi's style differs from that of his predecessors: he speaks in the first person, emphasizes the greatness of China, and quotes Mao. But if "control" is the keyword of Xi's style, this leaves little room for major political or structural reform. His top-down approach, which might be called "hard-line modernization," seeks to check irrational behavior such as corruption and runaway financing rather than to reform the key state economic actors. After doing away with the flamboyant Bo Xilai, his moves against so-called corrupt "tigers" have ensnared top-level elder leaders, who previously would have been a check on the authority of the general secretary: Zhou Yongkang, China's former security chief and a major supporter of former president Jiang Zemin, and the top two former military leaders, generals Xu Caihou and Guo Boxiong. At last count in March 2015, twenty-eight vice minister–level cadres have been purged, and some economic sectors—oil, coal, and increasingly steel—have been decimated: for Shanxi province alone, fifteen thousand cadres have been hit by the anticorruption campaign. Rumors abound regarding other top retired party leaders. Not since Mao has such a high-level purge taken place inside the party.

Xi has also neatly sidestepped Prime Minister Li Keqiang, who often looks like a high-level technical operative rather than a head of government; Wang Qishan, who runs the party's Central Commission for Discipline Inspection but has a strong economic and financial background, is much more in the spotlight. Xi is also ignoring statements about "low-profile" foreign policy inherited from Deng Xiaoping, and unabashedly claims a role for China as one of the world's two "big powers." He presides over an increasingly persistent assertion of China's regional claims. Indeed, Xi's China seeks strategic parity with the United States while pursuing a neighborhood policy based on China's superior strength.[1]

Even Deng Xiaoping had to contend with a large group of conservatives at the top of the party, from 1977 to 1984, and was increasingly unable to quell the infighting of different political factions after that date. Xi's power also exceeds that of Jiang Zemin, an underestimated leader who excelled in factional compromise and synthesis. It dwarfs that of his immediate predecessor, Hu Jintao, who increasingly hid behind the screen of collective leadership and ended his reign without a clear sense of purpose.

Xi's stature is clear from the functions that he immediately captured (including the important Military Affairs Commission); the support initially given to him by party elders; and the personal style that, unlike his predecessor, he does not hesitate to use. It is also clear from the disappearance of obvious political jockeying at the top and the silence maintained by many of his colleagues; the authority he is displaying over issues such as corruption; a "rectification campaign" of cadres; and the near disappearance of public dissent, whether from the liberal "right" of the party, from its nationalist and populist "left," or from the Chinese population itself. Criticism of Xi on China's social media does not cross a red line, and liberal editorializing in China's media, with the exception of some economic issues, has virtually stopped.

Xi's control of both the party and the military is also evident from a new turn in Chinese foreign policy. Before he took over, there was much talk about fragmented bureaucracies, indecisiveness at the top, and the pressures from activists and a supposedly powerful Chinese public opinion. But since the takeover, China's approach toward its neighborhood has become more rational but no less tough. In fact, since the People's National Congress session of March 2013, no one in China's vast military establishment has dared to go off-message. Anti-Japanese demonstrations and violence have been replaced by a more controlled campaign through newspapers and journals.

However, there are limits to Xi's power. Reformers and those loyal to Hu and Wen remain in the Politburo, where they are biding their time before the next party succession in five years. The price Xi has paid, willingly or unwillingly, for broad support from party elders and conservatives is an endorsement of major vested interests—above all, the state-owned enterprises or SOEs. To balance this, he has launched his massive and persistent anti-corruption campaign, which is also a tool to obtain compliance from an entrenched bureaucracy. Xi's Achilles' heel is the economy, which has been facing new obstacles as it meets the limits to growth and the buildup of vested interests. To bury factional debate, Xi has inspired, or at least tolerated, a revival of Maoist "mass line" politics.[2] But this reversion to the practices and rhetoric of the Mao era bolsters authoritarian leadership instead of preparing for a political transition.

It could also create foreign-policy problems. China's new Bismarckian reliance on bilateral partnerships requires strength on every front. There is now a long list of countries in China's neighborhood that have endured Beijing's hubris since 2010. Xi has arrived on the stage at a time when China no longer has "friends all over the world," as Mao put it, but does have interests all over the world, as Lord Palmerston once said of the British Empire. Yet China is not at the heart of a multilateral regime, nor does it have a single significant ally. It must permanently juggle a coalition of interests—which sometimes aligns it with developing countries, sometimes with other emerging economies, and also increasingly with the developed industrial societies whose political models it rejects. Above all, Xi faces a foreign-policy challenge as he seeks to combine assertiveness toward the neighborhood with a quest for an equal relationship with the United States.

HOW XI TOOK CONTROL OF CHINA

On the eve of the Eighteenth Party Congress in October 2012, there was open debate about the momentous choices faced by China. Reformers often talked of a crossroads, particularly on the issue of economic reform, where vested interests ran against more equity- and consumer-based growth. Liberal critics talked of a "lost decade" under the outgoing leaders, implying that their own predecessors before 2002 had actually been bolder in liberalizing China. Foreign policy and strategy was also openly discussed as nationalist activists and the fringes of China's defense apparatus challenged the indecisiveness at the top. There had not been such public debate in China since 1989. A symbol of this was the dramatic fall from power of Bo Xilai, China's most flamboyant politician, whose story reads like a contemporary martial arts novel.

However, that dramatic atmosphere has now vanished as Xi has taken control of China. Right before the February 2012 Chinese New Year, political liberals tried to revive their cause by suggesting in *Southern Weekly*, a leading party newspaper, that the "China dream"—a term used by Xi—included constitutionalism. But nothing could have been farther from Xi's mind than political reform and constitutionalism, and the article never made it into print. Since Xi took over, there have been no social protests as striking as the spectacular rural land protests or industrial actions of late 2011 and early 2012. Foreign-policy debates have also disappeared even as Xi has taken an even more aggressive approach toward Japan and India.

The turnaround that Xi has managed at the top of the party-state and also in terms of defining the limits of debate is impressive. It has generally been held that each generation of Chinese leaders was weaker than its immediate predecessor as it lacked either the revolutionary credentials or the experience of bitter "line struggle," as party factional infighting is often termed in China. "Collective leadership," which had become a credo after the disaster of Mao's personal rule, was all too synonymous with compromise and stalled decisions. "Fragmented authoritarianism" the trademark of the 1990s, had given way to the notion of bureaucratic "stove piping," with a diverse and corrupt system outgrowing the top-down political control that nurtured it.

Xi has defied those predictions and concentrated power. In addition to his three top posts—presiding over the party, the army, and the state—he directly runs at least six "leading groups" in areas that range from economic reform to state security, foreign and Taiwan affairs, and Internet issues. This was no fluke. Rather, it reflects a long-held ambition and was executed with a great deal of opportunity grasping. Xi has outmaneuvered his rivals, his colleagues, and even his mentors. His political style signals a return to personal power over "collective leadership," with strong ideological and campaign tools at his disposal. Hu and Wen wanted—but did not secure—a transition to a system of collective control in which "scientific socialism" and "harmony" would replace political decisions. Xi, on the other hand, has reestablished the primacy of the party. In lieu of checks and balances, or a constitutional separation of powers, Xi and the prime minister are streamlining the bureaucracy and emphasizing respect for rules set from above. There will be some freedom for individuals, NGOs, and market mechanisms, but the party will exercise even more control over officials and administrative institutions.

Xi has therefore moved decisively to recreate a political compact at the top. A corner was turned not long before the Eighteenth Party Congress. Xi's two-week disappearance from public sight right before the congress has never been explained, but in retrospect there is a strong similarity with Mao's ability to disappear from sight and launch counteroffensives. In the spring of 2012, some top-level party leaders and influential retirees had seemed to be unhappy with the way that then prime minister Wen Jiabao led the chase against Bo Xilai and his ideology—the mixture of Maoist "red songs," populist pork-barrel politics, and violent persecution of personal enemies. Bo was an earnest supporter of militarist and nationalist trends, and to conservatives he could be a "useful idiot" to counter liberal and legalist demands.

Both sides used the Bo case to their own advantage. Over the summer of 2012, Hu left Wen in the lurch and made his peace over the Bo issue in order to push for the appointment of his candidates—including CCP organization chief Li Yuanchao, reformist leader of Guangdong province Wang Yang, and the only woman at the top, Liu Yandong—to the Politburo to balance known hardliners and "red princes" (that is, the second-generation leaders from ruling families). But Xi put the first nail into Hu's coffin, when he and his backers—including eighty-six-year-old former president Jiang Zemin—suddenly shifted their stance and made the purge of Bo a major event before the Party Congress. In the same breath, a major supporter of Hu, his chief of staff Ling Jihua, was now denounced for the kind of family or political errors of which they accused their adversaries.

The conservatives then reverted to the oldest trick in the CCP's book: they assembled an "enlarged" Politburo, which includes veterans as well as regular members, giving "guidance" to a Central Committee plenum. It announced the expulsion of Bo for bribery, improper conduct, and "other crimes." The next move was against Hu's faction. A general close to Xi was appointed vice president of the Military Affairs Commission, while two of Hu's candidates were rejected. To show who was the boss, this was publicly announced *before* the Party Congress. At the Party Congress itself, Hu surrendered immediately his chairmanship of the Military Affairs Commission—the party-state's number one position since 1935 and the Long March.

The Politburo that emerged from the Party Congress is older than its predecessor: the average age of incoming Politburo members is sixty-three, compared to sixty-two five years ago. It is also dominated by "princelings": in a surprising instance of reverse genetic engineering, four out of seven members of the Politburo Standing Committee are either children of former top leaders or have a wife who is one. Xi, of course, is himself a "princeling" whose father served Mao and Deng. He may have lived for a while in a cave dwelling during the Cultural Revolution. But, in late August 2012, when the direction of the succession was in the balance, he is said to have remarked in frustration: "My family's house was taken over by strangers. Now they want to rent me back some rooms, but I want it all."[3]

XI'S STYLE

In order to understand how powerful Xi is and what type of China might emerge from his time in office, it is necessary to examine Xi's style, which differs greatly from that of his predecessors. Unlike them, Xi speaks in the first person, emphasizes the greatness of China, and quotes Mao. Drawing from the CCP repertoire of its "golden years" before the Great Leap and the Cultural Revolution, he extols the party as the core of the leadership and insists on Communist virtues. Hu Jintao, by contrast, always emphasized collective leadership and "harmony," made "peaceful development" into an official mantra, and designed "scientific socialism" as a compromise between different ideological choices.

Xi's speech to the press at the closure of the Eighteenth Party Congress announced what was to come. It was short, and two goals stood out. The first was that of "happiness," repeated twice. Guangdong province under its reformist leadership has had a "happiness index" for the past two years. The word suggests awareness of the aspirations of society, as distinct from party members and cadres. The other goal was the "great renewal of the Chinese nation," a formula implying that the country needs renovation and making "greatness" a goal in itself. After the congress, Xi made a well-publicized visit to Beijing's National History Museum, where the humiliations of the past are very much on display. There, he would explain the renewal in terms of "the China dream" and twice quote Mao.

Finally, Xi mentioned the need to "ensure that our party will remain at the core of leadership." That was a real play on words: instead of emphasizing the "core leadership" that has designated a collective group of leaders excluding factional wings, Xi's words put an emphasis on a monolithic party at the helm. This is a real change from the last decade. Instead of playing a balancing role between factions, Xi wants the party to unite around him, and he emphasizes cooperation, calling the Standing Committee members "colleagues" (*tongshi*). His own views may swing from one option to the other, but there can't be open debate, much less dissent, within the party's ranks.

In particular, Xi likes to quote Mao's poems from the 1943 to 1949 period and occasionally the poet Li Bai, whose poems were standard fare for Red Guards during the Cultural Revolution. In this sense, Xi has something in common with Bo, who also quoted Mao extensively. Of course, quoting Mao was also a standard recipe for political survival during the Cultural Revolution, and Xi might also be reassuring the older generation and conservatives who backed his victory. Xi's acceptance speech again included a Mao quote about "serving the people" and assuming a responsibility that is "heavier than Mount Tai." This is vintage Mao, revived during the Cultural Revolution and during Xi's formative years as a youngster.

Another significant element of Xi's style is his praise of earlier generations of CCP leaders. To Xi, the first thirty years of the PRC, from 1949 to 1979, are as worthy of praise as the thirty years from 1979 onward—in other words, the socialist construction era supervised by Mao is equal to the reform era ushered in by Deng Xiaoping. One cannot overdo Xi's loyalty to the founding families of the PRC: he has even received and heard out Hu Dawei, the politically liberal and activist son of Hu Yaobang, who was perhaps the most politically reform-minded leader of the CCP. Xi's generational and proximity sentiments may be genuine, but they may also blind him to the cronyism that the Chinese public so much resents.

These elements of Xi's style have implications for the possibility of reform. Reformists wanted the party to be subordinated to the legal system and a transition to a state of laws, if not to rule by law, and a democratization that started inside the party's selection system itself. But Xi has clearly halted the debate about such an institutionalization of the party-state and in fact is taking preemptive stands against its renewal. Immediately after the Party Congress, Xi emphasized party rules and due process—but not the legal system itself. During his Shenzhen tour of January, Xi castigated those who insist that "real" reform implies "embracing the universal values of the West," and claimed the right to choose "what to reform and what not to reform. There are things we have not changed, things we cannot change, and things we will not change no matter how long a time passes."

This is a strong leader who has an absolute sense of his individual, genealogical, and ideological legitimacy. Where Hu held out something for everybody in his speeches and thus set no real direction, Xi often expresses himself obscurely. One trend does come through: the return to the revolutionary era when the party controlled the state, without any prospect of transition to a normal constitutional state. On balance, and in this first two years of power, Xi's flow of words has shut more doors than it opens, and the resurrection of "mass line" politics and rectification campaigns hangs a sword over the party membership and government cadres. It is also remarkable that, since the handover, Wen Jiabao has not made any public appearance and Hu Jintao has appeared only once.

However, although Xi has a radical style, he is not encouraging any radical ideological theme and he occasionally stresses due process within the party. In fact, local cadres and governments have often been taken to task by the public in recent times, and a blackmailing industry is thriving around their private sins. The attack on corruption curbs conspicuous consumption of luxury goods, often financed in China by work units or bribes. It does not in itself roll back the private sector or legitimate business interests—and might in fact serve them. Neither can it empower them above party-state economic interests. In other words, if "control" is the keyword of Xi's style, this leaves little room for loosening the controls over the state economy. In 2013–2014, however, Xi launched a liberalization from below by freeing economic initiative in key policy areas.

FREEZING POLITICS AND REFORMING
THE ECONOMY?

This is the area where Xi's pro-establishment credentials clash with the need for an overhaul that would challenge vested interests. The key figure here is not Prime Minister Li Keqiang, who was not Xi's choice. In fact, Li was Hu Jintao's original choice for the top job until the collective leadership decided differently in 2007. Li is a reformer who once translated Alfred Denning's *The Due Process of Law* into Chinese. In 2012 he endorsed the World Bank's China 2030 report, which reads as a primer for fundamental reforms reaching well beyond the economy into China's power elites. The report's basic argument was that major reforms could not be delayed—in spite of its success, China's development model was unsustainable.

Instead, Wang Qishan, elevated at the head of the party's Discipline and Inspection Commission but a strong economic leader, actually plays a major role because the anticorruption campaign he runs with a steel grip has a huge role in persuading economic agents to comply with policy. And Xi Jinping has put himself at the head of a new Central Economic Commission, as well as on six to eight (depending on the sources) different "leading groups" at the top of the party-state.

Economic reformers had suffered setbacks at the Party Congress itself. Most notable is Zhou Xiaochuan, China's central banker, who had stuck his neck out for currency convertibility; he kept his job but did not get reappointed to the Central Committee. But they fared better in the spring of 2013, when China's semi-controlled legislature formally appointed a new government. Wang Yang, the former Guangdong party secretary, became vice prime minister for economic affairs. Lou Jiwei was promoted from the CIC (one of China's two sovereign investment funds) to the finance ministry. Liu He, an American-trained economist who was directly involved in the China 2030 report, was named head of the State Council's

Finance and Economics Leadership Small Group. Because Liu has been considered an adviser to Xi and is credited with coining "top-down reform" in 2010–2012, this is taken as a sign that there may be serious changes ahead. At first, the trend did not apply to control over state enterprises. Jiang Jiemin, the chairman of CNPC, China's giant oil firm, was named head of SASAC, the ministry-level agency that shares with the party's Organization Department control over top state-owned enterprises. Yet only months later, Jiang Jiemin was taken down for corruption, in a move that shook the important oil sector and set up the fall of Zhou Yongkang.

Since then, economic policy has confirmed the intention to rein in excesses and imbalances, even at the expense of growth—and this is being implemented more consistently than under Wen, who had initiated that policy. What is not clear is where the needle will stop between a further turn toward market and regulation and the preservation of a state-driven and top-down growth process in place since 2008–2009. China faces a real dilemma. So far, it is fast growth and its components—the export chain, pump-priming investment into infrastructure, top-down promotion of industry strategies, induced savings, and currency sterilization—that have made the reform era a success. A side result has been the unbalanced economy and society—an investment-to-GDP ratio of nearly 50 percent and a Gini coefficient that may be anywhere between a "low" estimate of 0.45 to an incredibly high 0.75. But inhibiting these trends certainly impairs growth in the short term. Reining in the state's not-so-invisible hand over the market may also produce wild speculative cycles. In fact, the central government may not even be certain that it can tie the hands of local governments.

Under Hu and Wen, macro-economic policy consisted of stop-and-go measures, with bank lending and bank deposit requirements as the key instrument instead of monetary and interest rate policies. Every time the government moved to stem runaway credit, it soon rescinded the move for fear of hurting growth. It signaled the intention to tax real estate, and in particular multiple home ownership, but mostly backed off because multiple home buyers were precisely the most attractive market for developers. China's borrowers—first and foremost local governments and their proxies, real estate and infrastructure companies, or firms in sectors where there is official encouragement—have used "shadow banking," including new wealth-management funds, to circumvent regulations. While China's central budget is balanced and foreign currency reserves reached an all-time high at nearly $4.5 trillion in mid-2014, the real scale of local government and shadow banking lending is not known with certainty, nor is there an assessment of hidden liabilities such as future pensions.

Occasionally, borrowers also find questionable sources of financing abroad. In 2013, China's hot money outflow of the second half of 2012, triggered by political uncertainties, reversed in appearance, thanks to a new scam. Export statistics at the beginning of 2013 suddenly showed huge increases (as much as 93 percent to Hong Kong year-on-year). In fact, the corresponding amounts are conveniently borrowed on new RMB markets abroad and repatriated to fuel the investment and real estate craze. Reining in central banking and credit is not sufficient to deter these new practices. Stamping them out, getting rid of overcapacities in industry and construction, will kill fast growth—perhaps only a statistical correction since that growth creates more and more unused capacities and buildings—but will also generate social tensions.

Like their predecessors, the new leaders have had one foot on the gas and one on the brake. In late June 2013, they acted much more decisively. A sudden curtailing of monetary creation sent short-term and inter-bank borrowing rates ballistic. The government quickly reassured markets that it would not starve the banks. That may seem like a replay of previous stop-and-go hesitations. But, like Federal Reserve Chairman Ben Bernanke's experiments with turning off the spigot of public bond purchases, the move does serve notice on China's informal borrowers that the good times of expansionary public policies will end. China's move, in fact, mirrors the Fed's own slow turn to restrictive monetary policies. For it is the current-account surplus and currency sterilization that have made it possible to finance China's runaway growth. Were the United States and Europe, China's main markets, to contract again, the margin for an expansionary policy in China would also shrink. In 2014 an export rebound, helped by demand from the rest of the world and a lower renminbi, fueled Chinese growth. In July of that year, China's trade surplus set a historical record at $47.3 billion. China's economy is simply not rebalancing as had been anticipated by most foreign observers.

This top-down approach by the central bank reflects a basic feature of Xi's domestic strategy: to check irrational economic behavior (corruption, waste, runaway informal credit). This is the priority, rather than reforming the key state economic actors, which might in fact emerge strengthened as a result. China's banks, state-run but with their own individual strategy, are caught in the crossfire because they have financed so much questionable development in China's gray economy or informal sector. Tightening money creation may also force more careful investment from China's big state actors—whether these are administrations or state enterprises. In 2013–2014, the government showed increased willingness to let some financial funds—especially those that were structured along questionable local lending—go bankrupt: this is also happening to local-level public firms.

It is of course very hard to immunize China's nonstate economy from a credit squeeze—whether it is small and medium-size firms, private companies without the privileged access to financing, or local speculators who are hurt.

The Third Plenum of November 2013 addressed these issues with such a bewildering array of economic measures that it is hard to believe they can all be enforced by a top-down administration.

Out of the two hundred-plus announcements from this meeting, most have the words "gradual" or "step-by-step" written in. Some of the more recent changes do suggest that Xi's administration will follow a two-track system—encouraging market developments in hitherto closed areas alongside the preservation of the state economy. One case stands out: the informal permission granted to a new web billionaire, Jack Ma, who earlier founded Alibaba, to launch a web-based money fund for private savers in China and Hong Kong. Alibaba has already become the world's largest online retailer and B2B company, with a turnover that exceeds that of Amazon and eBay combined. By cutting down on the healthy interest rate margin of official banks, Ma's new venture has collected more than $90 billion in eight months—shaking up the entire financial system. In a less high-profile decision, foreigners are now allowed to buy private banks, which could, if implemented, lead to genuine competition in the banking system.

The new leadership therefore has a two-track approach, neither of which should be discounted. As to the professed goal of reorienting the economy toward domestic consumption, as noted above, in July 2014 China broke its own record for a monthly trade surplus, and broke it again in January 2015, with a $60 billion trade surplus in a single month: in this case, falling world prices for oil and other raw materials, as well as a downturn for coal and steel production have actually pushed China's foreign trade imbalance even further. Talk about moving to free convertibility of the Chinese currency has remained just that—talk. Certainly financial authorities have launched all kinds of experiments that familiarize Chinese financial firms with capital markets and increase their numbers. But the basic restraints on convertibility remain in place, and most official pronouncements cite a delay of ten to fifteen years, if not twenty, for a changeover. Sitting on immense foreign currency reserves, China is already a world-class lender and financier. But this policy of monetary hoarding also implies that the renminbi itself has a very limited international circulation. To let the renminbi become an international reserve currency, China would actually need to reverse that policy and borrow abroad in renminbi. With a huge current account surplus, that is out of the question. So Beijing remains wed to a mercantilist policy, and foreign purchases of renminbi remain limited.

A TOUGHER, MORE RATIONAL FOREIGN AND SECURITY POLICY

The starting point for Xi's foreign policy is that China has arrived. The thirty-year period beginning with Deng Xiaoping has come to an end. Xi has dispensed with statements about "low profile" inherited from Deng and is clearly claiming a global reach that is no longer based on the idea of the "democratization of international relations" of which Hu spoke. Xi has immediately established a claim that China is a global power rather than what has recently been called a "partial power."[4] In his first trips abroad as president, Xi visited Russia, South Africa, two other African countries, and Latin America to demonstrate that he would not be boxed in by relations with the West. Meanwhile, China has deployed patrol boats near the Senkaku/Diaoyu islands and troops (armed with banners reading "this is our territory") beyond the so-called Line of Control with India, and it has sent a large oil rig close to the shore of Vietnam in waters that it claims as Chinese.

Xi's meeting with Barack Obama at Sunnylands in California in June 2013 superficially recalled Jiang Zemin's visit to President George W. Bush's Crawford ranch in 2002. That visit had been notable chiefly because Jiang signaled to Bush that he would not directly oppose a military offensive against Iraq at the United Nations. Instead, the meeting between Xi and Obama was as much a collision as a conversation: neither side ceded ground. This first summit with Obama was preceded by statements about a "large power relationship," and Xi said that "the vast Pacific Ocean has enough space for the two large countries of China and the United States." The phrase, which implies strategic parity, must leave the other Pacific nations wondering where they fit into this picture.

While calling for a "large power" relationship with the United States, Xi has also termed Russia as China's "most important strategic partner" (China and the United States do *not* call their relationship a "strategic partnership"). The declarations with Russia underscore respect for each side's "core interests," a phrase that China now seeks to promote with all of its partners. Minister of Foreign Affairs Wang Yi has also underlined that China will "build a new model of major-country relationship" and "take a more active part in the handling of international and regional hotspot issues."[5] These statements carefully balance a dialogue among equals with the United States without necessarily ceding ground on contributions to the global order and unspecified intervention into regional hotspots—a much more sensitive area.

Meanwhile, Chinese policy in the neighborhood has become even more assertive than it was during the last years of the Hu–Wen era. Xi was already in charge of one area of foreign policy before the succession last November 2012: in mid-2012, he was put in charge of the small group that runs maritime security and there are indications that he may have been put in charge of the response to Japan on the Senkaku/Diaoyu island dispute in September 2012.[6] If accurate, this is very important, as it puts Xi in charge of the most contentious area of Chinese foreign policy on the eve of his nomination to the presidency. He was also already vice chairman of the Military Affairs Commission. Since becoming general secretary, he has initially relied on Wang Huning as a kind of informal national security adviser—he is the only Politburo member without formal attribution. He then created a National Security Commission, which he heads and which fuses domestic security and military strategy. He has also merged five different maritime agencies (all active in the South and East China Sea) under the State Oceanic Administration. Xi is not shy about talking of the necessity to be prepared for war. One of his close personal associates, General Liu Yuan, is even more explicit. Overall, the battle against corruption now under way in military ranks is publicly justified by the need to build a war-capable army.

With Xi in charge, Chinese policy toward its neighbors has become more focused without necessarily moderating its course. China has maintained its hold over the area surrounding Scarborough Shoal, which has long been held by the Philippines but is now claimed by China. After a tense stand-off in June 2012, the United States encouraged a pullback on both sides—but layers of Chinese patrol units and fishing boats now maintain a grip around the islet. At the Asian Defense Summit in Singapore in June 2013, a PLA officer confirmed that its navy had sent vessels around Hawaii, into American exclusive economic zones (EEZs). Regardless of the final interpretation on the United Nations Law of the Sea, what matters here is that China is indeed claiming equal rights, if not parity, with the United States. In January 2014, it also proclaimed an Air Defense Identification Zone (ADIZ) over much of the East China Sea, compelling all air traffic to give advance notice of their flight paths through the zone.

Chinese neighborhood policy may be departing from the Hu era in two important areas. First, Taiwan is coming under increasing pressure—apparently from Xi himself—to submit any international move, such as free-trade negotiations, for the PRC's approval. Yet the Ma Ying-jeou government has gone very far to assuage the PRC. It used at least token violence (fire hoses) against Japanese custom boats around the Senkaku/Diaoyu, effectively carrying the challenge one notch higher. And Taiwanese fishermen have also been engaged in skirmishes with their Filipino competitors in the South China Sea, resulting in a single Taiwanese casualty. In effect,

Taiwan has often moved with China—but is apparently not being rewarded.

Second, Xi seems to be moving in the other direction with North Korea. In 2010, South Korea was bitterly angry at China for its refusal to side openly against North Korea. But, with its own dispute with Japan over history and territory, South Korea is now openly courting Beijing. New president Park Geun-hye (the daughter of late President Park Chung-hee, the anti-Communist modernizer of South Korea) did not hesitate to cancel contacts with Japan after Prime Minister Shinzo Abe publicly mishandled the war responsibility issue in May 2013. Ms. Park succeeded in getting from Beijing a joint declaration against nuclearization, and Chinese press reports hailing "the great emerging Korean nation" may be a sign that Beijing could finally contemplate reunification of the two Koreas in the future. The purge in late 2013 by North Korean leader Kim Jong-un of his own uncle, the regime's number two leader and reputedly close to China, accelerates the trend, with negotiations starting in 2015 on maritime boundaries and the EEZs of China and South Korea.

Two factors contributed to this shift. The first is an underlying belief in Seoul that American support is largely ineffective to resolve the issue—the Korean peninsula since 1991 has been a graveyard for international solutions to the North Korean nuclear issue. Conversely, China is persuaded that economic interdependence binds Korea to China more effectively than the strategic issues divide them. In sum, while Japan, Southeast Asia, and India are hedging against China by enlarging their US defense ties, South Korea is also hedging against potential American unreliability by getting closer to China. It doesn't hurt that this allows Xi to distance himself from Hu, who gave a very high level of public face to Kim Jong-il and even Kim Jong-un during his time.

Another development is also striking: the liberal, integrationist view within China's media and professional journals is diminishing. This concerns economic issues as well, which are supposed to be at the heart of China's convergence and cooperation with regional partners. Maoist hardliners and neo-leftist circles had been silenced as a result of the Bo affair. But there is now public intimidation of Mao Yushi, the elderly economic liberal who was a key architect of the first decades of reform. On foreign policy, the nationalists and hardliners seem to be rallying behind Xi, who fulfills their wish for a strongman. For example, in March 2013, leading nationalist general Luo Yan, who has ranted against "traitors," subscribed loudly to "the leadership of Xi."

THE CHINESE ANDROPOV?

Whether out of family, generational, or organizational loyalty, Xi has put the accent back on the party rather than on political transition and state institutions. Reforms, however urgent and important, are likely to be led by the party and not as part of a transition to another institutional setup. This means reformers have to choose: they either serve in their place or become political opponents. Whether in domestic or foreign policy, Xi wants to champion a line that might be called "hard-line modernization." Instead of separating party and state, he is reinforcing the primacy of the party. It means a return to the fusion of party and military leadership that existed before 1949, with the party—led by himself—directly in charge of the state.

One is tempted to invoke a precedent in Soviet history. Many conservative critics of the Hu–Wen leadership criticized the stagnation and indecision of the leadership team and suggested an analogy to Leonid Brezhnev's long reign. While sympathetic observers are trying at all costs to see in Xi a closet reformer—a Gorbachev in the making—he appears to be much closer to Brezhnev's first successor, Yuri Andropov. Andropov's reign, from 1982 to 1984, was abridged by illness, but he displayed some traits that could make him a role model for Xi. Very knowledgeable about the West thanks to his long tenure at the head of the KGB, Andropov believed both in a foreign-policy hardline to the West and party-led modernization in the original Leninist spirit of self-reform.

Xi is not an old and ailing leader and, unlike the Soviet Union in 1982, the party-state he leads is rich. He also appears to be a consummate political tactician, with one more trait that he shares with Mao: the ability to turn on a dime. In 2013–2014, Xi began turning against both party and PLA senior leaders. The long fall of Zhou Yongkang and two top generals as well as the rumored house arrest of at least one senior retired leader, Zeng Qinghong, are unprecedented actions since the end of the Cultural Revolution and Mao's death in 1978. Enabled by the anticorruption drive, this purge was unquestionably meant as a major deterrent against backstage sabotage of his policies of the kind that his predecessors endured from the retired elders of the party. But absent a further institutionalization of China's political system, this highlights even more the return to a personal leadership.

Nevertheless, Xi is taking big political risks. Putting children of former leaders in many top positions, confirming the party, if not its members, as above the law, hailing China's glorious past as the essence of the China dream is a feat of reverse engineering to bring back the revolutionary DNA, long lost in Chinese society. The gap with the outside world, and with a hypermobile society, may become even larger. His predecessors had built on Deng's very ambiguity by allowing for limited liberalization and opening to civil society—and for promises and hints that more was to come later. Held in check but allowed to persist at the grassroots, a viral information society in China would undoubtedly present a serious challenge to Xi's control if the economy were seen to tank. Nowhere is the risk larger than in foreign policy: any economic downturn would leave China exposed to the long list of its partners who have been unsettled by the country's affirmation as an unyielding great power in recent years.

Xi's ambition for China is a fascinating one, but it may ultimately prove anachronistic. In political terms, he is trying to recreate a militarized party-state as an effective builder of national sovereignty. In economic terms, he is trying to develop China from the top down rather than creating an individualistic and innovative society based on balanced institutions operating on legitimate rules. In foreign-policy terms, he is pursuing a neighborhood policy based on strength in which China subjugates small countries within its sphere of influence while pursuing a "big power" relationship with the United States and Russia. In short, it seems that Xi wants to combine nineteenth-century geopolitics with twentieth-century Leninist politics in order to gain the upper hand in a globalized twenty-first-century world.

NOTES

1. This concluding chapter has been adapted and updated from François Godement, "Xi Jinping's China," European Council on Foreign Relations (ECFR), 2013.

2. "Mass line" is a term from the Maoist era. It refers to the mobilization of the population to press for changes or to denounce and rectify party cadres or counterrevolutionary individuals and trends.

3. Interview with a leading Chinese political scientist, Singapore, December 2012.

4. David Shambaugh, *China Goes Global: The Partial Power* (Oxford: Oxford University Press, 2013).

5. Wang Yi, remarks at the World Peace Forum, Tsinghua University, June 27, 2013, available at http://www.fmprc.gov.cn/eng/zxxx/t1054783.shtml.

6. See Linda Jakobson, "China's Foreign Policy Dilemma," Lowy Institute for International Policy, February 5, 2013, especially note 33, available at http://www.lowyinstitute.org/publications/chinas-foreign-policy-dilemma.

Index

About the Author

François Godement is director of the China and Asia program of the European Council on Foreign Relations (ECFR), nonresident senior associate of the Carnegie Endowment for International Peace (Washington), and associate research fellow of Asia Centre (Paris). A historian by training, he has observed developments in China and East Asia over the last four decades. He was a professor at the National Oriental Institute in Paris until 2006 and at Sciences Po from 2006 to 2014, and is a permanent external consultant to the policy planning staff of France's ministry of foreign affairs. He is the author of *The New Asian Renaissance* (1993) and *The Downsizing of Asia* (1998). For ECFR, he has also published *The EU-China Power Audit* (2009); *A Global China Policy* (2010); *Beyond Maastricht: A New Deal for the Eurozone* (2010); *China: The Scramble for Europe* (2011); *China at the Crossroads* (2012); *Xi Jinping's China* (2013); *Divided Asia* (2013); *France's Pivot to Asia* (2014); and *China on Asia's Mind* (2014). He edits *China Analysis*, an e-journal from Chinese language sources.